BURFORD ROAD
FREE PASS
TICKET

SHAZAM!

THE HISTORY OF A REGAL CINEMA

EVERYONE'S THEATRE OF DREAMS

ROB HEMMING

First published 2008 by
Word4Word

CIP catalogue records for this book are available from
the British Library.

ISBN 978-1-906316-11-2

Printed and bound by Cromwell Press, UK

www.w4wdp.com

For Joyce Hemming

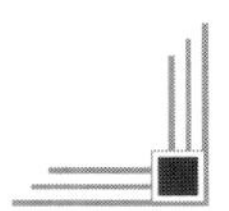

ABOUT THE AUTHOR

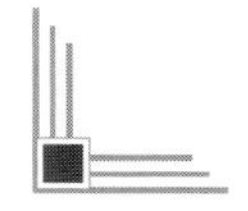

Rob Hemming was born in Birmingham in 1956.
Educated at Prince Henry's Grammar School, Evesham,
he dropped out of university and spent the next
twenty-five years in a variety of jobs including farmer,
local government officer, truck driver, salesman,
decorator, patio designer, classic car restorer,
personal trainer and printer before the penny finally dropped
that he was unemployable.

He therefore re-kindled an old love affair with creative writing
which now allows him to spend his days dreaming and talking
to himself. Besides, it's the one job in which his word is law.

Rob is the current chairman of the Malvern Writers' Circle,
occasionally contributes to the *Cotswold and Vale Magazine*
and likes to visit jungles, deserts and the back row of the flicks.
He has one daughter and lives in the Vale of Evesham.

To Kate
Best wishes
Rob Hemming

ACKNOWLEDGEMENTS

I would like to express my gratitude to the following people and institutions for their memories, anecdotes, photographs and other contributions:

Local historian Gordon Alcock and the Almonry Museum, illustrator Michael Barnard, Anne Bennett, Martin Bennett, the late Maurice Berry, Eileen Bowerman, Yvonne Brown, Ed Cohen, my pal Mark Daly both for his 'Foreword' page and for evoking the nostalgia of the Regal with great intensity, Barbara Dovey and the staff at Evesham Library, Pauline Fessey, Willy Ford, Tina Fortey, Bill and Joan Green, Ken Grove, John Hall, Martin Hammon, Russell Hancock, Brian Haywood, Norman and Margaret Holly, Brian Jordan, Phyllis Knight, Queenie Marcroft, Eileen Mustoe, Dave Nichols, former Regal Director Jane Peatfield, Stuart Peters, Diane Preece, Richard Price of solicitors Saunders Roberts, cinema historian Peter Thackeray, Joe Webb, and Terry and Anne Woodcock.

My gratitude also to Les Alexander, Linda Foxhall, Phred and Rob Newbury, Linda Radford and Mick Waseley for their enthusiasm, encouragement and practical help.

Thanks must also go to: The British Film Institute for facilitating the use of old movie images, *Evesham Journal* editor John Murphy, archivist Gerry Barnett and *Berrows Journal* editor Kevin Ward for allowing the use of photographs and information.

Special thanks to the *Cotswold and Vale Magazine*, particularly Managing Director Ian Tustin and editor Lynne Powell, for allowing me the initial opportunity of showcasing my 'Theatre of Dreams' project. Also to my colleagues in the Malvern Writers' Circle for their support and invaluable critique, especially Roz Wolseley-Charles who painted the gorgeous end-paper illustrations.

I would like to offer huge praise to Sue Richardson, Peter Chadwick, Cara Carey and the designers and staff of Word4Word Design and Publishing Ltd. for such a beautifully produced book, and to Sue Browning for the copy editing. Also to Graham and Lynn Cullimore of 'Pink Dylan' for the 'SHAZAM!' website.

I am particularly indebted to the following people for their many hours of absorbing reminiscences, plus photographs, which afforded me such fascinating glimpses into the past: former usherette Joan Butler, 'superfan' Tony Goodwin, master-projectionist Brian Houghton and his wife Mary, marvellously feisty former manageress Irene Mackenzie, Marilyn Small (daughter of Iris and Stan Jordan), projectionist David Stride and 'Spiderman' himself, the late, wonderful Bob Webb DSM.

I must say a huge "thank you" to my family: Mum Joyce, Dad Dave, brother Steve, daughter Hannah and Linda Otto for their support, common sense and for keeping my feet firmly on the deck.

Finally, the biggest "thank you" of all goes to my lady, Tina Carkeek, for her unstinting support, for withstanding the tantrums of a scribe when he has hit 'writer's block' and for the countless hours spent masterfully choreographing the text.

FOREWORD

Cinemas quickly joined the ranks of British small-town institutions and gained the particular quality of being much more personal than their big-city brothers. Like country railway stations, or early motor garages, the small-town cinema was always closer to its customers than movie houses in the cities. Community is a word now widely applied without much discretion, but if you lived or grew up in the small Worcestershire town of Evesham during the twentieth century, you were lucky enough to have a classic example of a community picture house on your doorstep – The Regal Super Cinema, 41 Port Street.

In fact, Evesham was lucky in having two cinemas, but the Regal was always more fondly regarded. While the Clifton cinema, spiffy and chain-owned, had the edge with first-run releases – it seemed to have a freehold on the early Bond movies, for instance – the Regal was much more a part of Evesham's life. *Shazam!* explains why. It is partly a social history, and partly the chronicle of a love affair, and like all good stories it is about people.

Although the Regal was an independent cinema, existing outside the major chains, the auditorium was anything but homespun. It was a large and stylish deco-styled 900-plus seater space dedicated unselfconsciously to entertainment. At the time of writing, early 2008, the building is still complete, although in grim disrepair. For anyone born after WW2 who goes to the pictures, the decline has been palpable. Cinema admissions in Britain fell from the 1950s, dipping below 600 million in 1959 and then down to 167.3 million in 2003, when the last film was shown at the Regal. It fought a long, valiant and enterprising retreat right up to the moment of its own Last Picture Show.

Rob Hemming's fascinating tale, which very hilariously nails down the details and personalities, also sheds light on some of the Regal's quirks. One of the biggest mysteries was the eccentric programming, still managing a three-changes–per–week routine into the late sixties. What was the story behind the Regal's inspired line in showing re-releases? Who programmed that collection of early Italian black and white sexploitation movies that ran in the summer of 1966? Why was the cinema packed for *The Dam Busters*, re-run as late as 1965? Brigitte Bardot turned up in *And God Created Women* (1957) ten years late, but it was delightful to see what the fuss had been about first time round. Does anyone remember any of those Audie Murphy/Elvis Presley double features run on Sunday afternoons, where the Regal's auditorium held a wild audience that seemed to teeter on the verge of anarchy? And on some insane weekday mornings in the 1970s Laurence Oliver's Shakespearian films were shown by special arrangement in a bid to sweeten the Bard for jaded GCE students. How did manager Ernie Highland make money from that?

There was marvellous innocence in the Saturday Morning Regal Chum's Club. It's good to hear about Terry and the Trojans, The Sapphires and The Wavelengths. Not many years later, for unknown thousands of adolescent Regal-goers, there was the usual illicit stuff – horseplay and sex and cigarettes – but if you liked movies you generally stuck with the film. For despite the many hundreds of extremely bad movies regularly shown at the Regal, it was clear to see that the people pulling the strings liked movies, knew their audience and fought to keep the cinema going. I always regret I never said thanks to them.

There were good movies too. I still congratulate myself on going there on my own, slightly underage, to see *The Wild Bunch* at a matinee first time round, staggering out afterwards into the shock of Bengeworth's unnatural daylight. I saw Hitchcock's last movie, *Family Plot*, on first release, at the Regal, and because of that, like the film more than it deserves. That's the catch, and that's part of the Regal magic. Cineastes may claim to savour purely the film, but can anyone truly separate a movie from the time and place they first saw it? You mostly go to the pictures when you are young, in unrepeatable lost-for-ever moments, and nostalgia is a treacherous emotion,

Even so, I can only think fondly of walking with my friends down Coopers Lane, turning into the pathway between the factory buildings, leading to the alley, which went past the air raid shelter (wartime S sign still intact). The alley then swung left into Port Street and with soaring expectation, we crossed the road to where the Regal was waiting.

Mark Daly

Freelance editor, *Jane's Defence Weekly*

South Nutfield February 2008

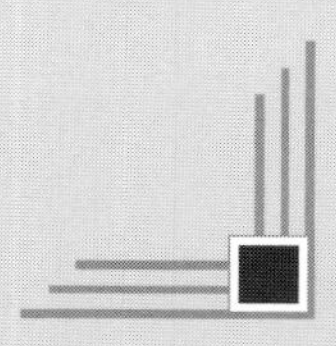

SHAZAM! THE HISTORY OF THE REGAL – EVERYONE'S 'THEATRE OF DREAMS'

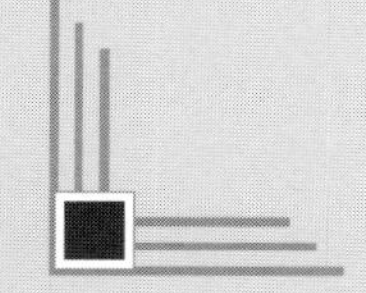

This book is more of a eulogy than a documentary. I could have chosen to write it entirely in the style of a local history volume, all sober facts and sensible description with only the many photographs preventing the reader from being bored rigid. However, the subject matter merits far greater artistic breadth because the Regal was Evesham's favourite conduit for the colour, flash and epic creativity of Hollywood and despite it now being defunct the old cinema has become iconic to the people of the Vale.

Like all local movie houses the Regal was built to make money by offering a very worthy service: the constant supply of fun, frolics, thrills, spills, frights, love and laughter, to anyone with the price of admission. Once those marble stairs had been climbed and a red velveteen seat selected, all we needed to do was watch and marvel. From the moment the lights dimmed, the curtains opened and that grainy black and white Board of Censors' caption bearing Lord Harlech's signature sprang out at us, we became mesmerised. The beauty of it was the sheer simplicity. Two or three hours in the dark, completely divorced from our humdrum existence, we could experience the whole panoply of the imagination, the brilliance of the movie makers taking us to the farthest edges of the universe or the most intimate reaches of the heart. No effort involved, save to keep your eyes and ears open, your jaw slack and to maintain a firm grip on the arms of the seat, or indeed your lover.

Once, every town had at least one cinema, usually referred to (affectionately) as the local 'flea-pit'. The Regal should never have been regarded as such because the term only really applied to lesser cinemas on which was lavished scant attention. But with a two-storey capacity in excess of 900 seats, although not Byzantine, she was no small theatre.

Certain buildings, whether through form, function or both, can be warmed to. I suspect that in time even a place which deserves Prince Charles' famous description as a 'monstrous carbuncle' may build a solid fan base. Thus, even in its current woeful state, this holds true for the Regal. Despite the lovely art deco interior with rococo scrolling, it was no Chrysler building, yet it possesses a certain unique cult status, a charisma if you will, which not even Clement Lichfield's imposing bell tower can match. I'm not suggesting they compare historically or architecturally; that would be ridiculous. But in terms of their effect on four generations of twentieth-century dreamers, there is no contest.

The 'Theatre of Dreams', as my father calls it, paraphrasing the Old Trafford soubriquet, was, until as late as the 1990s, the social hub of Evesham, its dark privacy the setting for many proposals, lovers' trysts, illicit meetings and simply pure enjoyment.

Well?
Which one is more fun?

The Regal's magic encompassed all of this, yet, besides the wonderful benefit to its customers, it built its own mythology through the people associated with its day-to-day running. Many of these ordinary folks became extraordinary characters who worked in the Port Street fun factory for decades and their tales prove that life really can imitate art. Truly, the Regal and its generations of staff are representative of all those deco picture palaces, large or small, ever to grace the planet.

As I researched this book, the more anecdotes I recorded and the more old photos came to light. I began to get some idea of how Howard Carter must have felt when he unearthed Tutankhamen's tomb. Yet my treasure was the colourful life of the 'Theatre of Dreams' related by the people who knew it so well. I could have continued to track down old fans and employees for years, each new tale and fact enriching the mix – enhancing this legendary piece of local culture – but the line had to be drawn somewhere. Thus, I offer my sincerest apologies to all those who may feel aggrieved that their tales have not been recorded, as I begin writing this book on Tuesday, 10 October 2006, the 74th anniversary of the opening ceremony, which seems wholly appropriate.

Hopefully, the blend of facts, stories, gentle lampooning and unabashed hero-worship will do justice to the history of an institution whose sole purpose was to hijack our emotions – to give us our money's worth of fun.

Please take your seats.

Rob Hemming

Carl Laemmle
PRESENTS
"ALL
QUIET
ON THE
WESTERN
FRONT"
WITH
LOUIS WOLHEIM
LEWIS AYRES
AND
JOHN WRAY
JACK WILHELM
a Carl Laemmle jr. Production
directed by Lewis Milestone
a Universal Picture

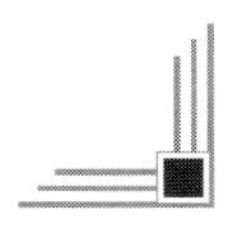
CHAPTER ONE

A THIRST FOR ENTERTAINMENT

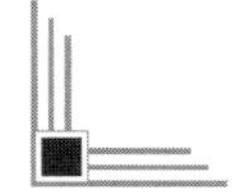

Movie roots

Ever since Napoleonic times scientists had striven to capture reality in a fixed image. By 1839 John William Herschel had coined the term 'photograph' and as the science progressed so did the desire to record the moving image. In 1872 Eadweard Muybridge began experimenting with photographing moving objects and we've all seen his typical subject matter – galloping horses, circus strongmen and even Victorian ladies divesting themselves of their many layers. This more 'racy' material was popular for decades on fairground 'flicker machines' usually presented under the title *What the Butler Saw.*

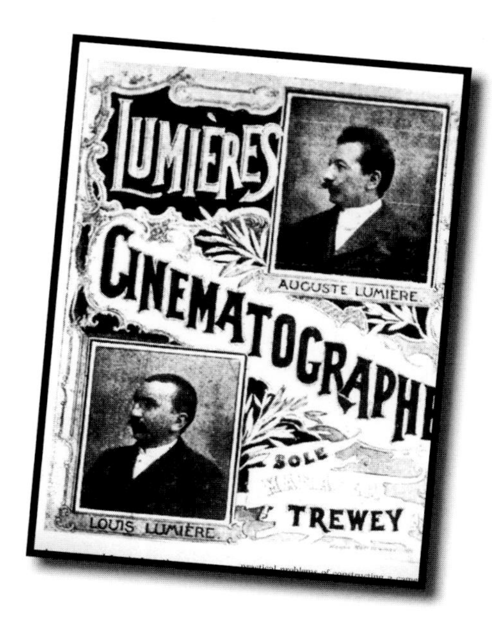

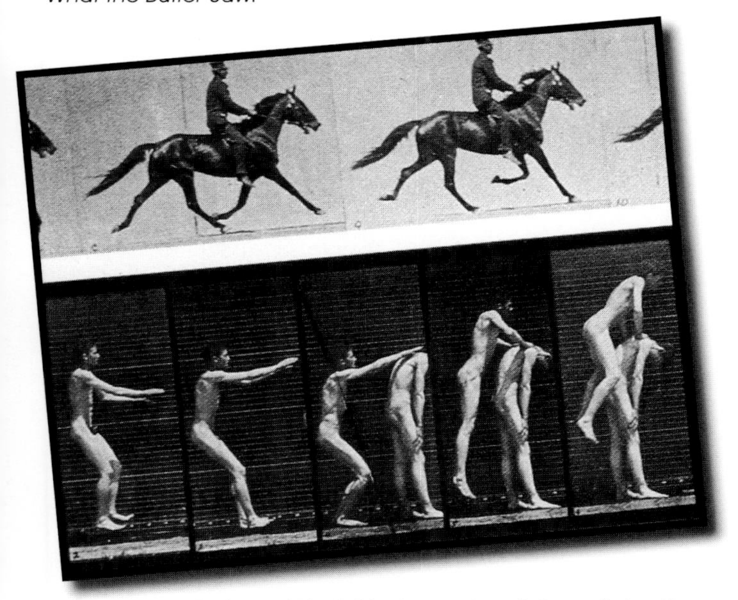

Eadweard Muybridge's experiments in capturing the moving image, eighty years before the infamous nude wrestling scene between Oliver Reed and Alan Bates.

By 1889 Kodak celluloid film roll was available and within two years Thomas Edison and W.K. Laurie Dickson had invented the 'Kinetograph', a camera for recording images, plus the 'Kinetoscope', a reciprocal device for viewing those images.

Many noteworthy names such as George Eastman, William Friese-Green and Louis Le Prince contributed to the burgeoning medium but by the middle of the 1890s four parties stood poised to claim the title of 'inventor of the modern movie film': Edison with his 'Vitascope', Max and Emil Skladonowsky with their 'Bioscope', Robert W. Paul with his 'Theatograph' and Auguste and Louis Lumière with their 'Cinematograph'. The Lumière brothers are generally reckoned to have won and their famous device gave its name to the movie makers' art form, cinematography.

By the turn of the twentieth century, moving pictures had progressed beyond merely capturing factual events and evolved into a whole new art form of fantasy story telling. The year 1902 saw Georges Méliès' experiment with special effects in his ground-breaking fourteen-minute film *A Trip to the Moon* and the following year Edwin S. Porter brought us *The Great Train Robbery*, which contained all the elements of the modern western.

The cinema industry made mercurial progress, which can be viewed in parallel with the development of powered flight. In 1903, as the Wright brothers were taking off at Kittyhawk, *The Great Train Robbery* was riveting audiences with its barely twenty minutes of action. By 1927, as Charles Lindbergh was piloting Spirit of St Louis across the Atlantic, Al Jolson's dulcet tones were being heard in *The Jazz Singer*, the first major full-length 'talkie'.

Meanwhile, back in the sticks

The English inventor Robert W. Paul was to give sleepy Evesham its first ever exhibition of 'animated pictures' in 1897 on his revolutionary 'Theatograph'. He had filmed the Derby at Epsom and Queen Victoria's Diamond Jubilee and was making a very fair living from exhibiting his newsreels all around the country. Alas, at bank holiday on the Crown Meadow, Mr Paul's show was a fiasco as a large crowd were disappointed by the indistinct imagery. So for entertainment, Evesham had to be content with the age-old travelling shows and circuses for a few more years.

There was, however, a frequent visitor to the Vale who stirred up much interest. 'Wadbrook's Electograph Show' would arrive in a train of gaudily painted caravans drawn by traction engines in the manner of a traditional circus. A stage was erected complete with dancing girls plus a barker in evening dress, top hat and rakish moustache, probably resembling Terry-Thomas, whose job it was to drum up interest in the show.

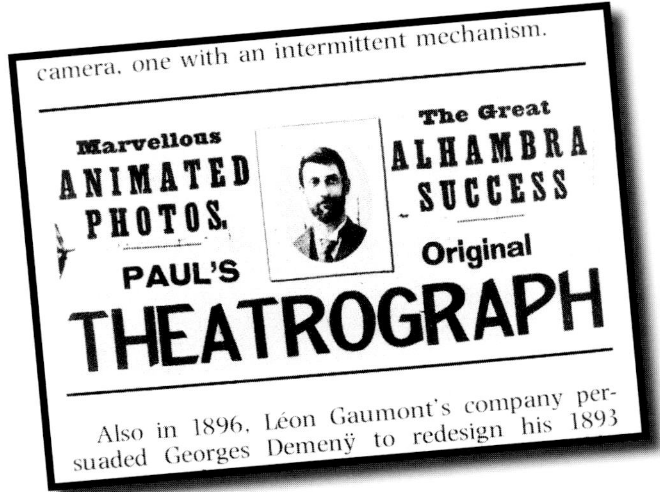

Ad. for Robert W. Paul's Theatograph.

When the crowd had reached fever pitch he would open the doors to a tiny theatre and nearly get killed in the stampede. For the princely sum of one penny (1d) all and sundry could enjoy half an hour sitting on wooden benches watching silent films of cowboys, travel and comedy, while the guy in the tux and top hat expanded on the stories, using a long stick as a pointer. Apparently, the most popular of these films was a French effort known as *The Bridal Night*, which showed a couple in a bedroom on their honeymoon. During it, the barker in the tux would merely lean on his pointer and forego any explanation, having no doubt reasoned that Asum[1] yokels knew all about the birds and the bees. And with no Board of Censors yet in operation to spoil the fun, a good time was had by all.

Eventually, in Britain, the powers that were felt regulation of the new medium was in order and introduced the 1909 'Cinematograph Act' as movies began spreading from the big cities to the provinces. Cinema was soon muscling in on the traditional territory of highbrow theatre and vaudeville or 'music hall' as it was known in Britain. (The latter had been a staple of entertainment for almost a hundred years and cinema would marginalise it within a generation.) In 1912, as the British Board of Film Censors was established, Evesham's first ever cinema, the Electra Playhouse, was erected on what was to become the bowling green adjacent to the Northwick Hotel. Under the proprietorship of, firstly, Mr Charles Senior and subsequently, Mr Frank Beach, its amenities were announced as a "large screen, comfortable seats, a sloping floor and electric light throughout". The interior walls were of a "distinctive and subdued red colour".

From the start, variety turns were mixed with the silent movies, as at many other theatres. So the 1912 opening programme blended the live singing talents of one Mr Evan Holland, 'The Derbyshire Miner Vocalist',[2] with the first ever silent feature films to be shown commercially in Evesham: *The Inner Mind*, billed as a 'superb drama'. This was supplemented with *Detective Jane* (a 'great comedy'), *White Brave's Heritage* (a tale of Indian life in the 'Wild and Woolly West') and *Spring Flowers* (amazingly, a duo-chrome COLOURED nature picture).

The price of admission ranged from 4d to 8d to 1/3d, which emphasised the chasm in wealth between those who sat in the 'cheap' seats and those who could afford four times the amount for the 'posh' seats.

The Electra was soon under pressure, with the opening of the Grand Cinema in Swan Lane in February 1913. This new theatre was advertised as the most up-to-date picture house in the Midlands, despite its initially being a spartan building with wooden bench seats. On 8 January 1914, the Electra ended its indecently short life and the Grand had the field all to itself.

It began under the managership of Mr Lew Davis and while the silent films played, the melodrama was stoked up by the frantic ivory bashing of Mr George Lowe, the resident piano/organ player. The first film at the Grand was an adaptation of *The Count of Monte Cristo* which showed to a capacity house of almost five hundred people. Films were changed twice weekly, on Mondays and Thursdays, and on the Sabbath it closed, except for charity occasions. There were two continuous shows between 6 p.m. and 10.30 p.m. and seat prices ranged from 6d to 1/6d.

In 1920, the managership was taken over by a certain Mr Frank Ridge, a lifelong cinema man who had moved from the Park Hall cinema in Cardiff and gained the distinction of eventually becoming the only individual to manage three of Evesham's picture houses.[3]

For ten years solid, the Grand was the only theatre in town, until 1923 when a group of local businessmen (including the directors of the Grand) formed the Super Cinema and Theatre (Evesham) Ltd. company, with the purpose of constructing a more modern film palace, the Scala. This was duly built in the town centre and opened for business on 1 October 1923, with a special engagement by something called Ernest Crampton's Company in a cabaret concoction called *Cigarettes*.
The Scala's admission prices showed a touch more equality, with the stalls available at 9d and 1/3d and the balcony 1/9d.

1 Colloquial pronunciation of Evesham.

2 The unfortunate Evan Holland was moonlighting to earn a crust during the 1912 miners' strike, so the Electra management felt compelled to stress that Mr Holland was "not one of the extremists" and although he had been on strike, intended to resume work as soon as possible. This proved to be sufficient to placate any disgruntled coal-starved yokels with chilblains, and by all accounts, Evan's recital went down a storm.

3 In the early days it became traditional for cinema owners to allow a yearly 'benefit' performance for the manager. This practice was continued until about the 1950s in Evesham and greatly helped the finances of a person who was usually popular in the town.

But private boxes were also available at 8/- and 10/6d which, at those prices, must have included champagne and caviar.

The Scala was designed to be a multi-purpose theatre, with facilities for film, stage shows and variety acts accommodated on its fully equipped 30 x 24-foot stage, complete with dressing-rooms. All the choicest films were shown at the Scala, leaving the Grand as the poor relation in the company.

From the mid-1920s, both cinemas came under the stewardship of Frank Ridge until 9 May 1931, when the Grand's final film, ironically entitled *Flaming Justice,* faded into oblivion, to the manic tinkling of George Lowe's piano. The owners had decided against splashing out on refurbishing the old place and installing new equipment capable of running 'talkies'. (The building had various uses over the next forty years, including as a billiard hall, grocer's, hairdresser's, ballroom and eventually a social centre, until its demolition in 1974.)

The Scala blossomed throughout the late 1920s with Frank Ridge at the helm and in 1924 became one of the first provincial cinemas to give Sunday performances as a matter of course. There was plenty of opposition to their initial application, but opinion was swayed by the staunch support for Sabbath movies of none other than the then vicar, the Rev. E.O. Burbidge,

who took an enlightened view that it might solve the problem of young people who had nowhere to go when they emerged from church on a Sunday evening and were tempted to get up to mischief. Where is the good Reverend when we need him in 2008?

Judging by the Scala adverts in the *Evesham Journal* in late 1929, Frank Ridge appeared to be deluding himself with regard to the imminent onslaught of talking movies, and it was rumoured that the Scala directors saw the 'talkies' as a passing fad. However, a full three years after Al Jolson's *Jazz Singer* heralded the age of sound, they unchained their wallets, sprang for a full equipment upgrade from Western Electric, and Evesham joined the modern era.

On Monday, 29 September 1930, the Scala screened the creaky musical *Sunny Side Up* and a packed house sat entranced as Charles Farrell warbled sweet nothings into Janet Gaynor's ear. For two solid years the Scala's ticket machine glowed red hot with demand but there was a shadow on the horizon in the form of the man who was to become one of Evesham's most celebrated businessmen.

Frank Ridge with his head in the sand.

Eyes on the prize

Victor A. Morrall's family came from Redditch and were business orientated. The Morrall family were founder members of the needle industries and the firm Abel Morrall existed until recent times. Due to his success and undoubted business acumen Victor's grandfather had been invited by Prince Albert to help organise The Great Exhibition of 1851.

Victor Morrall.

Victor Morrall served as a World War I pilot and afterwards worked for Austin Motors, eventually becoming a tester. By the mid 1920s, he and brother Frank had become two of the first AA patrolmen before establishing businesses in Evesham. Frank went into the fruit and veg trade but Victor had petrol in the blood and opened a garage.

Morrall was a natural entrepreneur who in later years would promote local boxing tournaments both on the Crown Meadow and in the Public Hall. During the 1940s, one such bout featured a youthful Randolph Turpin who would go on to wrest the World Middleweight Crown from the incomparable Sugar Ray Robinson in 1951.

The old Grand building, c.1974.

As talking movies began to make their mark in the late 1920s, the economic possibilities for the cinema industry became virtually limitless and when the Scala upgraded to sound in 1930, Victor Morrall couldn't ignore the potential for a rival cinema in Port Street, at the heart of a flourishing Bengeworth with its main bus routes out to Badsey and Broadway; and with Evesham's 1931 population up to 10,605, the market was obviously there.

Pre-Regal Port Street, c. 1920.

Morrall moved swiftly to secure the services of Birmingham architect Archibald Hurley Robinson whom he commissioned to design a state-of-the-art cinema. Victor owned the land on the corner of Port Street and the cramped Burford Road where stood the Morrall car showroom, a greengrocer's and a draper's shop. He intended relocating his motor business to the far more practical site at the junction of the Badsey and Broadway roads. This was to become the famous Motor House.

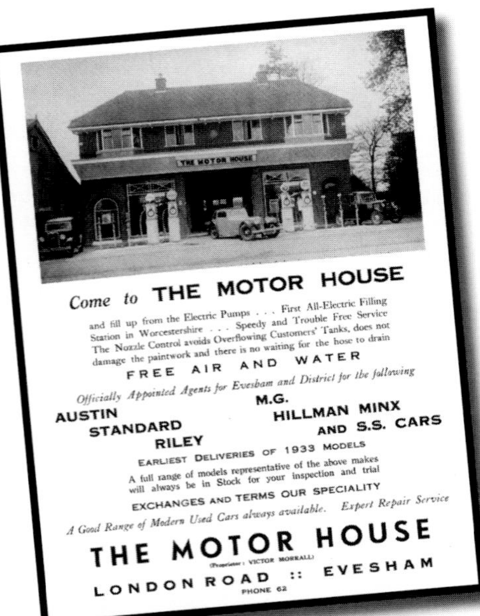

(I would prefer to believe that Victor built the Regal because he was a film fan from way back, bedazzled by Chaplin, Eisenstein, de Mille et al., but his true motive, of course, was always financial. He knew a gold mine when he saw it.)

Architect Hurley Robinson became something of a specialist in designing buildings which served a fun purpose and in the first half of the twentieth century was responsible for the creation of scores of cinemas, theatres and swimming baths. An unsung hero if ever there was one. Over seven decades on, it is fascinating to look at the austere old photographs of the original Regal luminaries, particularly Hurley Robinson, a man dedicated to the construction of buildings which, despite their technical brilliance and beautiful aspect, served as little more than 'fun houses' for the masses. He was no Christopher Wren or Frank Lloyd Wright and with his severe haircut, sensible glasses and no-messing stare, he looks the very image of the then establishment figure. He plied his trade in a time when social strictures were tight, discipline and law the order of the day. People knew their place, yet I'm not fooled. Under the starchy façade was a man who had caught the *zeitgeist* of the Jazz Age, which drove him to design pleasure palaces in vast profusion in order to show his love for the most broadly expressive art-form in history. He may have hidden behind the profession of architect, but his spirit was surely closer to that of Walt Disney than Normal Foster.

Archibald Hurley Robinson. Did this man moonlight as Harold Lloyd?

Through the winter of 1931/32 the plans for the new cinema came to fruition and were presented before the bench at Evesham County Petty Sessions in February 1932 by Mr J. Wythen Roberts on behalf of Messrs V. Morrall and F.M. Stubbs, two directors of the newly formed company, Regal Super Cinema (Evesham) Ltd. The meeting was adjourned for a fortnight while the town fathers considered this application for a cinematograph licence. Red tape and bureaucracy must have been thinner on the ground in times past because Victor Morrall's brainchild was rubberstamped within days and full-scale clearance of the Port Street site commenced.

What is almost forgotten is the second licence application presented at the same February sitting by Mr R. Hodgetts on behalf of the Super Cinema and Theatre (Evesham) Ltd. company who owned the Scala and the Grand. It was for yet another Port Street cinema to be built on the site then occupied by the Conservative and Unionist Club, with the proviso that the old Grand cinema would be subsequently discontinued. This application was unsuccessful, but the Grand became defunct anyway within two months. The stage would soon be set for Evesham's two-way rivalry between the Scala and the all-new Regal.

The Port Street gravy train

Victor Morrall decided the best way of financing the construction of the Regal was to offer share options to the other local businesses. At this time commerce in Port Street was buoyant, with Bengeworth like a small town in its own right, containing practically every type of shop or business. All flourished in that 350-yard stretch from the Swan Inn to Burlinghams by the Workman Bridge. Many local traders took up Morrall's offer, reasoning that a new cinema couldn't fail and that the spin-off trade from hundreds of individuals converging on the Regal would be considerable. Established Port Street traders such as Burlinghams, Dilworths, Hamptons, Pooles, Larners, Speeds, Stubbs, Webbs, Wheatleys and Wylds pitched in for cinema shares, and together with the financial input from Victor Morrall and the other directors, the target figure of thirty thousand pounds was achieved with almost indecent haste.

(Hamptons the newsagent/sweetshop/tobacconist directly opposite the Regal and Eric Poole's fish 'n' chip shop at the bottom of Port Street did particularly well from the new cinema by catering for many thousands of film fans down through the years. Until recent times smoking was de rigueur and no evening's entertainment would have been complete without six-pennyworth of fried spud. Eric Poole had the 'fast food field' to himself for many years because he was not obliged to compete with today's four Indian restaurants, two Chinese take-aways, a pizza parlour and a kebab house.)

Hurley Robinson's baby began to take shape as bulldozers moved in to demolish Morrall's old premises in April 1932.

The main stipulation from the local authority was that the front wall of the Regal must be set back four feet further from the main road than the previous building. The far-sighted plan was to widen Port Street to facilitate the inevitable increase in twentieth-century motor traffic, yet for some unknown reason this sensible scheme was never fully realised. The two buildings next to the cinema, Robbins the bakers and Goodwins hardware store, retained their original frontages while the rest of the lower part of Port Street complied.

Full marks, maybe, to the visionary thinking of Evesham District Council but the loss of four feet of space didn't make Hurley Robinson's job any easier in accommodating the seating requirements. So he designed a lower deck with a dish-shaped floor. This meant that the rear half of the stalls was facing downwards, while the front half was scooped upwards, giving the seats an impression of being part of a fairground ride. Some people loved to sit in the reclining seats with the big screen looming over them. I wasn't one of them. Around 1965, due to a packed house, I found myself watching the John Wayne circus film *The Magnificent Showman* in the very front seat. Never again. Even now, when I hear the word 'trapeze' I get a pain in the trapezius. A balcony man I became and shall e'er be.

Ready to support the gods.

It was rumoured that the first terraced house next to the Regal, No. 1 Burford Road, was to be demolished to lengthen the premises and solve the problem of cramped seating, but Robinson's original dished design sufficed and a total of 945 bodies could be accommodated.

(The Regal became one of only two cinemas in Britain with 'scooped stalls', the other being the Lonsdale in Carlisle. The general contractors for the erection of the Regal were Espley and Co. Ltd. of Evesham, using local labour, but most of the specialised jobs were undertaken by outside companies, mainly from Birmingham which, in 1932, was very much 'the land of a thousand trades')

Thus the thirty-grand palace was completed in less than thirty weeks, its construction having involved the removal of over one thousand cart-loads of earth, and the use of over one thousand tons of cement and concrete, a quarter of a million bricks and over one hundred tons of steel.

The most interesting part of the construction must surely have been the arrival, unloading and hoisting into position of the giant girder which was to support the balcony. At 6.30 a.m. on Sunday, 29 May 1932, a strange spectacle made its way up Port Street to where the steel shell of the new cinema was under construction. At fourteen tons in weight, sixty-eight feet five-and-a-half inches in length, and four feet eight inches in breadth, the huge girder seemed most precarious chained to the back of its fifteen-ton, six-wheeler transport.

It had been forged at the Crescent Iron Works by Messrs Jesse & Tildesley in Darleston and had begun its painstaking 8 m.p.h. journey at 1.00 a.m. in order to avoid any other motor traffic. According to the lorry driver, once south of Birmingham, he had encountered only one other vehicle. The load was greeted by just a handful of workmen, who had the unenviable task of shifting the giant beam without the aid of a crane. It took them an hour and a half to lever and shake it off the side of the lorry onto a waiting bed of railway sleepers. The noise and vibration must have awoken every Bengeworth resident enjoying a Sabbath slumber. Next, it was a matter of levering the girder onto rollers and shifting it into an appropriate position to be hoisted.

Very few people had witnessed the lorry's arrival, but by mid-morning several dozen people had gathered to watch the builders perform the delicate job of hoisting it off the rollers with blocks and tackle slung high up on the steel skeleton of the new building. One of the onlookers was the nine-year-old Joe Webb, now a sprightly eighty-five, whom many people will remember as the owner of the butcher's/grocer's at the top of Port Street, a long-established Bengeworth business inherited from his parents.

Joe's auntie, Stella Webb, had married Victor Morrall in 1923 so it was only appropriate that the Webb family had seized the chance to own shares in the new establishment.[6] Young Joe had been taken to watch the progress of his parents' investment on that Sunday morning and he related to me the excitement as he witnessed the builders pitting their wits against the massive inert length of steel. The chains and pulleys gradually took the strain and as the fourteen-ton monster cleared the ground it swung in a huge slow arc across the entrance to Burford Road and narrowly missed scything through the corner of the Bear Hotel. Port Street traffic, such as it was in 1932, had to be diverted until noon, when the girder had been hoisted into its permanent resting place.

In August 1932, when the balcony was completed, it had to be load-tested for safety, which was done by the laborious means of placing nearly four hundred sand bags, each weighing in excess of 120 pounds, evenly over the floor. It sagged by less than half an inch, indicating the required amount of strength/flexibility to accommodate a full house. The balcony was thus ready to support the several million people who would be sitting in it over the next seventy years and within a few short weeks the brand spanking new Regal Super Cinema was given a civic welcome.

Al Jolson.

6 Joe Webb was first cousin to my grandmother and as Vic Morrall was Joe's uncle by marriage, I am actually fourth cousin twice removed (I think!) to the man who built the Theatre of Dreams

"THE MOST AWESOME THRILLER OF ALL TIME"
the one and only
KING KONG
with
FAY WRAY
ROBT. ARMSTRONG
BRUCE CABOT
A MERIAN C. COOPER – ERNEST B. SCHOEDSACK PRODUCTION
FROM A STORY BY EDGAR WALLACE AND MERIAN C. COOPER
Chief Technician WILLIS J. O'BRIEN
DAVID O. SELZNICK
Executive Producer

CHAPTER TWO

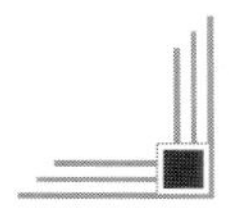

WELCOMING IN A GLORIOUS ERA

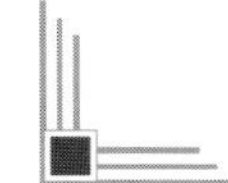

In less than thirty weeks Bengeworth had a new landmark to enhance its already vibrant trading base so it was only fitting that a fuss was made at the opening. The project had certainly created huge interest in the town and surrounding area and the local dignitaries pulled out all the stops when ushering in this new era of entertainment.

To mark the opening ceremony the new Regal Super Cinema directors produced a fine complimentary brochure for the occasion:

Souvenir Programme

OPENING

of

THE REGAL
SUPER CINEMA

EVESHAM

MONDAY, OCTOBER 10th, 1932

Proprietors:
REGAL SUPER CINEMA (EVESHAM) LIMITED

THE REGAL SUPER CINEMA, EVESHAM

TIMES OF PERFORMANCES:—

Evenings:

Continuous from 6 p.m. (Doors open at 5.30 p.m.)

Saturday continuous from 2 p.m.

Matinees:

Monday and Thursday at 2.30 p.m. (Doors open 2 p.m.)

Saturday at 2 p.m. (Doors open 1.30 p.m.)

Sundays at 8.15 p.m. (Doors open at 7.45 p.m.)

PRICES OF ADMISSION (including Tax):—

Weekdays:

Balcony **1/6**

Stalls .... **1/3, 1/-, 9d., 7d.**

Sundays:

Balcony **1/3**

Stalls .... **1/-, 9d., 7d.**

Children Special Prices.

Telephone: **EVESHAM TWO.**

The Management reserve the right to alter advertised programme and have the right to refuse admission to any person.

"REGAL" PERSONALITIES

V. A. MORRALL
Director

F. M. STUBBS
Director

H. F. KING
Director

S. HALL
Director and Manager

H. T. HODGKINSON
Director

HURLEY ROBINSON,
F.R.I.B.A., F.S.A.
Architect

Introducing the Personalities responsible for the conception and construction of Worcestershire's Finest Cinema

W. J. BOND, F.S.I.
Surveyor

Foreword and Policy

In asking your acceptance of this brochure as a Souvenir of the opening of the " Regal," the Directors hope that you will regard it as an expression of the very sincere welcome extended to you.

In the " Regal " they have endeavoured to provide Evesham and district with a home of entertainment which, for comfort, courtesy and convenience, will bear comparison with any other super cinema in the provinces.

It is hoped that a perusal of these notes, which give particulars of the construction and policy of the " Regal," will convince you that no effort or expense has been spared to provide high-class entertainment in complete comfort.

The " Regal " is a non-combine and privately owned super cinema, which enables the proprietors to study the individual and collective tastes of their patrons, and at the same time to promise that the best film productions will be shown (irrespective of cost or nationality). A list of some of the attractions which have already been reserved for early presentation at the " Regal " appears on another page. The very latest Western Electric sound apparatus and the most perfect projector-room equipment have been installed. In all such matters as these expense has not been spared, and everything possible has been done to ensure perfect reproduction.

Appreciation

The Directors of the "Regal " would like to express their thanks to His Worship the Mayor (Councillor Richard White) for his kindness in performing the opening ceremony.

They would like to express their appreciation of the courtesy and assistance received from the Magistrates, the various Council officials and to acknowledge the great improvement which has been effected by the setting back of the frontage.

They acknowledge the services of the Architect, the Quantity Surveyor, the many specialists engaged, and of the General Contractors.

The Structure

The Architect of the "Regal" is Mr. Hurley Robinson, F.R.I.B.A., A.I.S.E., who during the last ten years has been responsible for the design of over 55 cinemas and many other works of note, and who is at present engaged in planning the Kent Street and Sparkhill Baths—two of the largest covered swimming baths in the country.

The General Contractors for the erection of the "Regal" are Messrs. Espley and Co., Ltd., of High Street, Evesham, and, in passing, it may be noted that the rapidity with which the site was excavated and the theatre erected has been a matter of comment throughout the district. Less than thirty weeks ago the corner of Port Street and Burford Road was occupied by business premises, and even when these had been demolished there was still a tremendous amount of work to be accomplished before the actual theatre building could be commenced upon. Now the corner has become a landmark of the town visible from points at considerable distances away. Apart from other considerations, it is gratifying to witness the great improvement which has been effected at the corner itself through the erection of the "Regal." Sufficient space has been added to Port Street at this point to alleviate danger to pedestrians through stepping into the road at busy times, and the same factor has made the entrance to Port Street much safer for traffic. The quiet dignity and solid appearance of the theatre must appeal to devotees of almost every type of architecture. While modern tendencies are revealed, there is nothing about the exterior elevation which could be termed ultra-modern or in any way offensive to the eye of the critic, and it will be noticed that a successful attempt has been made to combine the artistic and the useful.

The design of the main facade reflects very creditably on the Architect, who wisely decided on a colour for the architectural stonework which harmonises with the general surroundings in a very pleasing manner. The two reeded columns each side of the main entrance which support the frieze possess a very dignified appearance, and a bold cornice decorated with a leaf design in high relief runs round the quadrant corner and caps two massive pilasters at each end. The architectural stonework was carried out by the Allied Guilds, Ltd., Tyburn Road, Erdington, Birmingham, in their well-known material

" Guildstone." This, unlike many other cast stones, is not an imitation, but a reconstruction, as a large proportion of the natural stone is incorporated in its manufacture. The ultimate result is that the beauty of the natural stone is still retained and many scientific advantages achieved; the two chief being that it is not affected by the smoke and grime of the atmosphere, and that it has no natural bed and cannot deteriorate through being incorrectly placed as is the case with many quarried stones.

The roof is covered with grey " Eternit " asbestos-cement diagonal pattern tiles, supplied and fixed by G. R. Speaker and Co., Ltd., " Eternit " House, Stevenage Road, Fulham, London, S.W.6.

The risk of fire is always an important consideration with cinema goers, and in this connection the patrons of the " Regal " can rest assured that everything possible has been done to protect them from this danger. Exits in excess of the number required by the exacting regulations have been provided, and the theatre can be emptied in less than two minutes. Furthermore, there is a minimum of timber and inflamable material incorporated in the building, and the roof is constructed of fire-proof slabs. The fire escape staircase at the rear of the building is constructed by Messrs. Lockerbie & Wilkinson (Tipton), Ltd., Staffs.

Messrs. H. Burlingham & Co., of Evesham, were responsible for the ornamental balustrade on the main staircase and the banister railing on the balcony staircase, both these items being constructed at their Evesham works by local labour. The collapsible gate at the main entrance is the work of the Acme Metal Works (1921) Ltd., of Brentford, Middlesex.

Special interest attaches to the camber of the floor in the auditorum. At the " Regal " the floor of the auditorium is not a continuous slope from the back of the building to the front as is the case in most theatres and cinemas, but the downward slope extends only to the centre, from which point the floor rises again in the direction of the screen. This is a new method of theatre flooring which ensures a much better view for those sitting in the auditorium.

In passing it is of interest to note that the building of the theatre involved the removal of over 1,000 cart-loads of earth, and the use of over 1,000 tons of cement and concrete, 250,000 bricks, and something over 100 tons of steel. Approximately 1,000 people can be seated with comfort.

THE GENERAL CONTRACTORS RESPONSIBLE FOR THE CONSTRUCTION OF THE REGAL SUPER CINEMA

ARE

ESPLEY & CO. LTD.

Building Contractors
Plumbers & Decorators

Offices & Works:
77 High Street
Evesham, and at
Broadway, Worcs.

ALL CLASSES OF
REPAIRS UNDERTAKEN
&
ESTIMATES FREE

Telephone:
Evesham 52
Telegrams:
Espleys, Evesham

The ORNAMENTAL BALUSTRADE
on the MAIN STAIRCASE

AND THE BANISTER RAILING
on the BALCONY STAIRWAY

IN THIS THEATRE WERE
MADE in EVESHAM by LOCAL LABOUR

BY **H. BURLINGHAM & CO. LTD.**

Electrical & General Engineers

EVESHAM

Established 1784

Telephone: Evesham 500
(2 lines)

Projection Equipment, Screen and Mercury Arc Rectifier

by

WALTURDAW

1896
to
1932

LONDON
46 Gerrard Street, W.1

BIRMINGHAM
37 John Bright Street

The Acoustic Solid Plastering, Granolithic Work and the Fibrous Plaster and Decorative Scheme in this Theatre was designed and carried out complete by

BRYAN'S ADAMANTA LTD.

Mars Works, Great Francis Street

BIRMINGHAM

Telephone : East 0332

Managing Director : Fred J. Bryan. C.R.P.

We have over 25 years' experience and have carried out more than 500 theatres and public buildings in the British Isles, and have a reputation to be proud of.

Management

Mr. Sydney Hall, who is a Director and General Manager of the " Regal," hails from Manchester, in which city his family can be considered pioneers of the film industry, having been connected with cinemas as far back as 1910. Mr. Hall's experience is wide and varied, and he has been in management and sole control of cinemas for the past twelve years; he has a sound technical knowledge of the industry and looks upon it from a scientific standpoint. He will appreciate constructive criticism and will always be ready to receive suggestions. His well-instructed staff will be equally courteous and eager to cater for patrons' comfort and satisfaction.

Decoration

The acoustic plaster-work, fibrous plaster and decorative scheme was designed and completely carried out by the well-known firm of Bryan's Adamanta, Limited, of Birmingham and Evesham, who hold a high position amongst the famous decorators of the British Isles, and who have been responsible for the decorative schemes of hundreds of theatres and public buildings throughout the country during the past twenty-five years. This firm employs artists and craftsmen of the highest class who, under the personal supervision of its Founder and Managing Director, Mr. F. J. Bryan, C.R.P., of Abbotswood, Evesham, make a minute study of originality in design and colour.

In the construction of the theatre every care has been taken to ensure that the acoustics will be correct, and in the application of the plaster-work, materials having acoustic values have been used throughout as a basis of the decorative scheme. All flat surfaces have been covered with " Brytex," a material which is the invention of Bryan's Adamanta, which counteracts any reverberation of sound, and produces colourful results. The fibrous plaster-work is designed on modern lines so as to relieve the otherwise rather heavy effects of the texture treatment, and at once becomes dignified and charming. The proscenium, organ grilles, flanking walls and the richly-treated balcony effectively tone with the concealed lighting features, and are all made in this remarkable material which is fireproof as well as highly decorative. The whole of the material was manufactured in Evesham by the firm's local craftsmen. The painting and colour-work have been designed to harmonise with the carpets and seating, which are in old gold, and the general treatment of the walls is in tones of old gold and rubbed ivory, with the ceiling in rich cream, turquoise blue and gold, a similar colour scheme being used in the massive proscenium frame, organ grilles and balcony front, etc. A "setting sun" surmounts the proscenium, the skilful brush graining in a warm oak colour of the doors and woodwork forming a tasteful contract to the scheme of the auditorium. It will be of interest to note that the carpets (which were supplied by Messrs. Fowler and Son, of Evesham) contain over 900 yards of material. All seating in the theatre is by Messrs. G. Pixton and Co., Ltd., of Newman Street, London, W.

The entrance hall, main staircase and foyers have been treated in somewhat similar lines with "Brytex" textured walls and rich fibrous plaster cornices, but the colour scheme is of a more vigorous character, and the introduction of cream, Chinese orange and gold gives the approach to the auditorium a warm inviting appearance, and demonstrates modernistic tendencies in the art of decoration.

Bryan's Adamanta are also responsible for the design and manufacture of the rich curtains covering the screen, which are made up in rep of old gold colour, with hand-painted scenic design in metallic lustrous paint, which picks up and reflects the concealed lighting of the proscenium frame and footlights, and results in a most effective splash of colour.

Electrical Equipment

In illuminating this cinema, no attempt has been made to follow the general trend of a blaze of coloured lights so often seen in the present-day cinemas, but rather to give a soft unobtrusive effect to harmonise with the general decorations. The whole of the wiring is encased in steel tubing. This, together with all the other materials used in the electrical installation, are of British manufacture entirely, and have been erected by The Etna Lighting and Heating Co., Ltd., of Birmingham, who have been entrusted (amongst other works) with theatre installations from the Shetland Isles to Land's End.

Heating and Ventilation

A feature of high importance in the construction and equipment of cinemas and other public buildings is the heating and ventilation system. In the case of the "Regal" Cinema this problem has received careful consideration in the light of modern requirements, both from the point of view of the safety and comfort of the patrons and the cost of maintenance. The matter was placed in the capable hands of Messrs. F. Evans and Sons, Ltd., Central Heating Specialists, 219, Heathfield Road, Handsworth, Birmingham, who have been responsible for the warming of a large number of cinemas in various towns, and the scheme they have designed and installed in the "Regal" Cinema has had the cumulative result of the wide experience of the Directors brought to bear upon it with highly satisfactory results. The heating medium used is low pressure hot water on the gravity circulation principle, two "Ideal" sectional boilers being installed in the basement. In order to make the basement absolutely watertight it is lined completely with Val de Travers foreign rock asphalte, with an external lining of brickwork to withstand the water pressure. Radiators distributed throughout the building are served with hot water by a system of piping circulations scientifically designed and properly proportioned to maintain an equable temperature of 60 degrees Fahr. throughout the cinema when the outside temperature is at freezing point. The entire scheme is designed to combine economy with efficiency, the whole pleasingly conforming with the general decorative scheme.

The air washing, heating, cooling, and ventilating installation, which is inter-connected with the central heating, is one of the features of the cinema, and is designed in accordance with the special requirements for the particular cinema into which it is installed. The necessary information required before any such plant can be designed being the cubical contents of the cinema and the number of persons to be accommodated. The capabilities of such an installation are as follows: During the summer season the correct volume of air is constantly being drawn from the atmosphere into the installation, where it is washed by a special process, cooled to the desired temperature, and forced into the cinema by means of an electrically driven fan. Electrically driven exhausters are constantly taking out the air from the cinema before impregnation occurs, and it will be understood therefore that a constant stream of fresh filtered air is circulating through the cinema. During the cooler seasons the same process occurs with the exception that instead of the air being cooled it is heated up to the temperature required inside the cinema. The Denton Sheetmetal and Engineering Co., Moorside Works, Denton, near Manchester, have installed these installations in many of the leading cinemas, where excellent results are being obtained in the summer and cooler seasons.

The bronze metal-work and ironmongery was carried out by Messrs. R. S. Mace, Ltd., of New Street, Birmingham.

The internal sanitary plumbing of this theatre has been designed and executed in the most hygienic manner by the well-known firm of J. S. Wright and Co., who have specialised in high-class sanitary plumbing, heating, ventilation and fire main installations for super cinemas throughout the country, including The Regal, Handsworth; The Pavilion, Wylde Green; The Pavilion, Stirchley; The Tudor, King's Heath; The Edgbaston, The Royalty, Harbourne; The Warwick, Acock's Green; The Adelphi, Hay Mills; The Tydsley Cinema, The Crown, The Mayfair, Tooting, London; The Regal, Newbury; The Empire, Aldershot; The Regal, Camberley; The Aspley, Nottingham, The Regal, Lichfield; The Bath, Leamington; etc., etc. The whole of the material used in this cinema is of British manufacture throughout. This firm has also been responsible for the installation of modern fire appliances under the guidance of the Evesham fire master.

Projection

The Ernemann projectors installed in this theatre are popularly known in the cinema world as the " Rolls Royce " machine. They are the perfect embodiment of engineering skill, designed on scientific principles which permits the passing of the maximum amount of light whilst the working parts are built of high-grade hardened steel and phosphor bronze bearings. A special feature of this machine is the hard steel ball bearings. Patrons will be interested to know that a patent safety device, which practically does away with danger from fire, is incorporated in the projectors. First in 1896 and still in the lead is the proud boast of the Walturdaw Cinema Supply Co., Ltd., Birmingham, to whom the job of " putting on the picture " was wisely given by Board of Directors.

THE PROPRIETORS OF THIS CINEMA
CAREFULLY CONSIDERED

YOUR HEALTH AND COMFORT

BY INSTALLING OUR PATENT

AIR WASHING, HEATING, COOLING
AND
VENTILATING INSTALLATION

AS INSTALLED IN MOST OF THE LEADING CINEMAS

We Manufacture

- DUCTWORK
- FANS
- VENTILATORS
- CYCLONES
- FILTERS
- TANKS
- DRYING CHAMBERS
- HUMIDIFIERS
- ETC.

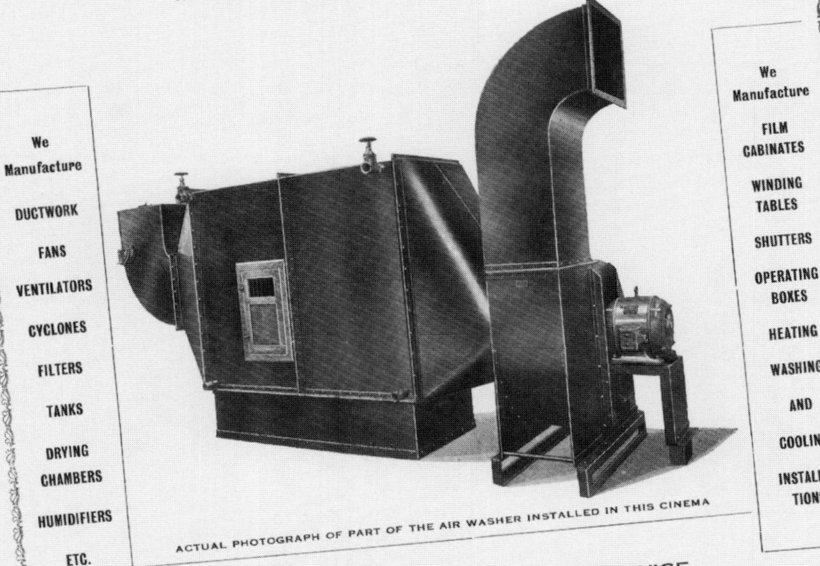

ACTUAL PHOTOGRAPH OF PART OF THE AIR WASHER INSTALLED IN THIS CINEMA

We Manufacture

- FILM CABINATES
- WINDING TABLES
- SHUTTERS
- OPERATING BOXES
- HEATING
- WASHING
- AND
- COOLING
- INSTALLA-TIONS

OUR EXPERIENCE IS AT YOUR SERVICE

THE DENTON SHEETMETAL & ENGINEERING CO.

MOORSIDE WORKS
DENTON, MANCHESTER

TELEPHONE: DENTON 2419

REGAL SUPER CINEMA, EVESHAM

Architect: HURLEY ROBINSON, Esq., F.R.I.B.A.

BRONZE METAL WORK & IRONMONGERY

carried out by

R. S. MACE LIMITED

CHAMBER OF COMMERCE BUILDINGS

NEW STREET, BIRMINGHAM

Telephone—Midland 2509

Telegrams—Macebearer, Birmingham

THE INTERNAL SANITARY PLUMBING, GASFITTING & FIRE APPLIANCES AT THIS THEATRE EXECUTED BY

J. S. WRIGHT & CO.

DALE END ... BIRMINGHAM, 4

SPECIALISTS FOR HEATING, VENTILATING, SANITARY PLUMBING AND FIRE PROTECTION FOR CINEMAS

PHONE { CEN. 1551
SOL. 0281

ALSO MILL LANE
SOLIHULL

F. EVANS & SONS, LTD.

HANDSWORTH, BIRMINGHAM, 19

HEATING SPECIALISTS

Contractors for Central Heating of the Regal Cinema

WE ARE ALWAYS PLEASED TO SUBMIT SCHEMES AND ESTIMATES WITHOUT CHARGE FOR HEATING, VENTILATING AND HOT WATER SUPPLY APPARATUS

PHONE: NORTHERN 1582

ALL CHOCOLATES AND CIGARETTES IN THIS CINEMA SUPPLIED BY

E. J. HAMPTON

High-Class
CHOCOLATES
of all descriptions

Confectioner, Tobacconist
Bookseller & Newsagent

FULL WEIGHT
BOXES
A SPECIALITY

LENDING LIBRARY

36 PORT STREET, EVESHAM

ESTABLISHED QUARTER OF A CENTURY

OPPOSITE THE REGAL SUPER CINEMA

For "EVERYTHING MUSICAL" go to

F. H. ALCOCK LTD.

London House
EVESHAM

Where Satisfaction is Guaranteed

LISTEN

To All Records Played in this Cinema
They are Supplied by F. H. Alcock Ltd.

THE PREMIER HOUSE *for*

PIANOS
WIRELESS
GRAMOPHONES
RADIO-GRAMS, Etc., Etc.

Write or Call for Lists
A Demonstration in Your Home with pleasure

All Instruments on Easy Terms to Suit Your Own Pocket

"PLAY WHILE YOU PAY"

STUBBS

ADJOINING THE "REGAL"

Special Autumn Display

AT NEW PREMISES NOW OPEN

We cordially invite your attendance, and a visit to our New Showroom will amply repay you

COATS GOWNS
MILLINERY

Distinctive and Exclusive numbers only entertained

LUTON HOUSE :: BENGEWORTH

THE WHOLE OF THE CARPETS IN THIS THEATRE
WERE SUPPLIED BY

H. FOWLER & SON

House Furnishers . . . Evesham

WHO SPECIALIZE IN CARPETS
AND ALL FLOOR COVERINGS

EXAMPLES OF VALUES

Axminster Carpets, 3 yards x 3 yards	57/6
Heavy Quality (just reduced in price) 3 yards x 3 yards	99/9

Entire Seating at the . . . Regal Cinema Manufactured and Fitted

by

George Pixton & Co. Ltd.
65 Newman Street
London W.1.

This Programme is Published and Printed by W. & H. Smith Limited, "Journal" Press, Evesham, who specialise in high-class productions of this character.

ENQUIRIES INVITED

THE REGAL
EVESHAM

ARCHITECT:
HURLEY ROBINSON, F.R.I.B.A., A.I.S.E., 6 Cherry Street, Birmingham.

SURVEYOR:
WALTER B. BOND, F.S.I., Newhall Street, Birmingham.

GENERAL CONTRACTORS:
ESPLEY & CO., LTD., Evesham.

SUB-CONTRACTORS:

Collapsible Gate—
ACME METAL WORKS (1921) LTD.,
Great West Road,
Brentford, Middx.

Decorations—
BRYAN'S ADAMANTA, LTD.,
Great Francis Street,
Birmingham.

Heating and Ventilation—
DENTON SHEETMETAL & ENGINEERING CO.,
Moorside Works,
Cricket Street, Denton,
Manchester.

Lighting—
ETNA LIGHTING & HEATING CO.,
275, Broad Street,
Birmingham.

Windows—
HOSKINS & SEWELL, LTD.,
Midland Works,
Bordesley,
Birmingham.

Seats—
GEO. PIXTON & CO., LTD.,
65, Newman Street,
London, W.1.

Artificial Stone Work—
ALLIED ARTS & CRAFTS GUILD,
Guild House,
Tyburn Road,
Erdington, Birmingham.

Sound Apparatus—
WESTERN ELECTRIC CO., LTD.,
Bush House,
London, W.C.2.

Lantern Lights—
WILLIAMS & WILLIAMS, LTD.,
Reliance Works,
Chester.

Projector Equipment—
WALTURDAW,
37, John Bright Street,
Birmingham.

Block Floor—
J. F. EBNER,
Stewart Street,
Cubit Town,
London, E.14.

Heating—
F. EVANS & SONS, LTD.,
219, Heathfield Road,
Handsworth,
Birmingham.

Terrazzo Pavings—
JACCONELLO, LTD.,
Peel Street,
Winson Green,
Birmingham.

Ironmongery—
R. S. MACE, LTD.,
Chamber of Commerce Buildings,
New Street,
Birmingham.

Steelwork—
J. TILDESLEY, LTD.,
Crescent Iron Works,
Darlaston, Lancs.

Exit Staircase—
LOCKERBIE & WILKINSON (TIPTON), LTD.,
Tipton, Staffs.

Handrails—
H. BURLINGHAM & CO., LTD.,
Port Street,
Evesham.

Roof—
G. R. SPEAKER & CO., LTD.,
Eternit House,
Stevenage Road,
Fulham, S.W.6.

Asphalte—
VAL DE TRAVERS, LTD.,
5, Lower Temple Street,
Birmingham.

Gasfitting—
J. S. WRIGHT & CO.,
Dale End,
Birmingham.

Carpets—
H. FOWLER & SON,
High Street,
Evesham.

Uniforms—
ALFRED HAROLD (UNIFORMS) LTD.,
22-22a Water Street,
London, W.

Printed by the " Journal " Press, Swan Lane, Evesham.

Let the fun begin. From l to r: Sydney Hall (Manager), F.M. Stubbs (Director), Victor A. Morrall (Director), Mrs White (Mayoress), J. Wythen Roberts (solicitor), Richard White (Mayor), E.J. Bomford (building contractor), Archibald Hurley Robinson (architect).

With the Union Jack fluttering proudly on top of the new Regal Super Cinema, a small group of well-dressed people gathered to strike a dignified pose for the camera on a quiet Port Street in the late afternoon of 10 October 1932. As the eight individuals stood quietly for this photograph on the new marble steps I am fascinated as to how they might have imagined cinema developing. Whether he realised it or not, the Mayor, Richard White, on declaring the Regal open, became one of the godfathers of Evesham's future entertainment – Vic Morrall being the father, Hurley Robinson the midwife and Sydney Hall the nanny. The film medium was now thirty-six years old, yet talkies were only just out of their infancy. Could they possibly have envisaged the evolution of movies from the clownish antics of Chaplin and Keaton to the pleasant whimsy of 'Robocop', the gentlemanly erudition of Eddie Murphy and the fey coquettishness of Sharon Stone? (Maybe I'm being too facetious. This generation had come through the trenches of the Great War, so perhaps a CGI gorefest like *Starship Troopers* would have seemed small beer.)

Whatever the future held, the compact new picture palace would provide refuge and escapism during a time of world-wide depression. The first night was a sell-out, and was to usher in twenty straight years of highly profitable business. The Regal's new 'sit up and beg' phone tinkled constantly as wealthier customers rang that magic number 2 to reserve tickets.[1]

By 5 p.m. the soon-to-be-familiar queue along Burford Road was approaching two hundred yards in length. Two ultra-smart commissionaires, the new manager in evening dress and a couple of the complement of ten usherettes, in their crisp new uniforms, steadfastly dealt with the surge of bodies in the foyer (or 'crush hall' as it came to be known) as people purchased their tickets and were shown through into the stalls (most of the balcony tickets were pre-booked).

Soon, a steady stream of limousines began arriving. These would park directly outside the cinema, whereby the first commissionaire would stride forward to open the door of each vehicle and escort its occupants up the steps to the beautiful art deco entrance, opened by the second commissionaire, where they were greeted by Sydney Hall. They would then make their way through the milling throng to the balcony steps.[2]

Many of the wealthier customers were the local market garden land barons – the so-called 'cabbage kings' who often resided in the plush houses at the top of town. Very soon, special occasions such as the screening of early blockbusters like *Gone with the Wind* would become labelled 'Green Hill films' because they would attract Evesham's more moneyed denizens, keen to enjoy a night at the flicks in their furs and tuxes. It showed the *status quo* of a generation: the nobs in the gods and the hoi polloi in the cheap seats. No one seemed to object.

The original ticket kiosk was tucked away to the right of the front doors in the space which would eventually be occupied by the sweet counter. For the first few years all joob-joobs came from the nearby Hamptons store and were sold from a tray into which was harnessed a young lad known as 'the chocolate boy'. Now there's a job title no one would own up to nowadays. In 2008, such a post would be called a 'mobile confectionary dispersal engineer'.

1 The Regal's phone number eventually became 6002 then 446002.

2 If the upper deck was ever fully booked, the best seats in the stalls could be reserved.

With the attendance touching four figures, it was down to the local bigwigs to herald the occasion. The *Evesham Journal* reported the grand event as follows:

The quiet dignity and useful appearance of the theatre must make a universal appeal. There is nothing that is ornate or superfluous in the erection inside or out and while the modern tendency in architecture has been exploited in many instances, the ultra-modern is fortunately lacking.

Inside, the building is delightfully decorated and radiating comfort and cleanliness. The screen is so placed as to ensure everyone an uninterrupted view and the talking apparatus is noteworthy for the clarity of its reproduction and elimination of mechanical noises. These and many other excellent features were noted and favourably commented upon by the big gathering at the opening ceremony and initial performance which was presided over by Mr J. Wythen Roberts. Supporting Mr Roberts were: The Mayor and Mayoress of Evesham (Councillor Richard and Mrs White), Messrs S. Hall, V.A. Morrall, H.T. Hodgkinson and H.F. King (directors), Mr Hurley Robinson (architect) and Mr E.J. Bomford (representing Messrs Espley and Co. Ltd.).

Mr Roberts said he was honoured by the invitation made to him to preside over that somewhat vast assembly and on their behalf he welcomed the Mayor and Mayoress (APPLAUSE).

It was not intended that the opening of the theatre demanded or warranted a full civic ceremony but at the same time it was such a unique occasion for Bengeworth and, in fact, for the whole town of Evesham that they thought it only proper they should ask the Mayor, in his official capacity to declare it open.

On the platform were the directors and some of those who had taken an important part in the erection of the building. He thought he could say they comprised the principal conspirators (LAUGHTER). The building was the outcome of the genius of Mr Hurley Robinson, the Birmingham architect (APPLAUSE) and it was mainly erected by the well-known firm of Espley and Co., represented by Mr E.J. Bomford (APPLAUSE).

The reason for the erection of the theatre was that the directors had been convinced for a long time that in the growing Evesham district – not only the town itself, but the wide district outside the town – there was an increasing number of picture 'fans'. Consequently, they considered themselves justified in making the venture. The theatre itself was very comfortable and every modern device had been incorporated in its construction. He (Mr Roberts) wanted to make it clear that the directors had no ulterior motive whatever for building the cinema. From their point of view it was purely a business transaction. They believed there was a demand for it and they set out to supply that demand just as if some person came into town to open a new shop. The effect of opening a new shop was that it was bound to cause some rivalry with other shop-keepers in the same trade and in the same way the opening of the Regal would also cause some rivalry. But he wished it to be distinctly understood that the directors and management wanted that rivalry – such as it was – to be of the friendliest character (APPLAUSE).

The Mayor spoke of the rapid growth of the Borough of Evesham, especially on the Bengeworth side of the river, within the last few years and he congratulated the directors of the theatre on their spirit of enterprise. There was a genuine need for a place of entertainment in Bengeworth. He expressed the hope that those people in Evesham and district who previously went to other towns in search of entertainment would patronise the amusements of their own town and he also mentioned the indirect help which would accrue to business people generally as the result of the theatre being erected. In declaring the Regal Cinema open, the Mayor commented upon the excellence of its design and decoration.

A bouquet was presented to the Mayoress by little Christine Knight. Mr Roberts thanked the Mayor for performing the ceremony and stated that the directors wished to mark the occasion by subscribing the sum of £25 for division between two outstanding Evesham charitable institutions – the Hospital and the Boys' Club (LOUD APPLAUSE). He asked the Mayor to accept the cheques for presentation to those two institutions. The Mayor thanked the directors and said how grateful the institutions would be.

Finally, when all the hot air was expelled, the dignitaries removed to their allocated spaces in the balcony, lit cigars and nestled their well-tailored behinds into virgin red-velveteen-upholstered seats.

The excited chatter subsided as the lights dimmed, the elegant curtains unhurriedly opened and one of the mighty Ernemanns began to roll, illuminating the brilliant white, twenty-four-foot screen. A thousand riveted yokels witnessed the Theatre of Dreams' first offerings.

The *Evesham Journal* described the opening programme:

A splendid feature film was chosen to set the ball rolling at the Regal. This was The Silent Voice *in which that great actor George Arliss gives a masterful interpretation of a great musician who, at the height of a brilliant career, loses his hearing and is flung into the depths of despair. He challenges the very existence of a merciful God and when he is on the verge of suicide, he is brought to a new way of thinking and great happiness. The story is original and clever. There is a wealth of wholesome sentiment without a suggestion of sloppiness and a moral which could not fail to get home. Supporting Arliss is a brilliant cast which includes Ivan Simpson. Simpson plays the part of gentleman servant to Arliss and this he does to perfection. Contrast of charm is to be found in Bette Davis as Grace, a young girl who believed she was in love with the musician, and Violet Hemming [no relation, honest! Rob H.] as Mildred, a widow. The film throws a spotlight on many aspects of human nature, but it is commendable that, for once in a while, these differences are merely differences of virtue and only that which is noble in man is portrayed. On the same programme was an English film entitled* A Voice Said Goodnight, *an ingenious murder mystery which is solved in a most unexpected manner. The acting in this picture is excellent and the River Thames near Teddington makes a perfect setting to the story.*

Jonathan Ross eat your heart out.

Over at the Scala, manager Frank Ridge paced the aisles nervously as the two cinemas began their forty-eight-year rivalry.

1936 cover of Film Pictorial, *featuring Gary Cooper*

British Lion
PRESENTS
NOEL COWARD'S
"IN WHICH WE SERVE"
Directed by NOEL COWARD & DAVID LEAN
Photographed by RONALD NEAME
A TWO CITIES FILM
NOEL COWARD · JOHN MILLS
BERNARD MILES · CELIA JOHNSON
JOYCE CAREY · KAY WALSH

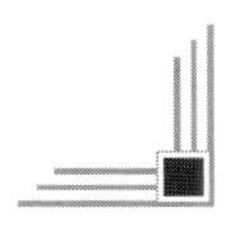

CHAPTER THREE

A GOLD MINE IN THE DEPRESSION

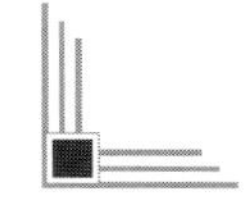

The ambitious Sydney Hall

The Theatre of Dreams at 41 Port Street settled into its highly profitable routine of entertaining almost ten thousand people a week in the course of ten full shows every seven days. It was managed for the first two years by Sydney Hall from Manchester whose family had been steeped in the cinema business since it first appeared at the turn of the century. Sydney's father owned several cinemas and as expected his two sons became involved.

First man in the hot seat.

In 1916, with World War I raging, the seventeen-year-old Sydney joined the Merchant Navy on a four-year apprenticeship. He returned to Manchester in 1920, his management and technical skills enhanced, to help run the family cinema chain. All was well until around 1930 when friction grew between the two siblings. With the advent of talking movies the two brothers had a major disagreement over which of the early sound systems would be suitable. So Sydney chose to broaden his horizons in the industry by leaving the family business and seeking management positions outside his home town. He finally arrived in Evesham where, impressed by his credentials, Vic Morrall offered him the skipper's job at the new Regal, along with shares and a directorship.[1]

The publicity photograph of the baby-faced Sydney, all Brylcreem-plastered hair and Arthur Askey specs, may make him look like some antediluvian Harry Potter but it belies the fact that he was a very professional man who ran the Regal like clockwork. However, he was also a very ambitious man who longed for his own picture palace.

By 1934 he had acquired sufficient finance to strike out on his own and build the New Cinema in Chipping Norton (later re-named the Ritz). Here he raised a family and became friends with George Arliss, ironically the first face ever to appear on the Regal screen in a major film, *The Silent Voice*. Despite the supercilious Kenneth Williams appearance, Arliss was a brilliant and respected actor in his day. Nicknamed 'the first gentleman of the screen', he made a successful transition from stage to silent screen to talkies, for which he won the 1929 Best Actor Oscar for his portrayal of Disraeli. He retired in 1937. Nowadays only dedicated film fans have heard of George Arliss. However, his co-star in *The Silent Voice*, Bette Davis, went on to become one of the most famous actresses of all time.

George Arliss. First face on the Regal screen.

1 His shares eventually passed on to his daughter Jane Peatfield but Sydney remained a Regal director until his death in 1981.

1934 Regal staff. Back row, l–r: Cynthia Wilson, Hilda Bandy, Iris Sale.
Front row, l–r: Barbara Dolphin, Elsie Williams, Frank Ridge, Mary Majors, Queenie Hale.

The genial Frank Ridge

By 1934 the Scala cinema was over ten years old and having had no refurbishment during that time, the huge smoky audiences of the period were taking their toll on the interior. It was now definitely the poor relation in Evesham's cinema rivalry and less charitable movie-goers gave it the moniker 'the old bug and scratch'. Therefore, it must have been particularly galling for the directors when Frank Ridge jumped ship to take over at their Port Street rivals. By all accounts, Vic Morrall didn't 'poach' him; more likely Ridge, as a proud pro, wanted the best in town and if the Scala bosses weren't willing to re-vamp their cinema, he seized his opportunity.

Like his predecessor, Frank Ridge was a dyed-in-the-wool cinema man and his move to Port Street meant that he was the only person to manage the Grand, Scala and Regal. Originally from Cardiff, he became a popular figure in town – the term genial often being used to describe him. He lived in Lime Street and would always wear a navy pin-stripe suit until the late programme when he would change to evening dress, his huge smile warming the customers as they surged in. He had the eccentric though endearing habit of gripping his lapels while holding forth on cinema matters, like some beaming statesman.

The classic staff photograph taken in 1934 on the middle landing outside the café soon after Frank's arrival gives one an indication of his personality. This is a man happy in his profession, a blend of Mr Micawber and Captain Peacock from *Are You Being Served?* while his seven usherettes exhibit the high standards of the time and the pride inherent in the industry. Their uniforms are green with gold braid trim and gold buttons. The manager would inspect his staff every day prior to opening time. All shoes had to be polished and any usherette with a button missing had to find a needle and thread, sharpish-like. They displayed exemplary manners to the customers in a time when such niceties were *de rigueur*. Frank was addressed as 'Mr Ridge' and he reciprocated formally with 'Miss' plus surname. Politeness was everything. What bliss.

On the far right of the back row is a young lady still some weeks shy of her fifteenth birthday, who was to spend more time at the Regal than any other person. Iris Sale (later to become Iris Jordan) began and ended her working life in the Port Street palace.[2] From 1934 to 1986 (with a break of about ten years after the war to raise a family) she would take the short walk from No. 9 Burford Road and has become something of a local legend. By the early sixties, she had gained the affectionate title 'Auntie Iris' from all the children who ever attended Saturday morning pictures and she came to exemplify the image of the Regal as a family place more than anyone.

John Hack: first spinner of celluloid

The first projectionists (or 'operators') in these heady days were John Hack (No. 1) and Alec Grant (No. 2).

Hack was yet another lifelong cinema man, having learnt his trade in Cheltenham alongside his brother. He was a quiet, systematic character, a stickler for routine and yet innovative – he knew the tricks of his trade. For example, the original proscenium arch was illuminated by a series of evenly spaced plain light bulbs (courtesy of Dilworth's) which John covered

2 The working hours for usherettes in 1934 were fairly strenuous but the pay good. For a six-day week of up to ten-hour days (approx. 1–11 p.m.) fourteen-year-old Iris Sale received 18/10d (94p!) which was actually higher than some of the local factory wages.

in various hues of cellophane to add a little colour. He would construct advertising features, such as the large wooden cross, again festooned with flashing cellophaned bulbs, that was used to draw in the customers to see one of the most controversial films of the early thirties, *Sign of the Cross.* One of Hack's cleverest tricks was to produce colour images on the screen showing a black and white film, using an ingenious little device which consisted of no more than a 12" × 4" strip of card with its centre cut out and replaced by three strips of cellophane, coloured amber, red and green. This could be moved back and forth through the gap between the running film and the flicker blade, giving the effect of background colour. Obviously it could only be used for the credits because it couldn't differentiate subtle colour changes as the action began, but in the 1920s and 1930s, where colour film meant extremely rare duo-chrome efforts, Hack's little idea was appreciated. Another innovation, particularly valuable during the war, when everything became scarce, was to re-charge the usherettes' torch batteries by connecting them, in some fiendishly clever way, to the house electricity supply. No question, John Hack was a useful fellow to have around.

A self-contained business

The self-contained family atmosphere of the Regal established itself immediately because almost every job was done in-house – from cleaning, and prepping films to maintenance, carpentry, painting and electrics, or even running errands for the directors. The daily routine kicked off around 9.30 a.m. and at 11 a.m. most staff would take a late breakfast, which would consist of tea and buns from the baker's next door. A Mrs Buxton set the standard for dedication to duty by scrubbing the marble steps from balcony to pavement every morning with pumice powder. Besides having to be the best-dressed man in town and learn how to touch his forelock, the commissionaire was required to keep the boiler filled with coke and monitor the heating system.

The hairiest job was changing light bulbs in the big octagonal house lights. This was done by the projectionists and involved gingerly negotiating the walkways inside the ceiling (accessible through a gable hatch opening onto the flat part of the roof) and leaning down into the light housings from above. Unbeknown to many, the panels of these were made of cellophane and not glass.

By 1936 the toilet walls were inevitably festooned with imaginative artwork and poetry, so the most junior member of the projection crew was dispatched with a six-inch brush and two gallons of jet black paint to cover the offensive hieroglyphics. It didn't help for long: crafty Kilroy abandoned his pencil and brought along a penknife instead.

One of the maintenance bugbears was a consequence of Hurley Robinson's lower-deck 'dish' design. The front few rows of seats in the stalls were angled backwards by some twenty degrees, their thin curved plywood backs therefore being put under strain by the greater proportion of bodyweight rammed against it. Every week some would have sagged or split and would have to be constantly re-secured with longer and longer screws.

If repairs couldn't be managed in-house there was usually some local business that could assist, such as Burlingham's, who would immediately dispatch their blacksmith if the boiler broke down. Equally important was the extractor fan which had to deal with the cigarette smoke from hundreds of parched throats. It did this by drawing the smoke through dozens of holes located around the proscenium arch where it was sprayed with fine jets of water and expelled into Burford Road.

Two jobs which needed the attention of specialist outside firms were the maintenance of the sound system by Western Electric and the cleaning of the screen curtains. These would accumulate so much dust from the smoky atmosphere, it could muffle the speakers behind the screen. The curtains were considered such a fire risk they required their own safety certificate. Modern multi-screen complexes have foregone the use of curtains (or 'tabs' as they were known in the trade), which is a shame. The one thing which stoked up excitement at the start of a movie, when the lights dimmed, was the faint whirr of a motor as the big drapes parted and the screen sprang to life. (You still get this twinge of excitement at the theatre, opera or wherever there is a curtained stage.)

Spick and span

The unsung heroines of the Regal were the usherettes, who had to handle the masses every day. Besides looking pretty and selling ice cream, at the end of the evening show they were required to clean up after a thousand people. They became accustomed to dealing with the usual detritus, but must have held a special dread for Friday nights during the 1930s and 1940s. Opposite the Regal, local butcher John Wheatley owned a shop where he would cook up the week's leftovers, such tit-bits as pigs' feet, cow heels, chitlins plus other visceral goodies, and sell them in greaseproof paper. A couple of hundred film fans would gnaw on these barnyard delicacies while gawking at Hollywood, before dumping the bones, gristle, fat and paper on the carpet. The poor usherettes must have thought they were cleaning out a charnel house.

I always remember this story when I'm at the pictures suffering taut nerves from the slurping/crackling/munching noises of gluttonous lard-arses who regard the modern cinema as a restaurant. These days, Joe Public is ONLY able to consume foot-long hot dogs, giant drums of popcorn, sackfuls of pick 'n' mix and gallon buckets of Coke instead of trotters, offal and fags. So I try to convince myself that times have changed for the better. It doesn't always work.

Usherettes in summer uniform on the roof fire escape c.1937. L–r: Queenie Hale, Mary Majors, Dorothy Heritage, Iris Sale, Cynthia Wilson.

Once the cleaning was finished, somewhere between 10.30 and 11.30 p.m., the staff would wrap up the evening with a little rota of chores: (a) check that the toilets were empty and all windows locked, (b) check for potential fire hazards, (c) turn out the gas pilot lights (these were the emergency lighting if the electric failed), (d) damp down the boiler, (e) lock the projection room, (f) water the three aspidistras on the first landing, (g) bring in the two bay trees from the pavement, (h) if the film programme was to change the following day, alter all posters and photographs in the outside display cases, (i) set up the steel security gates across the entrance, and (j) before locking these gates, turn off the main switch.

Finally, everyone could go home, although, popular as he was with his staff, Frank Ridge did have the annoying habit of sometimes talking shop long after closing time and keeping the projectionists hanging about. This mainly happened at the end of Frank's one night off per week when he would return from Cheltenham, full of Guinness and bonhomie, to check that the Regal was still in one piece. A true cinema junkie.

The way to the stars.

The projectionists' story

Like the cockpit of an aircraft, the projection room had a fascination for many people, who would request a visit to the 'flight deck' to see where the magic movies came from. I have the overriding regret that I never visited the Regal 'box' while a film was running. As a child I envisaged it as some kind of Frankenstein's laboratory – all flashing lights, crashing music and arcing electricity. Yet it was a sedate place, where film flickered through the projectors at a constant twenty-four frames per second and a calm demeanour was called for, not some manic baron harnessing the lightning. The people who worked there were the true back-room boys who made it happen, a mixture of engineer and nerd.

Behind the mysterious door saying 'Projection Area. No Thoroughfare' at the rear of the balcony was a flight of steps which led up to four rooms on the top storey of the building. The main room (about 15′ × 12′) housed the Ernemanns projectors (prior to 1947) which pointed downwards at around thirty degrees through two fifteen-inch-square holes in the rear of the balcony wall. These German machines were generally regarded as the best available in the pre-war period, extremely reliable and easy to maintain.

In the early days, films would be transported to and from the Birmingham regional studio offices three times a week by Regal director Ernie Evans. Usually, the lowest bods in the operators' hierarchy, the No. 3 and the 're-wind boy', would bring up the big flat zinc canisters (or 'tins') of film (perhaps a dozen, weighing 10–15 lb each) and the others would set to winding it onto the spools[3] in a small ante-room adjacent to the main box.

Each tin contained a section of film which would have to be joined (or 'spliced') onto the next in the correct running order. Each of the two projector spools could accommodate just over twelve thousand feet of film. At sixteen frames per foot, eighteen inches of celluloid was required to give you the twenty-four frames needed for one second of film. Each zinc tin contained around eighteen hundred feet of film (twenty minutes' worth). Therefore six or possibly seven tins could be spliced together at any one time, giving a continuous running time in excess of two hours before a fresh spool of film had to be installed. This would be ample for either a combination of news, adverts plus the supporting film or the whole of the

3 A procedure which the projectionists called 'lacing up'.

main feature. Not many films before the war had a running time in excess of two hours but if they did there would be an intermission, in which the projectionist could change to a freshly prepared spool (in later years the capacity of projector spools was greatly increased).

The term 'splicing' refers to the connecting of two reels of film by means of a small device which would literally weld the final frame of an outgoing reel to the first frame of an incoming one. One of the great nightmares of the projectionist was the breaking of an inadequate splice during a film. The image on the screen would disappear and a chorus of boos echo forth from the disgruntled audience. The back-room boys would scramble like Battle of Britain pilots, feverishly re-connecting the celluloid before they felt the manager's hot breath on the backs of their necks.

A far worse nightmare, however, was the connecting of reels in the wrong order. Film fans have, in their time, witnessed such anomalies as outlaws being shot dead only to be riding into Dodge the next minute, or whodunnits revealed before they did it (on a really bad day even the *Titanic* could have a happier ending). Mercifully, though, incompetent continuity was an extremely rare occurrence and all Regal films that I watched appeared seamless.

When the Regal programme changed (usually on Thursday, Sunday and Monday) all the film from the previous show would be cut down into roughly twenty-minute reels, 're-tinned' and swapped with Ernie Evans' latest acquisitions from Birmingham.

Before a day's performances began, the back-room boys had to make a sound-check, which meant ensuring all the speakers were working and that the volume was estimated at the correct level. Sound levels could vary greatly depending on the size of the audience, or even the weather – one thousand customers sitting in damp raincoats would muffle the sound far more than five hundred in light summer clothes. So, occasionally, adjustments had to be made early on in the film, depending on 'prevailing conditions'. There were buttons on both decks which rang a buzzer in the projection room if Frank Ridge wanted the sound altered. One short buzz would mean turn up the volume and two buzzes meant reduce it. A long continuous buzz would indicate a problem – such as the sound having gone off completely. The good operator soon learned to suss the acoustics without any need for juggling.

In order to project the image from such a small, densely detailed origin as a frame of film onto a screen of almost three hundred square feet a very bright light was required in the projector. The source of this was the highly efficient carbon arc lamp, a smaller version of that used in World War II searchlights. An arc of electricity is passed between two carbon electrodes set a specific distance apart against a reflecting mirror. The operator had to adjust the gap between the anode and cathode as they burnt away (a process known as 'feeding in') in order to keep the light constant. The reflected light would then go through a condenser, the film, the lens and onto the screen. The arcs required 100 volt direct current which was supplied by a device called a Mercury arc rectifier, housed in one of the smaller rooms next to the main projection room, which converted the 240 volt AC/DC house supply for the purpose. The rectifier had four switches which were turned one at a time gradually raising the ampage to the required power level.

The No. 1 projectionist had virtual control of the whole circus: the lights, the curtains, the sounds and the images.[4] Vic Morrall may have been the owner and Frank Ridge the manager, but John Hack was the guv'nor.

The major concern in the projectionists' box before the 1950s was fire risk from the actual film. Since the beginning of cinema, film stocks had been cellulose nitrate (nitrate-based celluloid) which was highly inflammable. Obviously with this material running through a projector using the intense heat of a carbon arc lamp, the back-room boys had to be on their guard, therefore the regulations required two projectionists to be in attendance at all times. The third-string operator and the re-wind boy allowed for flexibility in case of illness. The Theatre of Dreams never suffered a catastrophic fire but there were a few hairy moments when projectionists allowed themselves to be drawn into watching the movie through the observation portal as the nitrate film began smoking nicely. Their nose usually came to the rescue in the nick of time. Early in the 1940s, however, a gradual change to cellulose acetate 'safety' film (acetate-based celluloid) was under way and by the middle of the decade further refinement to the chemical base of film was achieved. But with this increased safety came drawbacks. Acetate film was subject to a greater degree of shrinkage which caused problems in printing and projection; it also had less resistance to tearing than nitrate-based celluloid and frequently broke during handling. Early acetate film was also more temperamental when being spliced, unlike the dangerous nitrate[5] stock whose low melting point allowed for an easy melding of film. However, by 1950 the industry finally got the chemistry right and introduced 'triacetate' film which had similar physical properties to nitrate but without the danger, thus cinemas benefited from reduced fire insurance as well as more user-friendly material.

Decomposing nitrate film.

Triacetate film was eventually replaced by the much thinner, stronger polyester film which is still used today but will inevitably soon be superseded by digital technology. The old-style projectors will become obsolete as pictures are delivered by laser from a disc similar to a home DVD.

There was one other device in the projectionists' domain: the slide projector, or 'epidiascope', which was connected to the side of one of the Ernemanns. This could be used for local advertising or static public messages such as warning the

4 One thing the projectionist had no say in was when an intermission could be called during a long movie. This was designated purely at the discretion of the film's director.

5 When the early nitrate films began wearing out or decomposing they were removed to the 'film dump' in Birmingham which was simply a patch of waste ground surrounded by a high corrugated iron fence.

war-time audience that the air-raid sirens had just sounded or that someone had left the crank handle in the front of their car. Also, personalised messages like birthday wishes or gooey stuff from courting couples could be beamed onto the screen during breaks in the programme. The slides used were walpamure-coated celluloid with the message scratched on. All the operator needed was legible handwriting.

Everything shown on the big screen, whether movies, news, adverts or slide messages, had to be recorded by the projectionists on a Performing Rights Sheet to keep the Regal on the rosy side of the then licensing, copyright and cinematography laws. This also applied to any music which came out of the speakers from the projection box record player. The sounds of the day have traditionally been played before the start of a programme or during an intermission, and for years the Regal borrowed records from Alcock's[6] music store in return for free screen advertising.

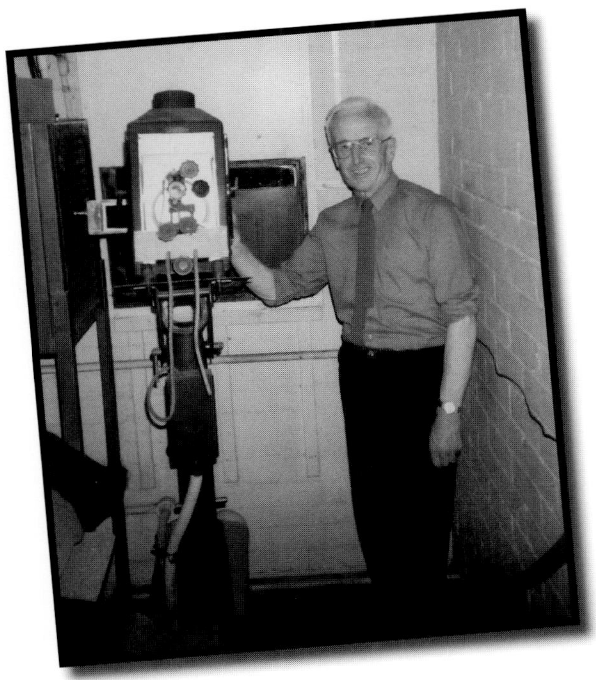

The slide projector or 'epidiascope' has remained in place throughout the entire life of the cinema. Here, projectionist David Stride is giving it a go in the 1990s.

A popular item on a Sunday afternoon was the music request slot which had locals dedicating songs to their loved-ones (sometimes accompanying a slide show) as a prelude to the films.

Radetsky Ridge

Manager Frank Ridge was a fan of marching music. Anything remotely military with a clompety-clomp beat would stir his blood and he believed it would induce a sense of excitement in the customers as they waited for their movie. Once, it was very nearly his undoing. Frank wasn't keen on the popular music of the 1930s; he thought jazz was decadent and unmanly and that the balladeers of the day warbled hogwash. Fair enough, but Ridge was not averse to telling the projectionists to change the record halfway through and put on something with a "bit more guts to it". One time in 1936, as Gracie Fields was beguiling a packed Regal, the manager stuck his head round the projection room door and told his staff to "take that rubbish off and put on something more exciting". John Hack knew the drill, so with a short screech of the needle, Rochdale's own vanished into the ether and the audience began to boo. By the time Frank Ridge had walked down to the stalls he was smiling, as the strains of Johann Strauss's *Radetsky March* echoed round the Theatre of Dreams. However, a thousand customers were going to make him pay for giving Gracie the bum's rush.

6 When Alcock's store closed, records were borrowed from Woolworth's.

Initially, Frank delighted in the reaction to a piece of music which would become a Proms 'clap-along' favourite but he was soon to receive a salutary lesson in the dangers of audience participation. Nearly a thousand people began stomping their feet in time to Johann's mean beat: Da da STOMP! Da Da STOMP! Da Da STOMP! STOMP! STOMP!

Frank Ridge felt a cold sweat break out as he looked up at the balcony vibrating like a bowstring, fine streams of dust issuing from its underside onto the heads of the people in the stalls. The world seemed to be now in agreement with Frank that marches were GREAT! He heard a structural groan as the giant supporting girder came under its severest ever test and when the plaster began to split, Ridge took to his heels like a jack rabbit. The portly manager rocketed up those stairs faster than Jesse Owens, setting the all-time Regal record for reaching the projection box from the stalls while wearing a tuxedo. He burst in pleading: "Turn it off, turn it off! Before they bring the bloody house down" – and with a short screech of the needle, Vienna's favourite son vanished into the ether to be replaced by our Gracie, which made the audience boo louder than ever. But their feet were stilled. The projection room staff stood in astonishment at the spectacle of Frank Ridge, marching fiend, bent double and gasping for oxygen, with his bow tie dangling from his neck like a dead bat.

Spiderman

The wonderful Bob Webb, who passed away in February 2008 at the age of eighty-nine, was one of those people who belied the accepted wisdom that age is something to be feared. A most intelligent and engaging gentleman, without whose input (stories, photographs, technical details) there would be a yawning chasm where chapters three, four and five should be.

Of all the denizens of the Theatre of Dreams, none has a more interesting tale than the man they nicknamed 'Spider'. Bob Webb grew up in Hampton and was a fine scholar, but forewent the chance of higher education, much to the annoyance of his parents, preferring instead to get out into the workplace and make a living. He agreed a compromise with his parents that he would attend night school from the age of twelve to fourteen while working as an errand boy for Mr Stubbs, a Regal director who owned both a clothes shop next to the cinema and a hotel on Green Hill.

In 1935, the sixteen-year-old Webb secured the job of 're-wind boy' at the Regal under John Hack's charge. The glitz and glamour of cinema's golden age soon grabbed him and for weeks he diligently carried out his duties rewinding the used films from the projector spools and cutting them at suitable lengths to be 're-tinned' and sent back to the studios. But, no way would this modest occupation satisfy him. He longed to work on the Ernemanns and asked the No. 1 if he could learn how to run them. This was a wholly reasonable request but John Hack turned him down flat. Hack's problem was that, despite being a highly competent operator himself, he was naturally guarded and had that dread of the 'new broom' – the young hotshot in the firm who is after your job. It was a dreadfully narrow attitude but in Hack's defence, he did have a point, because the young Webb was a particularly bright boy.

Bob refused to be put off and pleaded with No. 2, Alec Grant, for some tuition. Grant was more forthcoming and began showing him the ropes on John Hack's day off. Alas, the No. 1 came in one time unannounced, found his re-wind boy splicing the highly inflammable nitrate film prior to 'lacing up' (loading the projector) and called an immediate halt.

With aspirations flattened, Bob explained the dilemma to his father, who was still smarting over junior's decision to quit full-time education. Webb senior saw red, marched into the projection room and gave John Hack both barrels. The very next shift, the re-wind boy began training on the Ernemanns. He was a fast learner, pretty much had the job taped within a week, and moved up to the now vacant No. 3 slot.

Spider only had one serious glitch. As a young man enthralled by Hollywood he was prone to getting absorbed in the movie he was running. While glued to the inspection window, watching an old RKO film *The Lost Patrol* (about a British army platoon lost in the desert) Bob began to marvel at the lingering scene of the dazzling sun reflecting off the sand. His reverie was interrupted as the full house became restless and he was aware of John Hack's hot breath on his neck. The film had broken a minute previously and the dazzling sun was merely the light from the carbon arc lamp shining on the blank screen.

Nonetheless, John Hack recognised young Webb's abilities and was sad to see him depart in 1937 for a better-paid projectionist's job at the Scala.

A few months later, a chance meeting with John Hack saw Spider return to the Theatre of Dreams. The No. 2 post became available as Alec Grant had moved on and John asked Bob to apply for it. With the Scala due to undergo extensive refurbishment, there was a good chance Webb would be out of work for several months, so it was back to Port Street. With his technical abilities honed on the Scala's contrasting 'Kalee' equipment, the Regal directors were pleased to poach Bob back from their rival and offered him increased wages plus a guaranteed yearly pay rise.

Besides spinning movies, he would find himself doing much practical work around the place, such as converting the original ticket-office into a sweet kiosk[7] and even moonlighting for Vic Morrall by renovating the owner's dining-room. Bob began courting usherette Cynthia Wilson, got himself a pad (over the Port Street Milk Bar) and life was real sweet. Then along came Hitler.

In late 1939 Spider joined the Royal Navy and proceeded to live the type of war story which Nicholas Monsarrat would have been overjoyed to write (his novel *The Cruel Sea* was made into the famous 1953 film starring Jack Hawkins).

Bob was first drafted to the destroyer HMS *Scimitar*, which made six return trips to Dunkirk, rescuing 2,716 soldiers, before serving eighteen months of Atlantic convoy service.

In 1942 he trained in submarine detection (asdics) before joining the destroyer HMS *Quenton* on which he saw his finest hour. As Able Seaman Webb, he detected a U-boat from an asdic sounding, advised the bridge, and the *Quenton* proceeded to sink it. Bob was awarded the DSM for his outstanding skill and devotion to duty. Jack Hawkins eat your heart out.

The rest of Bob's war was no less adventurous. HMS *Quenton* was sunk under him by aerial torpedo but nothing was going to stop him getting back to England in 1943 to marry his beloved Cynthia. Returning to service, Bob joined HMS *Hydrangea* and undertook months more of Atlantic convoy duties.

7 This effectively eliminated the need for the 'chocolate boy'.

On shore leave in the West African town of Takoradi (Ghana) his old cinema skills came into their own. While taking in a movie at a services' cinema, Bob became increasingly agitated by what those in the trade call 'a ghost on the film'. This is when one or more white lines persistently waver from top to bottom on the picture. They occur if the projector flicker blade is out of sync with the intermittent motion (a sprocket which pulls the film through the projector). After a while, he could stand it no longer, marched into the projection area, told them who he was and pleaded with the operator to let him fix the mess on the screen. Synchronisation took all of five minutes.

As the war came to an end and cinema men like Bob Webb, DSM, who had been at the sharp end of the conflict, returned to their old jobs in the projection box, they must have enjoyed many a wry chuckle day after day watching Errol Flynn liberate Burma and John Wayne single-handedly take Guadalcanal. I guess that's showbiz.

In the 1930s it was a safe bet that almost all cinemas were doing a roaring trade. They were number one option in the limited possibilities for passive entertainment and many individuals would spend their hard-earned money at the pictures maybe three, four, or five times a week. Every week. Before the war the Regal was definitely top dog in the rivalry with the Scala. It had established an identity as 'the people's cinema', personal, warm, exciting, the place everyone wanted to go. Like Baby Bear's porridge, the Theatre of Dreams was just right.

Birth of the Clifton

After fifteen years of continuous use, the Scala was badly in need of refurbishment and came to the attention of cinema chain owner, Lord Clift, who snapped it up. Soon, the Scala was no more, as it underwent rebirth as part of the Clift dynasty. From May to November 1938 the entire interior plus the High Street façade was re-built and on Guy Fawkes night local MP Rupert de la Bere presided over its opening ceremony.

ADVERTISEMENTS 11F

THE CLIFTON CINEMA
in the HIGH STREET, EVESHAM

Continuous. Week-days 2—10 p.m.
SUNDAYS 3.30 till 9 p.m.
The premier and still the best house for entertainment. Where you are always sure of a good show. Recently rebuilt and modernised and now replete with every convenience. Earphones.

The new 'Clifton' was certainly impressive and in terms of location, space, access and equipment it probably had the edge on the Regal, its design being more in keeping with a big city picture palace than a small market town flicks. Its greatest advantage over the Theatre of Dreams, however, was the fact that it had now become part of a chain and would, therefore, have more clout when it came to booking the choicest films of the day on initial release. So, once more, game on.

I doubt that Vic Morrall and his co-directors were overly worried about the Clifton's impact on Regal takings during this time because the popularity of movies was at an all-time high. It was the golden age of the industry and besides, with dreadful events happening in Europe, cinema proprietors were probably more concerned over the possibility that the glitz of Hollywood would soon be replaced by ghastly Aryan propaganda films, if Adolf reached these shores.

4F
ADVERTISEMENTS
EVESHAM'S LEADING SUPER CINEMA
REGAL
The Cinema for Consistently Good Entertainment
Continuous Daily 2 till 10 p.m.
Sunday 3.30 till 9 p.m.
THE HOUSE OF COMFORT
COSY IN WINTER
COOL IN SUMMER

The Regal and new Clifton in 1939. Rivalry resumes.

SMOK

CHAPTER FOUR

OH, WHAT A LOVELY WAR!

It's one of the clichéd laws of showbiz that when times get tough, entertainment gets sloppy, so what with the depression then the war and its aftermath, times had got very tough indeed for a lot of people. Hemmed in by their lives, people needed to be reassured, to feel safe again, so they clung tightly to each other in the dark of dance-halls, or more comfortably, in the dark of the local picture house.

From the 1930s on, entertainment became bogged down in the Palais age – the golden era of the big bands and Fred Astaire musicals when everything was soft, warm, sentimental. The people needed make-believe like never before.

In the cinema, by 1934 the censors had clamped down on the more 'adventurous' proclivities of film makers (explained fully in Chapter Six) and with a few hard-hitting exceptions like *Angels with Dirty Faces* (1938), *Gone with the Wind* (1939), *The Grapes of Wrath* (1940) and *Citizen Kane* (1941) films were, for the most part, soft and safe and nothing to fret about. So, courtesy of the Wall Street crash, the censors and Herr Hitler, Evesham folk crammed into the Regal every night to lose themselves with Fred and Ginger, Laurel and Hardy, the Marx Brothers, Abbot and Costello or Hope and Crosby in the *Road to...* movies. The Theatre of Dreams was never more important than between 1939 and 1945, as people would seek escape there several times a week. Vic Morrall and his co-directors were coining it in.

To emphasise this notion of 'soft' entertainment, in 1941, Britain's darkest hour, the Regal screened a children's film of unbelievable sentimentality, *God Gave Him a Dog*. Forget about *Boystown* or *Mrs Miniver*, this avalanche of Hollywood slush had four hundred teenies, including my father, desperately ripping off their gas masks[1] to prevent themselves drowning in their own blub. It gets Dad's vote as the saddest film of all time.

Hear all about it!

Alongside the escapism, people in the provinces needed to be informed as to the progress of the war and without the window provided by newspapers, nightly radio broadcasts and the cinema newsreels, people would have been shuddering in the dark, awaiting the sound of jackboots. More than ten years before the advent of television, the Regal (and Clifton) gave Evesham people their only live-action glimpse of the carnage happening in the wider world. The jingoistic tones of commentators such as Bob Danvers-Walker expressed a carefully tailored optimism which kept the people onside, but if the truth about

1 Considering the amount of cigarette smoke swirling around the Regal for decades I'm surprised that gas masks didn't become a standard fixture during peacetime.

Michael J Barnard
FULL HOUSE
A memory of the "REGAL" Evesham
1944
REGAL
Coming Shortly
The Bells of St Mary's
Bing Crosby
Next Week Greer Garson in "Mrs Miniver"
Going my way
MATINEE
Regal Cinema - Port Street - Evesham - 1944
Michael J Barnard

England's plight in 1940/41 had been expressed in stark terms it would have crippled morale.

The cans of news footage from Pathé, Gaumont, Gazette and March of Time were shared between Evesham's two cinemas and it was usually the job of the re-wind boys to transport reels on their bikes between the Regal and Clifton with maximum speed in order to seamlessly maintain both schedules. As soon as a newsreel had been shown at one theatre, it was unspooled, canned and shoved in a saddle-bag or back-pack to be whizzed across town through the sparse traffic at breakneck speed, to be greeted by the staff at the rival cinema, where the re-wind boy would exchange cans and hurtle back to Port Street. He may have been the lowest in the projection room pecking order but during the war, the re-wind boy was the fastest man in town.

Thus, with new blackouts over the cinema windows and Frank Ridge ramrodding the Regal's war effort by boosting morale, Evesham awaited the arrival of the Yanks.

While researching this book I was shown a lovely ten-minute video filmed by students from BBC Wood Norton in 1982 during the Regal's fiftieth anniversary celebrations. It contains a short interview with Iris Jordan which gives a small insight into the clash of cultures, as England welcomed the American forces in 1942. Iris, who began work as a fourteen-year-old usherette in 1934, manned the ticket kiosk during the war and was less than impressed by the attitude of the brash young GIs who crossed the Regal threshold. "They would say things like, 'Keep the change, honey,' when paying for their tickets. I didn't like that," said Iris.

The thought of her, as custodian of the Regal's income, accepting cash from customers was abhorrent to Iris – even from the well-meaning Yanks, who would have been puzzled by the strange 'limey' currency. Besides the gulf in etiquette, it exhibited how much better off American servicemen were than their British counterparts, and such ostentation was frowned upon in the austere Evesham of the forties.

The illustrations opposite by artist Michael Barnard nicely capture the atmosphere of the time. One can sense the vibrancy of the wartime picture palace in early 1944 with American jeeps rolling up at the Regal as the nightly queue was forming to deposit those local girls lucky enough to catch the eye of an 'overpaid, oversexed' GI. The fact that they were here to help us repel the Nazi threat was regularly overlooked by British servicemen, with their baggy-arsed uniforms and subsistence wages, who became prey to the green-eyed monster. The Yanks had enough money to treat girls to a seat in the balcony and could also supply nylons, chocolate and cigarettes – decent ones at that, not the ghastly Turkish things which were virtually all the Brits could lay their hands on.

Rubberman

With the fuel shortage and general lack of cash, residents of the Vale were obliged to walk or cycle just about everywhere, including the nightly trips to the movies.
A certain Mr Merrett, who owned a small tobacconist shop on the other side of Port Street, some fifty yards down from the Regal, saw a sweet little business opportunity at this time which involved permitting cyclists to park their bikes in the comparative safety of his expansive yard for the princely sum of threepence (3d) per evening.

He would collect the money through a small window from where he could monitor the comings and goings. Despite his vigilance, however, at the end of many an evening, desperate jeep-less GIs were known to purloin the odd bicycle in order to get back to their billets at Honeybourne, Broadway or Pershore. The gruff Mr Merrett wasn't overly concerned; having provided his valuable service on the understanding that bikes were left at their owner's risk and with several pounds in threepenny-bits weighing him down, he wasn't the ideal person to sprint after any thieving Yanks. In any case, Mr Merrett and his wife were probably sympathetic to our American cousins, having had to relocate to Evesham in 1941 after the Luftwaffe put paid to their jewellers' shop in London.

Merrett's place was one of those strange little establishments which, although ostensibly a tobacconist's, sold various oddments of hardware like batteries, penknives, puncture repair kits and the like, plus one commodity of vital importance, the purchase of which had traditionally required more courage from young men than the war itself. Yes, the young bloods of the day could discreetly buy 'something for the weekend', no questions asked – Londoner Merrett being that more enlightened creature from the wider world – and whether he realised it or not, this made him an important person. Without Merretts, all young men had to undergo the horror ritual of buying contraceptives from the chemist. Around this time, Evesham had one particular chemist (he shall remain nameless) who was never going to win any popularity contests. He would stand tall and implacable in his white coat, a wall of professional condescension and a formidable obstacle between spotty teenagers and their aspirations of carnal extremis. This scenario has long since become something of a hilarious cliché but in the forties, if this pillar of the Asum business establishment decided to adopt a puritanical stance, the kids were stymied.

> *"Are you married, young man?" he might enquire, in lofty tones – which was tantamount to telling you to bugger off. If you were quick-witted enough you might decide to bullshit: "I'm engaged. We're planning to get married next year." But this could elicit further questions. "Ah, I see. And what is the lucky girl's name?" He would be beaming inside with a tsunami of evil glee. "Julie." "Julie who? Perhaps I know her parents…", etc.*

A young man needed to be of considerable character to ride *these* rapids and would often bottle out, settle for a quarter of herbal tablets, and kick the first stray dog he encountered.

(By the late 1950s, when teenagers were beginning to flex their economic and social muscles, a local Teddy Boy found himself making the old tentative request for rubbers from our notorious chemist. When asked if he was married, the Ted exploded: "What the f**k's it gotta do wi' you?" at which point his exit was requested. He leaned across the glass counter, gave the witch doctor a ferocious V-sign, spat on the floor and stomped out, taking his Jimmy Dean complex with him. He didn't bother with the herbal tablets but did receive a visit from the law.)

Yet there were two even WORSE scenarios for the randy

forties' dude. If the chemist was absent he might have left his female assistant in charge. She would either be some fearsome iceberg resembling Rosa Kleb, devoid of empathy, having long since been disconnected from the joys of nature's icky sport; or (worse still) the most beautiful woman in town, whose dazzling smile and engaging demeanour negated all chance of your even intimating that you were hell-bent on leg-over. Either way it was herbal tablet time.

Therefore, one can appreciate the sheer importance of Mr Merrett's establishment and how, even if he did let a GI nick your wheels, it would have been unwise to administer a bollocking, lest he be tempted to cut off your supply of Johnnies. (The Regal's influence on this aspect of life is further explored in Chapter Ten, 'Rites Of Passage'.)

The Regal rake

Despite the perceived decadence of the Americans, manager Frank Ridge remained a traditionalist who liked to run a tight ship. He was no puritan but somewhat patriarchal as far as his female staff were concerned and would tolerate no 'hanky-panky' between the ten or so usherettes/cleaners and the male employees (four projectionists, two commissionaires and the poor old chocolate boy). That's not to say it didn't go on right under Frank's nose. If boys and girls want to play in the workplace they will usually display the necessary animal cunning to avoid the boss. Thus, a system of signals was devised between the staff to warn any 'fraternising' couple of Frank's approach. (To Mr Ridge, the term 'fraternising' encompassed all interaction from prolonged conversation to, God forbid, a quick kiss. To the best of my knowledge he never had to break up any orgies in the projection room.) If a look-out was posted on the balcony landing, by the time Frank had hauled his portly frame up the marble stairs, the alarm would (quietly) have been sounded and whoever was somewhere they shouldn't have been could quickly be somewhere else, such as the projection room, the toilets or hot-footing it down the rear fire-escape and back in through the side doors.

However, Frank Ridge was anything but daft and it came to his attention that he had a naughty boy in his midst. Les Roberts was a high-spirited young guy who probably felt a greater affinity with the heroes of the screen than any other Regal employee and yearned to be as cool as Humphrey Bogart. Consequently, he would ape the actor's manner, dress, speech and the way he smoked. It was only to be expected that a junior operator should be heavily influenced by the glorious flickering images that were his trade, but Les took it to a whole new level and I suspect for a good reason: the skeleton in his cupboard. A few years previously he had begun his cinema life as the lowly 'chocolate boy' – the very nadir of cool, ponced up like Buttons in *Cinderella*, harnessed into a tray dispensing joob-joobs to the punters. But now he was rocketing up the ladder and would soon make No. 1 operator before moving on to the Clifton, eventually becoming manager at the end of the 1940s.

The photograph above of Les Roberts (alongside his

Les Roberts' attentions until the louche operator had moved across town to the Regal's great rival. Finally, Boss Ridge could breathe a smug sigh and feel proud to have upheld Miss Dolphin's honour. Pointless. Babs and Les rode off into the sunset to get married.

Frank Ridge was to leave the Regal before the end of the war. He was in poor health, having contracted diabetes, but was to ride off into the sunset himself and marry his girlfriend Catherine Farman, having skippered the Theatre of Dreams through a memorable decade. The managership was taken over by chief projectionist John Hack in 1943.

The other Humphrey Bogart. c.1950.

projectionist pal Ray Ballard) was taken on the roof of the Clifton around 1950 by fellow projectionist Norman Holly and portrays Les at his sartorial best: sharp pinstripe duds, rakish air, the cigarette held just so. From Chocolate Buttons to Sam Spade in less than a decade. It's easy to imagine how Frank Ridge regarded Les as a mischief-maker because along with the ersatz-Bogart charm came a taste for the ladies. The particular apple of his eye was the lovely Barbara Dolphin and Frank nearly ran himself ragged shielding the chastity of his pretty usherette from

Iris and Violet on the Regal steps c.1940.

Flower power

Soon after the outbreak of war, Iris Jordan was joined at the Regal by big sister Violet. 'Auntie' Vi Woodcock (née Sale) decided the local picture palace was the place to allay her fears, earn some cash and brighten up the grey times while husband Ralph was away on active service. She was born at 9 Burford Road (the family home for a hundred years) and was the eldest of the four 'floral' Sale sisters, Violet, Iris, Ivy and Rose. Between them, Vi and Iris became more synonymous with the Regal than Vic Morrall himself.

Many people will remember Violet as the lady with the patch over her right eye, who worked mostly in the sweet kiosk from the 1960s onwards. During the war she took in evacuees of all ages, one of whom turned out to have a murky background. This was revealed late one night when the police came calling to arrest a suspected spy. Vi never did glean full details of his actions but needless to say, her fifth column lodger never got to walk up the marble stairs again.

I couldn't uncover many photographs of Violet who, by all accounts, was conscious of her patch, having suffered the truly dreadful experience of being blinded in her right eye on her twenty-first birthday by falling on a broken bottle in Evesham Park. She became one of the quartet of long-serving women (Vi, Iris, Elsie Tandy and a bit later Irene Mackenzie) who gave the Regal its unique family atmosphere. 'Auntie' Vi retired in 1986 at the age of seventy-eight and passed away soon after the Regal closed in 2003 at the grand old age of ninety-five.

I feel I have been indecently brief in penning this chapter, considering the importance of the Regal during the war years. Despite my research, the anecdotes were thin on the ground. There is no question that its significance as a social hub (like all cinemas) was never greater than during those dark days from '39 to '45, as a whole generation congregated in the dark, fearing for the future – girls holding the hands of their squaddie boyfriends or husbands until their knuckles blanched, trying to derive succour from the flickering images on that twenty-four-foot screen.

I encountered several stories which were difficult to confirm but have since passed into local folklore – such as the great flood of 1941 which may or may not have reached the Regal steps, or various punch-ups in the Regal concourse, as British servicemen took exception to the attentions paid to their girlfriends by our affluent American allies.

The Americans must have been puzzled, if not horrified, at the comparative poverty of Evesham and the dour nature of many of its residents. One particular usherette, Phyllis Knight from Hampton, whose husband was fighting in Europe, appeared so unmoved by the Yankee exuberance that it earned her the title of 'the girl with no smile' (which struck me as unfair because when I met her as a spry eighty-three-year-old she beamed all the time).

The best legends, however, are the ones about where various bombs landed around Evesham. Many people have different accounts. Put them all together and bombs apparently fell at various times on the Crown Meadow, near the station, at the top of Green Hill, in several orchards... My favourite story is of a bomb which exploded close to town, the force of which literally jumped the mighty Ernemann projector off its mount during a matinee. When the audience's panic subsided they were greeted with a blank screen and noticed that Walter Pidgeon was now smooching Greer Garson on the side wall.

But this was a time of myth and as the forties wore on, customers no longer had to evacuate the building as the sirens sounded; blue skies beckoned and Regal fans thanked the Yanks for both Hollywood and the enduring freedom in which to watch it.

Valerie's clothes shop, next to the Regal, in early 1946. The war was over and the Dior 'New Look' on the way.

Van Johnson in Thirty Seconds Over Tokyo.
(Illustration by Michael Barnard)

SUDDENLY YOU REALIZE MURDER IS AT YOUR ELBOW!
— and there's no way out!
SPENCER
TRACY
ROBERT
RYAN
M·G·M's SUPREME SUSPENSE DRAMA
BAD DAY AT BLACK ROCK
A
CO-STARRING
ANNE FRANCIS · DEAN JAGGER · WALTER BRENNAN · JOHN ERICSON · ERNEST BORGNINE · LEE MARVIN · RUSSELL COLLINS
ScreenPlay by MILLARD KAUFMAN Adaptation by DON McGUIRE · Based on a Story by HOWARD BRESLIN · Photographed in EASTMAN COLOUR Directed by JOHN STURGES Produced by DORE SCHARY
An M·G·M Picture

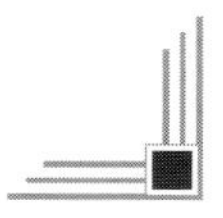

CHAPTER FIVE

THE POST-WAR YEARS: WINDS OF CHANGE

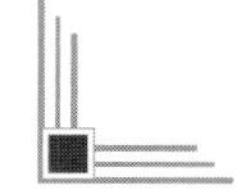

Business as usual

By late 1945, as World War II began to recede into the history books, the Regal cinema continued on its own merry way. Not too much had altered since 1939 except an increased turnover of young staff, the removal of the blackout curtains and the fact that bananas and chocolate were beginning to reappear. John Hack was managing the business in his systematic, careful way and the projection room was being bossed by a young man named Basil Cook. During the next few years many projectionists came, went and often returned, mainly due to the machinations of national service, and I apologise for not being able to expand on such characters as Basil Cook, Norman Roberts, Basil Care, John Kilby, Les Brown, Dennis Brown, Maurice Dore, Cyril Keen, Reg Birch and Trevor Scaysbrook.

Alas, as with most industries during the war, the British Film Industry (BFI) had taken a battering, having not been able to supply much quality product plus being unable to compete with the huge influx of excellent popular movies from Hollywood. Cinemas were thus ordered to fill their programmes with a minimum of one-third British films, with no more than two-thirds of combined American and European output. The Clifton's pulling power was making its presence felt and it became difficult for the Regal to secure enough good home-grown movies to fulfil its commitment to the BFI. Thus, the temptation to occasionally ignore this undemocratic ruling and indulge customers with more than their 'fair share' of Hollywood was ever present. (The advantages of chains over independent cinemas is explained fully in Chapter Six.)

In January 1946 a de-mobbed Bob Webb arrived back in Evesham. He turned up at the Regal with a view to getting his old job back and having witnessed the stark realities of war, the prospect of being once again immersed in the dreams and fantasies of movies must have seemed very appealing. The directors offered him the post of No. 2 projectionist to Basil Cook, but Bob wasn't wearing that. After having his life disrupted by the war and becoming a highly skilled, decorated naval technician, he insisted on the No. 1 position. In fairness to Basil Cook, the directors were prepared to create two positions as No. 1 projectionist, but Webb stuck to his guns on the grounds of his experience, seniority, technical expertise and the fact that it wasn't his fault Hitler had fancied a crack at world domination.[1]

Besides, two bosses in such a small space was a recipe for disaster. He won his argument and became sole boss of the projection room on around £6 per week, much to the chagrin of Basil Cook who was demoted to No. 2. But this was 1946, industrial tribunals didn't exist and Cook and the rest had to lump it.

1 In 1946 Sam Goldwyn produced the classic film *The Best Years of our Lives* which highlighted the difficulties of servicemen returning from the war and attempting to adjust to their old jobs in Civvy Street. Many found themselves having to start again on the bottom rung of the ladder as did three stars in the film. Bob Webb was determined not to suffer a similar experience.

However, Bob had no intention of being as curmudgeonly with his expertise as John Hack had been to the inquisitive young Webb in 1935. So Bob devised several innovations to improve the skills of his junior operators. He taught them the ins and outs of the electrical and sound systems by using self-drawn schematic layouts as an aid. This increased their knowledge and interest and kept them focused. It also negated any resentment over his appointment and things soon settled back into the familiar friendly Regal atmosphere.

Staff on the Regal roof, c.1947.
Back row l–r: Bob Webb, Ida Lampitt, Grace—, Joan Knight, Mary Keen, John Hack, Les Brown, Ted Newbury.
Front row l–r: Margaret Lampitt, Eileen Griffiths, Margaret Griffiths(?).

By 1947, the effects of the war were still being felt as spare parts for the German-made Ernemann projectors were no longer available, courtesy of the Royal Air Force, so the Regal directors were obliged to unchain their wallets and spring for two new projectors from Western Electric. The old Ernemanns had given fifteen years of sterling service and as cinema was soon to go through big changes, Vic Morrall couldn't complain about the necessary investment. The new state-of-the-art Westar machines (specifically, for all the nerds out there, Westar 2001/A 35 millimetre with 2002 optical sound heads) eventually generated far more revenue than their predecessors by showing films right up until the closure of the cinema in 2003.

The carbon arc lamps (essential for illuminating the film) had always produced a fine white ash which hung in the air and did staff lungs even more harm than the passive-smokers' nightmare of the main auditorium. With health and safety issues gradually becoming prominent in the workplace, Bob Webb insisted that the ash/dust problem be addressed. Burlinghams were duly sent for and fitted an extractor connected by six-inch-gauge flexible tube to the carbon-arc housings.

Bob Webb and John Hack had been friends for years but it didn't prevent a certain niggling rivalry between them. When the Westars were installed and the Western Electric engineers had brought Webb and the rest of the crew up to speed on their usage, manager Hack found his old operator's instinct kicking in and longed for a go on the Regal's new toys. John began sniffing around the projection room whenever possible and eventually asked the No. 1 for some tuition, to update him on the new technology. Bob Webb refused him point blank, saying, "You're the manager now, so get and manage". This may seem mean-spirited but Bob was remembering his first few months in the job and John Hack's stultifying attitude towards him as he thirsted for knowledge. Revenge was sweet.

Bob Webb and Norman Roberts with their new toys in 1947.

Bill Stickers and his buddy Holly

For many years the only ways the movie industry could advertise its product was either through its own medium in the form of 'trailers', which ran before the main feature, the local newspaper or posters stuck up on boards all round town. Being a 'poster boy' (in the days before it meant male model) was one of those nice jobs that teenagers could do, so much more glamorous than a paper round or delivering for the local butcher. After all, you had a handle on Hollywood's latest thrills and could slop paste around with a long brush. Three times a week, when the Regal programme changed, the poster boy[2] would set off on his bike with a bag full of rolled-up posters to strategic sites in the area as far flung as Hampton and Green Hill. The running order would be something like: Colston's sweet shop, waterside, Birlingham's billboard, Shakespeare's fish 'n chip shop, West Street, Evesham Station billboards (for both the GWR and LMS), Cambria Road shop, down to Monks garage (now Bredon Motors), the railway bridge billboard at Bengeworth (Hampton) station and Hampton post office. Plus, many shops in town agreed to display posters in their windows in exchange for free tickets. Alas, by their very nature, posters were as expendable as yesterday's newspaper, and hardly anyone thought about saving them. They were either pasted over or torn down and binned, which is tragic, because they are now in great demand by collectors worldwide. Anyone who has a decent original of *Casablanca*, *Gone with the Wind* or pretty much any famous old film can now start a bidding war on eBay. Most of the old Regal staff I have encountered still bemoan the loss of this opportunity.

During the post-war period 1946–60 the personnel in the projection room tended to change regularly, as the young

2 Both of Bob Webb's sons, Alan and Maurice, became 'poster-boys' during the late 1950s and early 1960s.

men were called up for national service and many better-paid jobs became available. In 1947 the operators' line-up was: No. 1 Bob Webb, No. 2 Norman Roberts, No. 3 Maurice Berry (a mere fourteen-year-old) and the re-wind boy, the splendidly named Hilton Green, known to all as Bill (also fourteen).[3]

Bill Green first became a Regal poster-boy and would also charge to and from the Clifton on his bike swapping newsreels, before being ensconced in the projection box as a part-timer (5–10.30 p.m. for four nights on the princely wages of £1 per week). A year later he became full-time on £1/10 shillings (one pound fifty pence) and although he liked the job, realised it was a case of dead men's shoes and that vast riches would not be forthcoming. However, the now sixteen-year-old Bill had his eyes on another prize: pretty usherette Joan Westwood. (In a workplace mix of men and women there are always romances and this was no less true of the cinema. It seemed that for every usherette there was a white knight spinning celluloid in the box, even though the ratio was about two-to-one against. A whole string of couples were to get together at the Theatre of Dreams: Bob Webb and Cynthia Wilson, Les Roberts and Barbara Dolphin, Trevor Scaysbrook and Madge Oakes, Norman Holly and Margaret Westwood and Bill Green and Joan Westwood.)

Bill became so enamoured with Joan that he would even come into work on his days off, dressed to the nines in crisp white shirt and dickey bow, in order to be near her. The ever-cautious John Hack, fearing for the efficient running of his cinema, stepped in like a true wet blanket and asked Joan to leave. But neither kill-joy Hack nor two years' national service could stop this love affair. Bill and Joan married and they remain happy to this day.

Norman Holly getting wrapped up in his work in the 1950s.

Paralleling them was another cinematic tryst between Bill's great friend Norman Holly (a Regal part-timer who worked mostly as projectionist at the Clifton) and Joan's sister Margaret. Their romance spread across both Evesham cinemas but was mainly conducted at the Clifton and came to the attention of its gruff northern manager David Johnson who, like Frank Ridge before him, was protective of his female employees.

3 Up until the late 1950s, when 'adult' films were shown (18X), junior operators were required to have time off until the programme changed although, I suspect, many of them snuck in regardless, for an illicit thrill.

"Ah hear ya courtin' Norman 'olly, Margaret."
"Uh, yes, Mr Johnson," replied Miss Westwood.
"Well, ah'll 'ave no bloody messin' about," he ordered, and as an afterthought, "Ah think Norman is too gay for you." (!)

Now this was the early fifties and the term 'gay' had yet to evolve into its current manifestation. Johnson was alluding to the fact that Holly had a bit of a reputation with the ladies and he was therefore concerned for young Margaret. (In 2006 I asked Norman Holly if his reputation had been justified. He threw up his arms and insisted he had been the victim of gossip – but his eyes were twinkling.) Nonetheless, patriarchy is no match for love's young dream and they soon married. Along with Bill and Joan Green, Norman and Margaret are the most pleasant couple you will ever meet and as an incurably romantic writer I put it all down to the influence of the Theatre of Dreams.[4]

Norman and Margaret Holly.
Still haunting the Theatre of Dreams in 2003.

By 1950, if one envisages a snapshot of the Regal, one sees a business enjoying success almost comparable to the pre-war years, with ordinary folk enjoying better-paid work and therefore with more cash to spend. However, the Clifton's booking strength was beginning to make itself felt and the Regal's interior was becoming jaded after eighteen years of almost continual full houses: nearly a thousand bodies per show, with maybe half of them smoking. Nonetheless, as long as the queues down Burford Road persisted, Vic Morrall and the directors were content to let things roll on. On a really good day, the walkways at the rear of the stalls and balcony would fill up with customers (perhaps a hundred or more) who would be stuck with 'standing room only'[5] until a seat became available, at which time the usherette's torch would finger its way along the rows to indicate the vacancy for the next in line.

Very often, couples had to be content with being split up into seats which were rows apart, if they wished to be seated. No one complained, the movies enthralled them and the till jingled. But there were bumpy times ahead for the Theatre of Dreams.

In late 1950 John Hack fancied a change of direction, resigned as manager and went off to run the Sherbourne Arms in Northleach with his wife. No. 1 Bob Webb had been pencilled in to replace him, but didn't fancy the hassle of the manager's job, being content to spin celluloid in the box. Besides, Bob had also been making plans to leave the Regal for pastures new. In 1951 he went to work for British Rail but was to rekindle his love of the cinema by moonlighting at the Clifton from the late 1950s until the mid-1960s as a part-time projectionist, which he worked into his BR shift pattern.

4 Ironic indeed that Iris Sale, of all Regal stalwarts, was to meet future husband Stan Jordan while visiting the Clifton on her night off.

5 Modern Health and Safety rules would never allow this today.

Spiderman preparing to 'lace-up' Lawrence of Arabia in 1962.

Operation Petticoat

Everyone expected Vic Morrall to install a professional manager from outside, yet he and his co-directors concurred with John Hack's recommendation that usherette Eileen Butler succeed him. Women were the poor relations in the workplace at this time, so it was quite a coup for Eileen to secure the top slot. It's possible that Morrall may have been a more enlightened soul but more likely he had an eye on his High Street rival who had installed Joan Mackenzie as manageress and was doing very nicely. For her part, Eileen Butler was a feisty and determined character whom, I suspect, Vic Morrall hoped would bring fresh energy and dynamism (and glamour) to the role, in contrast to the cautiously efficient John Hack.

Eileen Butler warmed to her job but, conscious of criticism from some members of the staff, set about shoring up her defences. She seconded a junior operator, John Kilby, to give her tuition on the Westars during down time and became reasonably proficient at spinning the celluloid.

Roof-top glamour.
L–r Beryl Taylor, Joan Sanders, Eileen Butler c. 1954.

The projection box team on the roof in 1952. L–r: Basil Cook, Maurice Berry, Basil Care.

Norman Roberts replaced Bob Webb as No. 1 but was soon to leave, so Maurice Berry was subsequently promoted to Chief, with Bill Green as his deputy. Bill became top gun for about twelve months but, while Maurice returned to the projection room when de-mobbed, Bill decided that the lure of the cinema wasn't strong enough to merit his trying to live on the three-pound-odd per week wages.

Maurice Berry, who sadly died in late 2006, insisted that the Eileen Butler era was the happiest time of his working life. She bossed the Regal with a spirit of *laissez-faire*, was never overbearing to the usherettes/cleaners, didn't complain if the projectionists bent the occasional rule, such as eating fish 'n' chips in the box while working, and even turned a blind eye to junior operator Alec Jelfs bringing in a couple of bottles of potent home-made wine on Saturday nights. (The projectionists did have the good sense not to start imbibing until the main feature was well under way!)
So, during the early 1950s, the Theatre of Dreams was a marvellous place to work, but storm clouds were forming over the industry and small independents such as the Regal were going to catch the brunt of it.

A break from cleaning to smile for the camera in 1953. Top: Joan Sanders. Middle l–r: Madge Robbins, Jeanette Lippett, Jean Holland, Margaret Bayliss. Bottom l–r: Joan Blake, Beryl Taylor.

Female staff outside the Regal in the mid-1950s.
L–r: Shirley Knight, Pansy Knight, Doreen Green, Joan Sanders.

When recommending Eileen Butler for the managership in 1950, John Hack couldn't have realised that he was catapulting her into a time of upheaval in the cinema. By 1952 the Regal takings were down on previous years, for the first time ever. This was partly due to the Clifton, whose superior muscle as part of a chain allowed it to secure the top films soon after their initial release. However, more significant in the long run was the impact of the little square box appearing in the corner of more and more living rooms. The BBC was now broadcasting programmes for several hours during the evening. In 1952 only a small proportion of households possessed a television set but it was obvious that they would soon become as essential in the home as food. Year on year, sales of TVs began to rocket and, like cinema owners everywhere, Vic Morrall began to feel the pressure. The cracks really started at the end of 1952 when, for the first time since the Regal opened, the total premiums paid to shareholders fell way below thirty thousand pounds. This figure had been the original cost of the place and was something of a benchmark which the shareholders had become used to receiving during the previous twenty years. Some of them, believing television to be the dread writing on the wall (a belief not entirely unfounded[6]) panicked and offloaded their shares onto their more stoic fellow investors.

The next clout came in 1954 as, with Regal takings still declining, the Clifton struck back against fluctuating audiences by installing 'cinemascope' (complete with state-of-the-art magnetic stereo sound) which the industry had introduced for just this purpose. Vic Morrall began pondering the possibility of complete meltdown in the industry – it did seem reasonable to assume that television would decimate cinema audiences within the decade. If you imagine its impact in this time of post-war austerity and rationing, television must have seemed like the eighth wonder of the world; moving pictures, with sound, at the flick of a switch in your own home. With the possible exception of the motor car, television was the ultimate 'must-have' item. Its effect must have been comparatively far greater on the consciousness of people in the fifties than either video on the far less naïve consumers of the eighties, or DVD and computers on the jaded palate of today's techno-savvy market.

In 1954 Vic Morrall received an offer for the Regal from Miles Jarvis, owner of the Kings and Queens cinema in West Bromwich. He teetered on the brink of selling but refused Jarvis's offer,

6 In 1953 , when the BBC announced its intention to screen the Queen's coronation live, it triggered a huge surge in demand for television sets.

reasoning that a booming industry couldn't disappear overnight. The following year ITV came on stream, completing a triple 'whammy' for the movie industry and Morrall committed the Regal to an upgrade by ordering cinemascope.

CINEMASCOPE was a technical innovation made possible by the introduction of a special 'anamorphic' lens on the movie camera (the term simply means 'changing the shape'). Cinematographers could now film a scene approximately two-and-a-half times as wide as it was high and the image was then squeezed into ordinary 35mm negative film. A similar anamorphic lens on the projector swelled the scene out of its original shape. Cinemascope completed the illusion of 'being there' with stereophonic sound, with four tracks printed onto the 35mm film to provide left, right, centre and ambient audio channels.

Cinemascope movies were to become very popular over the next decade. They usually consisted of big budget/cast of thousands, religious/historical epics such as *The Ten Commandments*, *Ben-Hur*, *Spartacus* or *Cleopatra*, all filmed in glorious Technicolor and beautifully showcased by the wide-screen format. The first ever cinemascope movie was *The Robe* (Richard Burton, Jean Simmons and Victor Mature) which

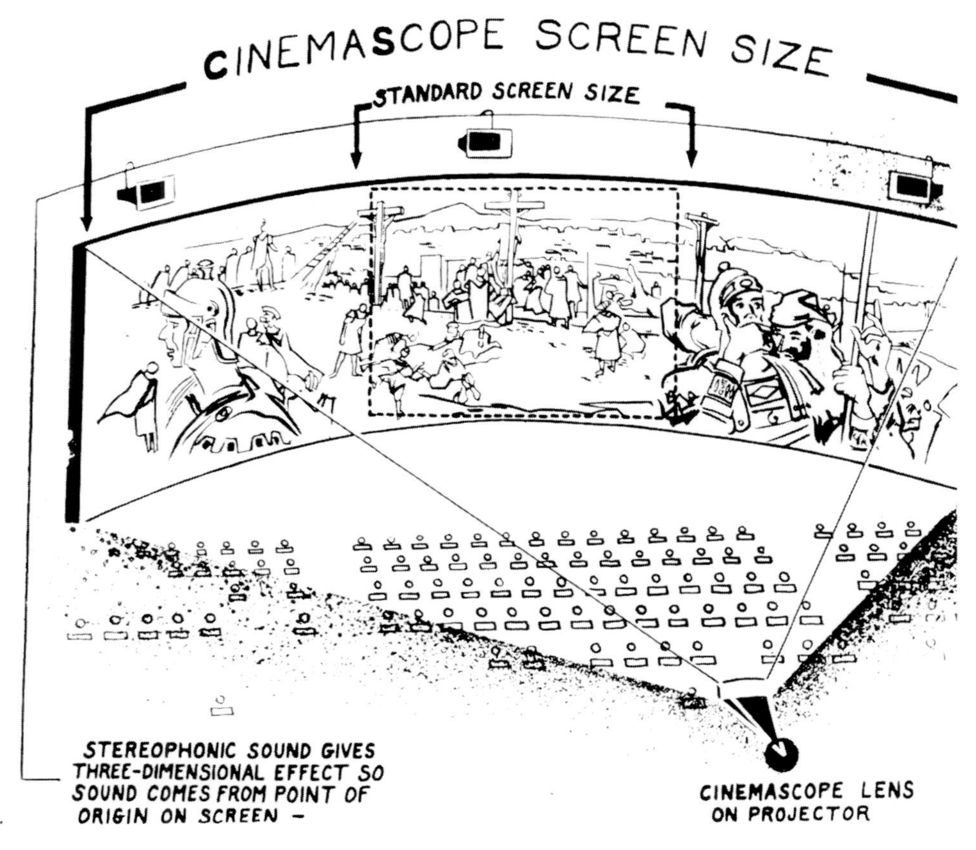

How cinemascope works.

played at the Clifton in November 1954.The introduction of a wider screen required a few adjustments in the Theatre of Dreams. The proscenium had originally been in-set close to the very back of the two angled walls which meant that to increase the width from its original 24 feet to the necessary 30 the whole arch would have to be moved forward by almost three feet. This would then allow the 24-foot screen to be increased to the cinemascope size of 26′ × 11′6″. It further necessitated the removal of the front two rows of seats in the stalls, which were now too far forward, thus reducing the seating capacity by 98 from 945 to 847.

The worst problem, however, was the re-positioning of the Westars. To make the screen more agreeable to customers at the front of the stalls it had been lowered by almost two feet; therefore, in order to target the screen accurately, the two projectors (now fitted with their new anamorphic lenses) had to be tilted at a downward angle increased by some five degrees. Alas, because of the then unusually wide gangway between the front row of seats and the balustrade in the balcony, people walking along it would quite easily obstruct the projection beam. This problem was eased by restricting the area in question to occupants of the front row only, by constructing a false balustrade three feet back from the existing one, then removing the top from the original and covering the gap with a chamfered panel.

Finally, with admission prices at this time varying from one shilling (5p) at the front of the stalls to 3/2d (16p) in the gods, on Monday, 30 May 1955, 847 seated, plus dozens of late comers crowded into the rear walkways, enjoyed Tony Curtis and Janet Leigh in the Regal's first ever wide-screener, *The Black Shield of Falworth,*[7] and Vic Morrall began to believe there was still life in the Port Street pleasure palace.[8]

A second innovation which Hollywood came up with as a panacea for the ills of the industry was 3D and, like all cinemas, the Regal gave it a lash. The idea of projecting 'natural vision' had been around for years but it was an independent 3D-film called *Bwana Devil*, shot in 1952, which kick-started Hollywood's interest. It was basically a crude jungle story but it promised 'a lion in your lap', which more or less summed up its limitations, in that 3D came to be used as a gimmick. With audiences being assailed by sensational moments involving bullets, boulders, bodies, cars and fierce creatures coming 'out of the screen' at them, they were frequently distracted from the storyline – the 3D gimmicks becoming the *raison d'être* of the movie.

As well as earning a reputation for being contrived for the sake of the effects, 3D movies suffered other disadvantages. Firstly, the audience had to wear special spectacles to get the effect. Secondly, screens had to be specially treated and thirdly, two projectors were required to operate in synchronisation; thus the poor operators needed to watch them like hawks lest they slipped out of sync and the effect was ruined.

By the mid-1950s audiences were gripped by cinemascope which offered both depth and breadth and did not require Polaroid specs. (I'm still baffled as to why they didn't iron out the problems with 3D. There were a couple of half-hearted attempts to resuscitate it in the 1980s, such as *Jaws 3D*, but it died a death again. However, its undoubted potential now appears to be being re-addressed by digital technology.)

7 This medieval romp became famous for the line "Yonda lies the castle of my fodda" delivered by Tony Curtis in his best Brooklyn accent.

8 Vic Morrall was either very shrewd or too tight with his cinemascope investment in opting for a fudge, by keeping the Regal's original sound system and not installing four-track stereo like the Clifton. However, as no one complained and audiences stabilised he must have regarded it as the correct decision.

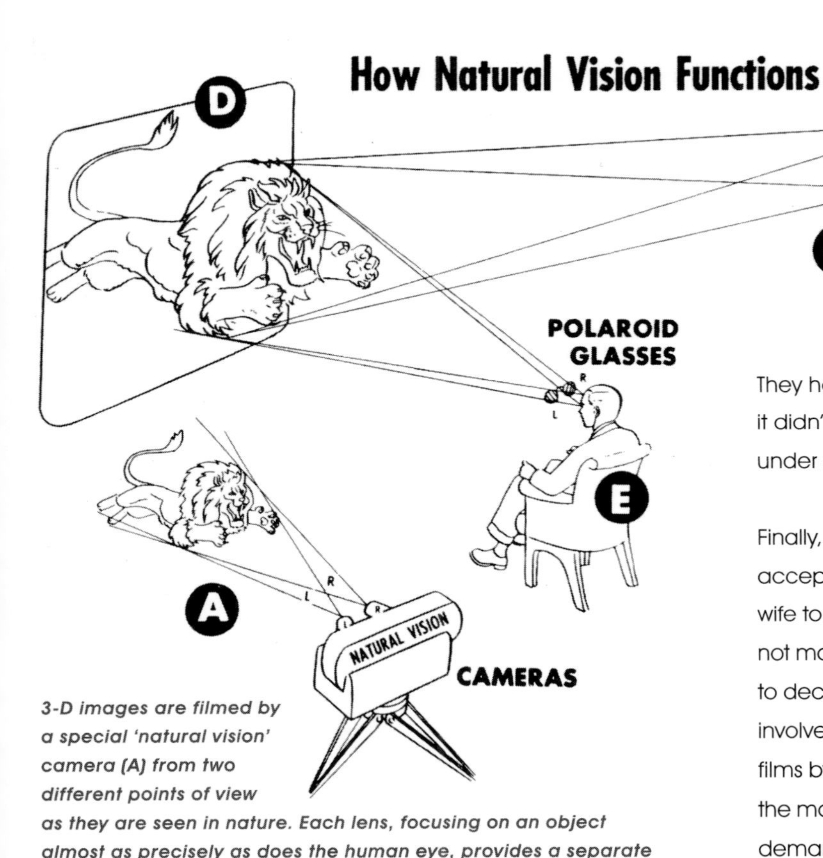

In the cinema two separate pictures from two (conventional) projectors (B) are superimposed on the screen. Right and left images pass through Polaroid light filters (C). The two images are reflected back to the viewer who is equipped with Polaroid spectacles.

3-D images are filmed by a special 'natural vision' camera (A) from two different points of view as they are seen in nature. Each lens, focusing on an object almost as precisely as does the human eye, provides a separate and complete two-dimensional picture.

The Regal staff were not oblivious to the downturn in cinema business and realised that future pay rises might become few and far between. So Maurice Berry pulled a crafty flanker on behalf of the projectionists. When the re-wind boy (fourth in the pecking order) left in 1955 he suggested to Vic Morrall that only three staff were required for the successful running of the box – the re-wind boy was a bit of a dogsbody. So instead of hiring a new No. 4, the three operators would take on all the tasks, providing they could share four wages. Morrall saw the sense in sweetening the pot for his projection staff without it costing him more money, and agreed to Maurice's request.

They had to keep the deal secret from the usherettes and it didn't endear them to manageress Eileen Butler who was under severe pressure to keep the place ticking over.

Finally, in late 1955, Eileen Butler had had enough and accepted an offer from former manager John Hack and his wife to work at their pub in Northleach. The big studios had not made the job any easier for Eileen. As the industry began to decline, they had introduced the 'weighting system' which involved clawing back extra revenue from the more popular films by demanding a greater share of the takings. The hotter the movie (i.e. the greater the 'weight') the more return was demanded and if cinemas didn't agree they were bypassed. No way could a small-town independent argue the toss on this matter. Eileen Butler had attempted to ease matters by contracting for films to lesser rental companies in the hope that some of the 'cheapies' would prove popular. This tactic only worked to a certain extent and tended to clog up the Regal schedule when the chance came to show bigger movies.

Vic Morrall was now committed to the Regal's future, having inherited shares from former directors, who wanted out (his original stake had been 52 per cent which gave him controlling interest). He saw little choice but to try to entice a battle-hardened cinema professional into the manager's job to bring the business back on side against a sea of problems.

A PETER ROGERS PRODUCTION
SIDNEY JAMES · HATTIE JACQUES · KENNETH CONNOR · CHARLES HAWTREY · ESMA CANNON · LIZ FRASER
Glamcabs
CARRY ON CABBY
'U'
with
BILL OWEN • MILO O'SHEA • JUDITH FURSE • AMBROSINE PHILLPOTTS • RENEE HOUSTON • JIM DALE
Produced by PETER ROGERS · Directed by GERALD THOMAS · Screenplay by TALBOT ROTHWELL · Based on an original story by S. C. GREEN and R. M. HILLS
From ANGLO AMALGAMATED
for WARNER-PATHE release

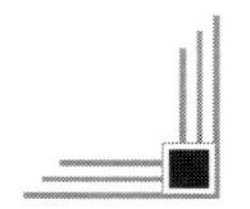

CHAPTER SIX

WHEN THE GOING GETS TOUGH...

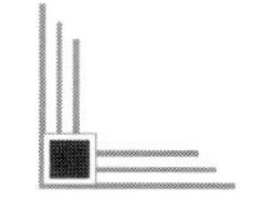

With the upgrade to cinemascope, Vic Morrall had struck his first successful blow against the creeping menace of television and the slide in Regal attendances. His cinema now had the largest screen in Worcestershire and, like its town centre rival, could show any film in the world in all its glory. What he now needed was a person with vision, energy and commitment to rejuvenate the building and encourage the crowds back, thereby once again sweetening the premiums for the shareholders.

The Brummie on the bike

In January 1956 Morrall advertised for a new manager to replace Eileen Butler. A couple of weeks later a motorcycle emerged through the winter murk and drew up onto the Burford Road pavement. The driver removed his gauntlets and shook hands with an expectant Vic Morrall, who thanked him for braving the elements on his journey down from Birmingham. Ernest Frederick Highland, the man who eventually became known as 'Mr Regal', cast his eyes over the marble-floored entrance and knew that the land of a thousand trades would no longer be his home.

Ernie, a Brummie born and bred, had joined his local power company straight from school in 1927 at the age of fourteen on an electrical engineering apprenticeship. Alas, within two years the company folded as the country lurched into the Great Depression, but Highland's grounding proved invaluable as he secured a job at his local cinema as a projectionist. Within two years he was promoted to manager, having become hooked on the movie business. The war years saw a hiatus in his career while he served in the Fleet Air Arm, but it failed to keep him away from the film world completely. Using movies provided by the NAAFI he organised shows at various naval bases and on the aircraft carrier *Victorious*.

During the two decades either side of the war, he would manage picture houses in West Bromwich, Cannock, Stoke-on-Trent, Brierley Hill, Coleshill, Leicester and Derby. But it was Evesham that snared him for good. He commented on how fresh the air quality was in the Vale compared to the Black Country. Remember, this was a time when traditional industries were still very much to the fore in Britain, and the smoke and smog of the second city could not have contrasted more with a shire town containing few motor vehicles, surrounded by market garden land and fruit trees where, during blossom time, Evesham actually smelled of scent.

'Mr Regal' in his office in 1982.

Ernie Highland walked around the building, then had a quick look in both the stalls and balcony. His mind made up, he informed Vic Morrall that he would very much like the job. Morrall didn't hesitate – he had found his man, and offered him a decent package, including shares.

Ernie hit the ground running, determined to bring the jaded building and faltering business up to scratch, but almost from the word go ran into a major snag. Replacing Eileen Butler with this brash out-of-towner went down like the *Hindenberg* with several of the staff, who promptly walked out. It's easy enough to understand. Highland did have the look and energy of a big city clubland impresario and as the Regal's charm had always been its slightly insular family atmosphere, when a dyed-in-the-wool pro was parachuted in with a new broom, it inevitably created suspicion and resentment.

For a few weeks, Ernie found himself busier than a one-armed bill poster in a hurricane as he, at various times, ran the kiosk, sold ice cream, swept the floor, helped the short-staffed projectionist and probably wondered what sort of parochial backwater he'd blundered into. But a job is a job and the Regal had a hatful of vacancies, so as soon as the locals sensed that Highland wasn't some corporate ogre, they began to realise that the Theatre of Dreams was still the place to work.

Ernie's first appointment was Violet Woodcock (née Sale), who had originally worked there through the war years as an usherette, and now that her family commitments had eased, fancied returning to Evesham's favourite venue.
Vi was an essential contact for Ernie, because she knew so many local people. Soon she would entice her sister Iris Jordan back for another stint, firstly as an usherette, then as Ernie's assistant. Violet and Iris, the grand old dames of the Regal, would go on to clock up an astonishing seventy-eight years' service between them.

Once he had enough bodies back on site, Ernie began working on some key innovations. First he organised a rota of contract cleaners. In the past, the staff had all pitched in to help with the sundry jobs, particularly cleaning and maintenance. So this professional touch was much appreciated by the beleaguered usherettes, who no longer had to remove the crushed popcorn and melted ice cream that they had sold to the customers three hours previously.

Bob Fisher in attendance in late 1956.
Who needs John Wayne? The girl in the ticket kiosk is Joan Sanders.

The Fisherman and The Refugee

Other memorable figures arrived to work in Ernie's new empire, such as Bob Fisher, for many years a commissionaire, and the formidable but lovely Elsie Tandy, who was cashier until the 1970s.

Bob Fisher was a good guy. I can state this categorically because of one experience I had as an eight-year-old in 1964 while attending the Saturday Morning Regal Chum's Club. My older brother Steve and his friends would take me with them on the bus and looked after me well, but as the junior of the bunch, I was apt to get teased occasionally. A couple of them were ensconced in the row in front of me and during a break in the programme decided it would be fun to turn around and pull faces. For some reason I thought an appropriate response would be to kick the back of their seats. This only elicited more gurning and I was soon giving the seat in front some thunderous wallops. Finally, with a resounding crack, my little boot went straight through the thin curved plywood, tearing the red felt upholstery. There was a ghastly second, as the stalls hushed and I looked to my left to see Bob Fisher's stern expression twenty feet away, his crooked finger beckoning me hither as if t'were the lifeless arm of Captain Ahab when roped to Moby Dick. I was terrified and clumped up the aisle with leaden legs to the waiting doorman and a fate I dared not contemplate. With his smart uniform and peaked cap, he represented a most dreadful authority and bent down to ask me the obvious question: "Now, why did you do that, son?"

> *"D-don't know," I blubbed, my face now a tomato and lower lip wobbling like a Gerry Anderson marionette.*
> *"Well, are you going to behave yourself from now on?"*
> *My head nodded wildly as I sensed reprieve.*
> *"Go and sit down then," he said softly.*

And that was that. A less tolerant man would have bounced me into Burford Road.

One day while checking the balcony at the end of a performance, Bob Fisher found a £350-roll of banknotes. In the early 1960s this was a king's ransom so after he and Ernie had checked the amount it was stowed in the Regal safe to await the return of some white-faced customer. The policy was always to hold misplaced valuables for a week before handing them to the police. Sure enough, the next day in marched a miserable-looking gentleman who had lost a substantial amount of cash. Ernie and Bob checked out his story and when convinced that he was the rightful owner, handed over the loot. Ernie then suggested he might consider a good tip for the honest doorman, which seemed wholly reasonable. The man grunted, handed Bob a ten-shilling note (50p) and left. Standing there with his one-seven-hundredth commission, commissionaire Fisher must have felt inclined to facilitate the gentleman's exit with a size-ten boot.

It is Elsie Tandy's story which, for me, sums up the value of the Theatre of Dreams more than anyone else's. Originally she was Elsie Abraham, a Jewish German girl from Hanover who, as a teenager, witnessed the rise of the Nazis. Her father, a solicitor, became aware very early on of the growing anti-Semitism in the country and realised there was little choice but to get his three children out of Germany as soon as possible. Elsie's parents made a heartbreaking decision to send her to England and in 1935, at the age of eighteen, she landed in Brighton, a refugee, where she was interned for several months.

As World War II raged, her family were not so lucky. With the exception of one of her brothers who escaped to South America, the rest became concentration camp victims.

Eventually Elise arrived in Evesham, began a job at BBC Wood Norton, met and married Jim Tandy from Hampton and raised a family in their home along Burford Road.

In 1956 Elsie Tandy became part of Ernie Highland's Regal renaissance and soon secured the job in the ticket office which she ran with typical German efficiency. Although a delightfully kind soul, Elsie brooked no nonsense. Her affection for the place was no less great than those grand cinema sisters Iris Jordan and Violet Woodcock. She would help with the cleaning in the morning, go home at lunchtime to feed the kids, then it was back to face the customers in the evening.

I remember her in the late 1960s as she cast a suspicious eye over the gangly eleven-year-old shuffling awkwardly as his father bought tickets for *Bonnie and Clyde*. This was then an adult film but I managed to slip under Elsie's radar. The same day, my friend Moray Porter wasn't so lucky. He was about six inches shorter than me at the same age and Mrs Tandy refused him entry. Moray's Dad tried his best: "He's not afraid of a bit of blood and guts," he remonstrated, but Elsie wasn't wearing it. As far as I could tell, I was the youngest person in a packed house where I fell unashamedly in love with Faye Dunaway as she introduced me to the intoxicating concept of bad girls. Thank you, Faye. Thanks, Dad. And thank you, Elsie.

Elsie Tandy's one problem at the Regal was the screening of war films which would remind her of those dreadful days in the thirties. However, such movies could be easily avoided and the Regal embraced her as a family member. It seemed somehow fitting that Elsie should work in an industry in which fantasy is everything because considering the harrowing experience of her youth, reality was something she could very often do without.

Elsie Tandy. Burford Road, 1959.
The Boys have made an alien for a Saturday matinee competition.

Courting the Reps

By April 1956 Ernie Highland had won round his new staff, streamlined working remits and convinced himself that the cinema wasn't a basket case. So he began to tackle the main problem: the product.

From the very beginning of Highland's tenure he had insisted to Vic Morrall and the directors that he wanted a *carte-blanche* mandate on film booking. With Ernie's experience, Morrall saw this request as wholly sensible and trusted him to untangle the haphazard booking arrangements he had inherited. Highland now had to prove his worth and began cultivating good working relations with the reps from the major companies as he had done in his previous management positions. This bore fruit and very soon he was back onside with most of the distributors.

(The notable exception being United Artists who went on to produce the James Bond movies. Until the mid-1960s, if you wanted to be shaken, not stirred, on 007's initial release, then it was off to the Clifton. Ernie didn't crack this lucrative franchise until the late '60s. Astonishing also that Disney (notoriously protective of their work) never featured on the Regal menu on initial release until Darby O'Gill and the Little People (ironically, starring a pre-Bond Sean Connery) was secured in 1959. It's fortunate that the Disney classics such as Snow White and Pinocchio became eternal box office winners and could therefore be shown every few years to a new generation.)

Before the late 1970s, when smaller cinemas began to close due to falling attendances caused by pressure from video, other expanding media outlets and entertainment diversity in general, the main film studios, although based in London, had important regional distribution centres in the larger cities. Ernie Highland and his predecessors would primarily do business with their Birmingham offices.

One of Highland's contacts at the MGM studios in Birmingham was Pauline Fessey who worked there for about five years during the mid-1960s before being made redundant when the branch closed and operations were centralised in London. Pauline gave me a brief insight into the workings of the regional studio office at this time. Mondays were spent on the phone to all the cinema managers in her area and recording the weekend's takings on whatever MGM productions were doing the rounds. These figures were then passed on to head office in London. The rest of the week would be spent dealing with individual cinema requests for movies and the drawing up of contracts (agreeing percentages of the takings, dates the films were to be shown, collection times, etc.).

All MGM stock was delivered and collected by the Film Transport Service (FTS), then once back at the Birmingham office, used movies were inspected, repaired and stored ready for future use.

The most exciting part of the job was attending the advance screenings of the blockbusters of the day, such as *Dr Zhivago*. These were specifically for members of the press and television but many of the stars often attended too. Afterwards, it was off to the Albany Hotel for a huge post-movie bun fight. And if Omar Sharif could be dragged along for a gin and tonic, all well and good.

The Regal in chains:
combating the power of the studios

As I've already touched on, The Regal, being an independent cinema, was more vulnerable to the dynamics of the industry and, during the late 1950s, still subject to the 'barring system'. This worked through the desire of the big studios (MGM, Paramount, Columbia, Warner Brothers, 20th Century Fox, Universal, United Artists, Rank, etc.) to screen their films initially in venues which would bring in the fattest returns. That is, the cinema chains in the cities and larger towns where ticket prices, population and therefore potential revenue were greater. Thus, minnows such as the Regal would have to wait sometimes for several weeks before securing a copy of a movie for screening to lesser audiences at their lower ticket prices. This effectively 'barred' the independents from cashing in on the initial publicity and popularity of major films. Add to this the burgeoning threat of television and the fact that the Regal had a sizeable 'chain' rival in Evesham High Street and one understands that during the late 1950s Ernie Highland had his hands full with his run-down charge.

Most of the blockbusters of the day, such as *Shane*, *The Ten Commandments* or *Bridge on the River Kwai,* were initially only screened in the Clifton, while Ernie had to untangle a legacy of contracts with certain lesser rental companies which mostly secured films with limited potential. Not many people would have chosen to watch some duff black and white British 'B movie' when they could marvel at a Charlie Heston spectacular on the other side of town. This is not to say that Highland didn't have a modicum of success during his first year. Any first-class movie, featuring either John Wayne, giant menacing creatures, the Second World War or sexuality above and beyond the conservative standards of the day would virtually guarantee a turn-out in excess of seven hundred per show.

There were other occasional victories during Highland's struggle to turn the Regal around, particularly when the Worcester, Cheltenham or Redditch cinemas got their homework wrong and dismissed a movie, believing it to be a potential box office flop. The cinemas in question were required to make a declaration to the distributors that they did not wish to show it and the film would move down the food chain to the Regal, where it often generated good business.

Nonetheless, the big four British cinema chains (ABC, Gaumont, Odeon and Rank) appeared to have the system sewn up. With their hundreds of picture palaces granted initial viewing privilege by all Hollywood and most foreign studios, they had their own distribution network and kept films 'in-house' as far as possible to minimise their 'cost-base' and suit their own agendas. Rank, in particular, was a very powerful player because it made its own quality films so had a grip on the industry from the first inkling in a screen-writer's imagination, right through production to marketing the completed movie. Little wonder that small independents felt like the poor relations of the film world, beholden as they often seemed to be to the whims of first, the studios, then the big cinemas, then the pulling power of the actual movies. Only when audiences finally began to wane in the larger cinemas would the film 'trickle down' to the smaller rural cinemas. If the film in question was a real smash-hit, this might not happen until the third or fourth week. It all went to emphasise Ernie Highland's task of bringing the Regal back up to standard and overcoming the advantages enjoyed by the Clifton.

The percentage takings for the Regal varied depending on how skilfully Ernie Highland could negotiate a contract. The studio distributors would normally insist on around eighty per cent of the takings for the first week of a big film, falling to around seventy per cent during the second week, if the movie merited it. But Highland would only change the time-honoured weekly rota (Monday to Wednesday, Thursday to Saturday, with Sunday for one-off shows) if the movie on offer was 'hot' enough. If the film was a box-office mega-hit (*Ben-Hur*, *West Side Story*, *Sound of Music*, *Dr Zhivago*) the distributors would insist on perhaps ninety per cent of the first week's takings, plus eighty per cent of the second, but with the Regal ticket machine 'chinging' wildly due to terrific demand, Ernie Highland would have been unwise to complain. Exceptional films could be held over for a third week, but this was rare. In the case of Sunday-only films, the distributors usually charged a flat fee. Between 1956 and 1970 this ranged between £5 and £15.

By 1958, Ernie Highland had buttressed the Regal business, now holding its own against the Clifton, but could not quite generate the cash needed to fulfil his ambition of a complete refurbishment. That same year the Clifton underwent extensive alterations to its façade, which allowed for the building of several offices. The bulldozers moved in after the last showing of *Bridge on the River Kwai* on Saturday, 12 April 1958 and the Clifton remained closed until Monday, 7 July the same year. This gave the Regal a full twelve-week period as the only game in town and subsequently attendances increased, giving Ernie Highland's coffers a welcome boost.

The Master Operator

However, a simple method of sustainable revenue increase was suggested by a young man destined to become a true cinema stalwart and unsung hero to those of us in awe of the mysterious characters in the box at the back responsible for actually putting the movies on the screen. Brian Houghton was Evesham born and bred and became the Regal's longest serving projectionist, running celluloid through the two mighty Westars, on and off, for forty-five years.

He began his association with films in 1954 as a junior operator at the Clifton and things weren't easy. Brian had to wear callipers for several years in his youth and carrying the heavy reels of film up the cinema steps to the projection room was quite a struggle. Many of his colleagues assumed he would not survive in the job, but he proved to be a tough young hombre and eventually overcame his need for leg braces.

In his first years at the Clifton, Brian was assistant to his friend Norman Holly, who taught him the ropes until 1957 when Holly left and was replaced by Ray Austin (I've given this guy a fictitious name), an experienced operator from Leamington Spa. Austin proved to be that one person whom we have all met in the workplace – Hell-bent on making life awkward for someone because they feel they have the authority to do so. Brian became his main target, probably because his taciturn manner was never going to make him sufficiently deferential to the new boss. Nonetheless Ray Austin cracked the whip unfairly. Most people would be miffed on finding themselves feverishly 'prepping' a zillion feet of celluloid in time for the next performance, while the man in charge was casually drinking tea without offering to lend a hand. "If I'm going to do the work of two assistants, I should be entitled to higher wages," grumbled the young Houghton hopefully. But Ray was oblivious. He had digestives to dunk. Brian's blood pressure mounted daily with Austin's lack of assistance and guidance, but through his own trial and error he actually learned the projectionist's job brilliantly. He was nothing if not positive and with his skills becoming honed, found it easier to deal with Ray Austin's awkwardness. Alas, the projectionists' domain is geographically finite, and with the best will in the world, if your boss is out to get you in a confined space, he'll usually succeed. One 'put-upon' too many did the trick when Ray insisted that Brian bring up and prep the latest film while he indulged in some serious tea-drinking.

"It's a gripping jury-room drama. You'll enjoy collecting that and winding it on for me," said the No. 1 sarcastically. Thus, Brian Houghton exited the Clifton in a steaming temper, having advised Ray Austin to shove *Twelve Angry Men* up his arse and trudged across town to where Ernie Highland's warm welcome soothed his savage breast. Brian was made deputy to Highland's chief projectionist Norman Hill.

All in the best possible taste

It puzzled Brian Hougton why the Regal wasn't adopting the same strategy as the Clifton by showing more hard-hitting films on a Sunday. It appeared that Ernie Highland was being unnecessarily cautious with his choice of single-day programmes on the Sabbath, no doubt wary of the wrath of the church and the local authority. However, Evesham in the fifties wasn't QUITE Salem in the seventeenth century, so he needn't

Brian Houghton 'prepping' a movie in the 1980s.

have been so concerned. Thus, on Houghton's suggestion, he ordered a batch of twelve older movies comprising Lugosi/Karloff/Chaney horror classics and other shockers, the scariest creature features available, plus a couple of French/Italian cheapies containing sub-titles and the promise of low-grade sexual titillation. All tame stuff compared to modern times when our ten-year-olds sit through *The Fly* and Channel Four's *Big Brother* without batting an eyelid, but stimulating for their time.

They proved to be a big hit with the locals and boosted weekly takings by close to three figures, which may sound like chicken-feed nowadays but in 1960 it allowed Highland the finance he needed to plan a complete refurbishment of his Theatre of Dreams.

There had long been restrictions on the showing of particular material on Sundays (although strictures were easing by the late 1950s). Even if the censors awarded a film a general release certificate, it was at the discretion of the local authority whether it made it to the screen in their towns and cities. If the content was perceived as blasphemous, the church would move heaven and earth to block it; and if sex ever came into the equation moral guardians everywhere would wet themselves, bombard the local newspaper with complaints and inform the cinema manager(ess) that he/she was a disgusting pervert.[1]

Now, I am talking about the period from 1930 to the early 1950s when the church was still hallowed and sexual explicitness in the cinema was defined by a fully clothed man kissing his wife in bed while NOT having ONE foot on the floor. Nowadays, this may sound as bizarre as the old Sunday trading laws, but this kind of stultifying nonsense held sway as the censors' 'leg-over yardstick' until late in the 1950s, when British film makers began to inject some gritty realism into their work with the emergence of the so-called 'kitchen sink dramas'.

The Americans were also obliged to keep it clean and pious during this period and if they weren't being paranoid about 'reds under the bed' they were being scandalised by the osculatory gymnastics between Burt Lancaster and Deborah Kerr on the beach in *From Here to Eternity* (1953) which drew gasps of outrage from the moral crusaders in

1 I would like to stress that to the best of my knowledge this never happened to Ernie Highland or any other Regal manager(ess) but it certainly occurred in other towns and cities in Britain, not to mention the wider world.

the Bible belt. Funny how it cleaned up at the box office and the Oscars.

Okay, it all seems laughable now but however enlightened British cinema proprietors of the time were they had to watch their step. Pornography and homosexuality were illegal and any hint of such degenerate filth being available for public consumption was roundly condemned by worthies everywhere. Bless 'em, they couldn't possibly have known that the young Ken Russell was already sharpening his beautifully painted claws. As for the Holy Rollers in Dixie, not even Elvis, Flower Power, Vietnam or Watergate could prepare them for Monty Python's *Life of Brian*.

I mentioned, flippantly, in Chapter Two that Vic Morrall and those who sanctioned the presence of the Regal in Evesham could not have imagined what they had become party to, inasmuch as within two generations the silent, clownish antics of Charlie Chaplin would have been superseded by the pleasant whimsy of *Robocop*, the genteel erudition of Eddie Murphy and the fey coquettishness of Sharon Stone. Yet ironically, before 1934, many films were produced with a harder edge. Nudity, suggestive language and violence were surprisingly common in the 1920s, but censorship soon clamped down hard until the late 1950s. This taming of decadence in America was due to the 'Production Code', a batch of rules drawn up by a team led by Senator William Hays, who sought to keep in check what they perceived to be the excesses of the movie industry. Hays and his moralising cohorts regarded Hollywood as a West Coast Sodom and Gomorrah, and their code would act like a kind of *Ten Commandments*. Depictions of sex, alcohol, infidelity, racial integration, Communism – you name it, Will Hays smothered it.

In Britain, we had the British Board of Film Censors (the BBFC) who drew up a similar charter of movie taboos, no less puritanical, unenlightened, racist, bigoted or politically correct than that of the Americans'. These censors got to work soon after the introduction of sound in the late 1920s and by 1934 the 'Production Code' was fully effective.

To balance this debate on censorship, I suppose some new strictures were inevitable to protect the decency of the medium. Quite honestly, if the four horsemen of the apocalypse (sex, horror, violence and blasphemy) are permitted to run riot, the quality of the movie usually suffers, as the excesses swamp any subtle craftsmanship. However, before Senator Hays stuck his oar in, cinema seemed to be having a leisurely march in that direction and many pre-'Production Code' films were later edited to protect the sensibilities of the public. Consider the 1925 version of

Senator Will Hays: Spoilsport.

Ben-Hur, shot in duochrome technicolour with its scene of many bare-breasted young nubiles casting roses upon the strutting charioteers. And yes, you could see the nipples. Then there was the scene in *King Kong* in which the big ape is actually chewing a native. Shocking. So both *Ben-Hur* and *King Kong* had to be doctored, along with many other films from the twenties and thirties.

Mae West presented a more subtle problem for the censors. Although her whole screen persona was based on overt sexuality, she never actually disrobed, swore or said anything directly erotic. Her timing and innuendo were all she needed and Hays' code seemed ineffectual in curbing her vulgarity. But the sneaky senator finally made her toe the line and by 1940 Mae West's films were about as titillating as Evensong.

One notable film escaping emasculation despite its remarkable mix of erotic fantasy and religious fervour was Cecil B. De Mille's 1932 *Sign of the Cross*, for which Regal original John Hack had painstakingly constructed a large illuminated cross as an advertisement. De Mille was possibly the only film maker in Hollywood who, because of his standing with the clergy and his high moral reputation, could get away with scenes such as the one where actress Elissa Landi is tied naked to a post and ravaged by a gorilla. Great stuff.

Setting aside the artistic licence of film makers, there was a pervasive air of unreality in movies for thirty years. The Regal, like all picture houses, was, after all, a 'Theatre of Dreams' and not a 'Theatre of Perfect Reality'. No matter how violent gangsters were with their machine guns barking, no blood ever gushed. Fist fights could last for five minutes but no one ever suffered a busted nose or multiple contusions – worse than that, their hats always stayed on. And just WHAT WAS supposed to happen after that first jaw-breaking kiss? (No tongues please,by order of Senator Hays.) Consequently, films were obliged to achieve excellence with clever, witty scripting, minimalist direction, actors with true charisma and actresses with cloaked sexuality shoe-horned into outrageous dresses. It DID work much of the time and hundreds of classic films were created as less often became MORE. To hide the cracks in cheaper movies, particularly forties *film noir* stuff, the script-writers did brilliant things, creating intense gaggy dialogue so engaging that you forgave the censors for not allowing us to see the bullet holes appear in a wise guy's zoot suit when he caught a slug.

The stars, too, were legendary without over-kill. Even now, no modern actor can match the brooding menace of James Cagney, whose very presence evinced mayhem and rape yet not once did he swear, fart or flash his bottom (à la Richard Gere) though granted, he DID ice a lot of suckers and stool pigeons.

The Watch Committee: my dream job

During the post-war period until the late 1990s, if a controversial film was on general release, Ernie Highland was obliged to invite a small group of local worthies, known as 'the Watch Committee' for a private, advance viewing. They would usually consist of a local magistrate, a policeman, a councillor or two (or three or four), perhaps a doctor, probably a teacher, definitely a vicar and at least one solicitor. Moral guardians all, they would stretch out in the balcony and while Ernie's staff plied them with tea and biccies, pontificate on whatever brutality and licentiousness the movie industry felt tempted to bombard us with, before reporting on its suitability to the powers that were. Highland would have his fingers and toes crossed that the committee didn't give a film the thumbs down and ban it because the more controversy generated, the more bums on seats.

As jobs go, being on the Watch Committee was right up there with being a Miss Wet T-Shirt judge, although they did only manage to extricated a mere £5 each expenses from the Regal directors. Now, I have never liked the idea of somebody controlling what I watch and hear, no matter how appalling, but on the other hand, I wouldn't have wanted my children to have sat through *The Exorcist*.

In fairness to the members of the Watch Committee, they generally displayed liberal judgement and gave the green light to many controversial films of the day, such as *Soldier Blue*, *Bonny and Clyde* and *The Wild Bunch* (all criticised for violence), *Women in Love* (nudity and sexual content), *The Wicker Man* (nudity, sexual content, blasphemy) and Ken Russell's playful production *The Devils* (nudity, sexual content, blasphemy, violence, language, horror, degradation and Oliver Reed's bloody acting).

(In 1960 an equivalent Watch Committee in Warwickshire insisted that two love scenes be deleted from *Saturday Night and Sunday Morning* on the grounds that they were too explicit and that they glorified marital infidelity. British Lion executive David Kingsley was outraged and said, "We are not prepared to agree that a film of outstanding importance and merit should be re-edited by the Mrs Grundys of Warwickshire County Council. It is fortunate for the world that Warwickshire's greatest and often bawdy son, William Shakespeare, was not subject in his day to the restrictions of prim and petty officialdom." Neither side relented and as a consequence the film was never shown in the county. Up on his cloud, the bard must have been shaking his head with astonishment.)

The Regal Watch Committee did have one or two flutters in the early 1970s with, firstly, *A Clockwork Orange*, with its amoral brutality and bizarre style. The watchers must have been shocked but let it pass in its entirety. I sneaked in to see it as a confused sixteen-year-old and two hours later wandered down the marble stairs, nodded a 'thank you' to Ernie Highland and swaggered up town with a deranged grin on my face. By the time it had whipped up a nationwide storm of controversy, director Stanley Kubrick pulled it out of circulation in a fit of pique. No one could get to see it either at the pictures, on video or DVD until it was re-issued almost thirty years later and once again packed out the Regal with a curious new generation, plus me again. My opinion didn't alter much. It was still an anarchic masterpiece but I could sense the pull of middle age because I thought the Drooges' white jumpsuits, fitted with codpieces, were pervy.

Next in the controversy stakes was *The Exorcist* which, although deeply shocking, had become such a world-wide smash by the time it hit Evesham that to ban it would have been farcical. Not to mention that the loss of potential revenue would have had Ernie Highland putting out a contract on the Watch Committee. (In the end it didn't make any difference to Highland, because the Clifton grabbed it first.) But perhaps the most heart-stopping moment for them was the screening of *Straw Dogs* in 1971, after an outraged customer had complained bitterly about what he perceived was being done to Susan George on the settee. Our moral crusaders scrambled for a second viewing, decided that the miffed punter certainly had a point and feverishly debated whether or not to pull the film. However, as it had been showing to good audiences for several days without further complaint, they decided to bite the bullet and let things take their course – a bit like Susan George had to.

ASSOCIATED BRITISH-PATHE Presents A HAMMER FILM Production
ONE MILLION YEARS B.C.
A
Starring
RAQUEL WELCH · JOHN RICHARDSON
with
PERCY HERBERT · ROBERT BROWN · MARTINE BESWICK
Special Visual Effects Created by RAY HARRYHAUSEN · Music and Special Musical Effects Composed by MARIO NASCIMBENE · Screenplay by MICHAEL CARRERAS · Adapted from an original screenplay by Mickell Novak, George Baker, Joseph Frickert · Associate Producer AIDA YOUNG · Produced by MICHAEL CARRERAS · Directed by DON CHAFFEY · TECHNICOLOR · Released through WARNER-PATHE

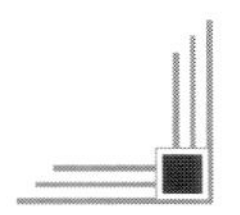

CHAPTER SEVEN

THE IMPORTANCE OF BEING ERNIE

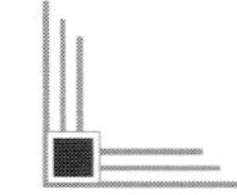

With just a few condensed facts and a healthy dash of hero worship it is easy to regard Ernie Highland as some messianic figure who swept into the ailing Regal in 1956, sprinkled cosmic dust around and had the place back to its gleaming, successful, pre-war best. The truth was, the advent of television had put paid to the golden age of cinema which had seen packed houses every night, seven days a week, the Clifton was proving a formidable rival and the strictures of an industry under pressure squeezed the independents like never before. Thus, it took Highland a full seven years of hard graft to generate enough cash for a complete overhaul.

During this time he had to utilise all his experience and try every trick in the book to get the customers through the doors. From the word go he smarmed, cajoled and manoeuvred around

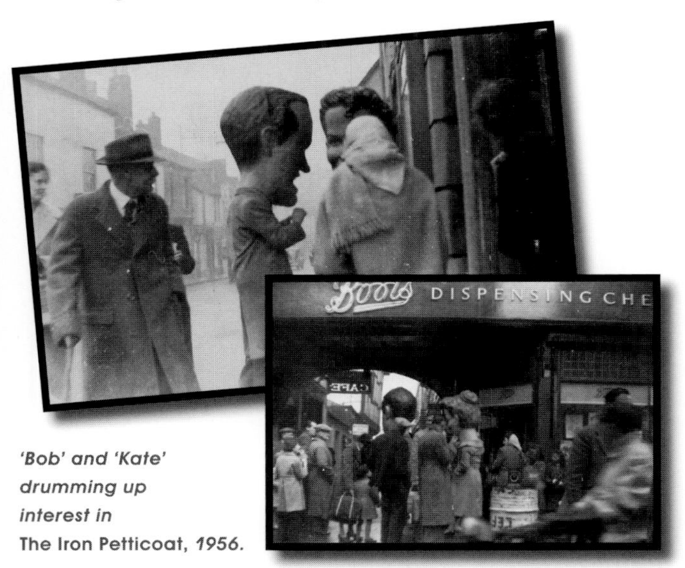

'Bob' and 'Kate' drumming up interest in **The Iron Petticoat**, *1956.*

This photo of Joan Sanders and her friend Jean Richmond on the Regal steps illustrates the difference between the England of 1956 and the present. Joan is holding a blue canvas bag containing the week's takings and is about to walk across town with it to deposit it in the bank. Nowadays such a task would have to be undertaken by two thickset gentlemen in an armoured truck.

the studio film reps for better film deals and even boosted ice cream sales during intermissions by turning the spot lights on the usherettes as they stood with their trays at the front of the cinema. Just for the record, the first usherette to be put under No. 1 Maurice Berry's spotlight and subsequently besieged with requests for Mivis was Joan Sanders, who regards it as the hardest fifteen minutes' work of her life!

Joan, who became chief cashier, was also seconded into another of Ernie's innovations. To advertise a forthcoming 1956 movie, *The Iron Petticoat* starring Bob Hope and Katherine Hepburn, Highland obtained large, hollow papier mâché heads of the two stars and asked Joan to accompany him around town, he as Hope and she as Hepburn (see photos). She succumbed to his princely bribe of ten shillings for the task and later cursed herself for not holding out for a quid.

By 1963 the Regal finances were secure enough to merit splashing out on long-awaited refurbishment. With Vic Morrall's blessing, Ernie began researching how best to decorate the Theatre of Dreams. He first struck a deal with a Walsall cinema for their second-hand seats, in excellent condition, trimmed in red velveteen. Highland then became enamoured to the point of obsession with the ceiling of a Birmingham picture palace, the Gaumont in Steelhouse Lane, which had a dark blue ceiling sporting myriad tiny lights, resembling stars, but when he researched the cost of emulating it in Evesham, he back-pedalled, pronto.

The decorators arrived in the last week of May and as the interior scaffold was removed on June 17, the Theatre of Dreams gleamed red, gold, burgundy and navy. Ernie Highland beamed with a corn-cob smile. Yet, although the old place looked brand new, almost all the original character had been retained inside. Windows had been installed in the curved wall of the manager's third-storey office and the balcony fire escape had been blocked off: the stairs were rotten and the Fire Chief concurred that it was an unnecessary feature.

Tony Goodwin tiling in 1965.

The appearance of the Regal entrance was radically altered, however, as the two Cotswold stone supporting pillars and outer block façade were boxed in with wooden shuttering, cement rendered and painted.[1]

A packed house, including a seven-year-old yours truly, delighted in the fresh paintwork and new seats as it watched the first feature to be shown after the re-vamp: *Jason and the Argonauts*.

Ernie the character

The man who became known as 'Mr Regal' was a high-energy individual, a bit larger than life, who I always felt had stepped from a black and white British movie. A shrewd, old school, big-city operator, not overly creative, just straight and passionate about his profession. He was traditional, a bit right-wing and liked the monarchy. How many of us have stood through the national anthem at the end of an evening with Ernie Highland blocking the exit until the last note? Usherettes would be rebuked if they began tilting up seats during 'the Queen'.

Despite having this starchy facet of his personality Highland was a sucker for a dare. An usherette once hinted that he would be afraid to do her job so, come the next intermission, Ernie was harnessed into her tray, flogging lollies. Another time he spent the whole morning cycling around town in his suit with a cinema advertising board slung under its crossbar. He was scared of precisely nothing.

Apparently he didn't like Christmas much but by all accounts did have a yen for the ladies and would be charm personified in female company. He was long-time friends with jazz pianist

1 Around 1965 the entrance was adorned with twelve-inch-square panels of small black and white tiles which gave it its definitive look. Leastways, it was the one I grew up with.

Winifred Atwell,[2] whom he met in the Caribbean while on active service during the war. Once, in 1986, while I was exiting the Regal after seeing *Jewel of the Nile,* he asked me if I had enjoyed it.

> *"Wow, Kathleen Turner has a funny effect on me," I enthused, but not so loud that my girlfriend heard. "Yeah, nice isn't she?" he agreed, then stepped forward to speak in conspiratorial fashion. "You know who really does it for me? Jenny Agutter," he confessed softly, and even as his knees buckled slightly at the thought, I saw the lust shining behind the big dark-rimmed specs.*

Ernie the professional

The teetotal Brummie was, in many ways the archetypal cinema man. Exuding huge bonhomie, he could hustle with the best of them but the customers always came first. Highland's remit was simple: the creation of the perfect, profitable family cinema in which all were welcome and everyone felt at home. One old lady who lived locally would visit the Regal regularly in her slippers, stating that it was as familiar to her as her living room.[3]

He had tightened up procedures since Eileen Butler's tenure and expected a disciplined attitude from Regal employees but he was no martinet and remained popular and good humoured. Certain pranks could sorely test his patience, such as when an unidentified usherette released an inflated condom over the stalls while the audience was engrossed in a tender love scene, but on the whole Ernie was indulgent with his staff.

Throughout the 1960s, however, the hardest part of the job by far remained Highland's constant battle to secure the hottest films as near as possible to their release date while in competition with his High Street rival. Ernie and Clifton manager David Johnson actually had a good relationship. They were both cinema pros who knew the score, enjoyed a working friendship and even agreed an arrangement whereby staff from each cinema could visit the other for free. However, the relationship Ernie had with the Clifton's film buyer, Ken Jones, was like that of Cain and Abel. Man, they hated each other. There began a low-key battle between them that would last for years and usually took the form of petty one-upmanship involving film selection.

For example, in 1959 when Ernie secured the Hitchcock thriller *North By Northwest* Ken Jones countered with *Northwest Frontier* (starring Kenneth More). A year later, a similar thing happened, the Clifton screening *Oscar Wilde* (starring Robert Morley), billed as 'the most talked-about film in the history of the cinema', and the Regal striking back with *The Trials of Oscar Wilde* (starring Peter Finch), billed as 'a film to make cinema history'. Highland and Jones outsmarted themselves with this latter duel. Because of the prurient interest attached to Oscar Wilde in those days both cinemas were packed, although as the Regal held their film over for six days and the Clifton only four, I suppose Ernie could claim victory.

2 Highland was a fine pianist in his own right and had more than one piece of music published. His favourite self-penned offering was a thing called 'The Mini Blues' which he composed during the sixties in praise of Mary Quant's famous skirt.

3 Ernie followed the tradition of Regal managers by changing into evening dress on Saturday nights. Only once was he obliged to greet customers in his usual duds after tickling Irene Mackenzie under the arms while she carried a twenty-four pack of Kia-ora drink cartons. These hit the deck and detonated in an explosion of orange juice all over Highland's tux.

Best of all, in early 1971 the rivalry plumbed new depths as Highland screened something called *The Body* which could be loosely classified as a sex-education film. This stirred up huge interest and Ken Jones began trawling for suitable opposition. He found it in a thing called *Love Variations* which was a similar 'instructional movie'. I was just shy of fifteen at the time and despite being well under age for their adult rating, determined to see both (as did every kid in the area). However, the prospect of facing down the formidable Elsie Tandy in the ticket kiosk made me hesitate. (Under no circumstances could you ask your parents to take you to gawk at stuff like this.)

While I was dithering, Ernie Highland had a change of heart and pulled *The Body* after a couple of days. According to long-time Regal usherette Irene Mackenzie, he felt his professional credibility was under threat, screening such licentious garbage, and while seeing his twenty-eight-foot screen festooned with sweaty, fleshy unmentionables he lost his temper, stomped up to the projection box and ordered operator Brian Houghton to "Take that filth off and let's put on a decent movie." The horny youth of Asum let out a collective groan and Ken Jones capered with delight on hearing that Highland had blinked first. Attention shifted across town to *Love Variations* so I, plus around a dozen mates, plucked up courage, caught the bus to the Clifton and took our chances with their box office battleaxe. We reasoned that, regardless of the adult certificate, they wouldn't turn away so much trade in one go. It worked – we were in! We sat with bated breath, poised to be exposed to far, far more than the usual glimpse (I had seen a topless Mexican girl in *The Wild Bunch* the previous year). You guessed it – it was hogwash. Some spawny-eyed doctor sat behind a desk explaining what an impossibly bored, thirty-something Scandinavian couple were supposed to be doing, as they flopped naked on each other. I'd been more aroused by Maths homework.

Regal V Clifton:
Who can show the dirtiest movie?

Despite the glitch with *The Body*, which was a big hit while it lasted, Ernie Highland's aim was always 'bums on seats' at whatever cost to the art form. He professed to liking certain movies such as *Ben-Hur* or anything with Elvis or John Wayne in it, but he didn't really care just so long as a queue formed down Burford Road. He gave the people what they wanted and with the exception of a few midnight movies in the late 1950s/early 1960s (e.g. *Inn of the Sixth Happiness*) plus some one-off all-ticket speciality productions such as Verdi's *La Traviata*, he kept it simple. He wasn't about to risk the Regal finances by getting creative and screening a Jean-Luc Goddard 'art-house' season when the core audience of unreconstructed hillbillies, like me, wanted to see gun-ups on main street. Monsters, mayhem and madams – marvellous. Or put another way: T. Rex, tanks and tits – terrific!

Highland always cultivated good working relationships with the film studio reps based in Birmingham and one of the perks for the Regal staff was the chance to accompany him to the second city to preview new movies and suss their box office potential. Iris Jordan would often go and take her son Brian. Now HE was a young man to be jealous of, because as well as these premières, he claims never to have had to pay to get into the Regal in his life. However, he also claims the dubious honour of being targeted for rowdy behaviour and ejected by his mum more than any other individual, whether he was guilty or not. Iris obviously believed that privilege came at a price.

Projectionist Brian Houghton, who replaced Norman Hill as chief operator in 1963, became rather good at spotting the potential of 'cheapies' otherwise slipping under the radar screen, which would invariably clean up over a week at the Theatre of Dreams. Stuff such as *Hercules Unchained*, a dubbed Italian, technicolour, sword and sandals effort starring former Mr Universe, Steve Reeves. Corny and creaky, Ernie paid peanuts for it and it packed the place out.

Hard-wearing fan

Goodwins, the hardware store, two doors down from the Regal had a long connection with Ernie's empire and one member of the Goodwin clan, Tony, could rightly claim to be its number one fan. A true cinema junkie.

When I first contacted him to ask if he wished to contribute to this book he was very cagey, concerned about the Regal's history being portrayed accurately and with requisite worship. He took some convincing that I was also a huge fan and not some 'stitch-up' merchant, but has since been most forthcoming with photos, stories and information.

Tony's interest expanded to old cinemas in general and he became a member of the CTA (Cinema Theatre Association) but his heart belonged first and foremost in Port Street. Specifically in seat F9 of the balcony, where he always chose to sit – an aisle seat which afforded optimum viewing pleasure. If Tony ever arrived late for a movie and F9 was occupied, that customer would become aware of an icy presence until suitable alternative repose had been selected. Only once did Tony choose not to grumble, when he steamed in to find Vic Morrall himself sitting in his seat.

Ernie and Tony became mates for thirty years with the Regal providing much work for the Goodwin family firm. Tony became proficient on the Westars and would stand in as a projectionist whenever needed. He also enjoyed trips to Birmingham to preview forthcoming attractions, adding his voice to the decision-making process on which films to select. Once, in the late 1960s, he pitched in with a suggestion which has embarrassed him ever since. At this time, the long-running serial

Sacred seat, F9.
Only a true fan will understand.

The Forsyte Saga was the most popular programme on television so Tony espoused the screening of the 1949 Greer Garson/ Errol Flynn version of John Galsworthy's famous books.

"You can't miss with this one, Ernie. It'll pack 'em in for sure," he chirruped with great pride in his perspicacity. Alas, the locals never got the message. At the first showing Tony Goodwin settled himself into F9 with a sense of unease as sagebrush swirled down the aisles and Greer Garson's dulcet tones echoed round the vast emptiness of the Theatre of Dreams. He was a man virtually alone until a perplexed Highland rested a reassuring hand on the shoulder of his scarlet-faced friend. "We all have our off-days, son," he opined philosophically, through gritted teeth.

When I first met Tony Goodwin I naturally bombarded him with all manner of questions on the Regal's history. One such query was what happened to the old wooden, glass-fronted cases on the outside walls which displayed photos of scenes from current and forthcoming movies.

"Ah," he said, "come with me." He led me into his back yard and, joy of joys, there it was: a lovingly renovated, illuminated display case. To top it all, it was fitted with stills from my favourite film.

Ernie the Tough Guy

With his hugely personable nature and his liberal distribution of free tickets earning him the moniker 'Mr Complimentary', it would have been easy to make the mistake of regarding Highland as little more than a warm-hearted benign individual. No one's patsy, but no ogre. When I was little I always viewed him as a kind of middle-aged Milky Bar Kid. Yet, when it came to the pinch he was just about the toughest guy in town. Although,

Tony Goodwin with his display case.

only of average size, his strength-to-weight ratio defied the laws of physics. He wouldn't tolerate bad behaviour in his cinema under any circumstances and REALLY bad behaviour would be met with biblical wrath. There was a multi-stage procedure for dealing with unruly customers – a kind of 'three strikes and you're out' system, if you will. If the errant youth of the day, or anyone for that matter, was making a noise and wrecking the ambience, the initial action would be for an usherette to shine her torch on them and request a bit of hush, thank you. This normally sufficed, particularly if it was either Iris Jordan or Irene Mackenzie wielding the torch. However, if the ruckus continued Ernie would step in with a similar, though sterner demand for quiet, thank you, again. If matters still persisted, the offender(s) would be asked to leave and if they refused, an octopus grip would manifest itself on their arm or collar and the miscreant would be propelled, with awesome power, right out of the door. Thank you and goodnight. This happened to many people during Ernie's thirty-one-year tenure and unlike the recipients of today's ASBOs, I doubt if anyone, young or old, regarded their ejection from the Theatre of Dreams as some badge of honour (although one particularly rough bunch known as the Blockley gang almost became celebrity evictees).

Some individuals managed to transcend the usual procedure by going from stage one (torch, friendly request) to stage three (removal) in one step, such as the young couple in the rear of the stalls who had been asked politely to tone down their snogging grunts. The young lady complied but with smooches no longer forthcoming and with her boyfriend's hormones crashing the red line, he decided on a different approach. "Get your hand out of my knickers!" she suddenly screeched like a fishwife, making five hundred film fans leap higher than they did when the head fell out of the boat in *Jaws*. Romeo and Juliet were immediately bounced.

You didn't necessarily have to make a noise to merit getting chucked out. Highland once spotted three of his usherettes giggling at a scene transpiring in the gloom of the stalls (back row, of course). Two gay men were kissing, thereby exhibiting a drastic lack of common sense (this was 1960s Evesham). The usherettes were sent scurrying as a morally indignant manager applied his vice-like grip on the collars of two well-tailored jackets.

If a fight ever kicked off in the Regal, Highland would spring into action by quickly removing his specs and either stowing them in his top pocket or thrusting them into the hand of his nearest usherette as he stomped into the fray. He would adopt the classic swift gait favoured by many old actors. Think Jimmy Hanley in *The Blue Lamp*, jaw set in grim determination as he closed in on George Dixon's killer – the slight forward lean, the arms pumping downwards and across. Likewise, Ernie would propel himself into a rumble and nullify it within seconds. No modern bouncer could effect redress more efficiently.

To the best of my knowledge only one individual ever received a lifetime ban. During the late 1950s, this particular gentleman managed to purchase a ticket without it being noticed that the smell of alcohol on his breath was strong enough to melt titanium. Somehow he located a seat on the lower deck (he would never have made the balcony) where he continued to imbibe from a hip flask until cross-eyed paralytic. Through the fog of inebriation nature made a call and he staggered to his feet for an heroic, though fruitless, attempt at locating the men's room. Pissed beyond comprehension, with compass shot, he had little option but to unzip himself and let fly in the aisle, to the horror of the audience, many of whom were women and children. Ernie Highland just happened to be nearby and descended on the hapless soak like an avenging angel, his face resembling something which, 'tis said, only appears at full moon. The drunk's world must have taken on a kaleidoscopic slant as he was lifted like a feather and bundled out of the stalls, leaving a little trail of droplets in his wake across the marble foyer. With a final mighty flourish, Ernie literally booted him out of the front doors where he sprawled like a rag doll, now beyond all pain and suffering, on the Port Street slabs.

Little Miss Feisty

Along with that of Iris Jordan, Violet Woodcock and Brian Houghton, Irene Mackenzie's service to the Regal spans more than half of its history. Yet, as is often the case, it was only by chance that she began her long stint. In the summer of 1962 while watching *The Young Ones* she fell foul of Ernie Highland's 'three strikes' rule for high-jinks and general rowdiness. Irene and a couple of her friends were duly ejected from the stalls with Cliff crooning to his leading lady. I can understand her restlessness on this occasion because a Cliff Richard musical could make an Elvis one seem like *West Side Story.*

So, kicking her heels on the Port Street pavement the penny dropped that it might just be time for her to seek gainful employment. Thus, a couple of days later Irene and her friend Pat Payne found themselves at the Employment Exchange (then situated in Port Street), their futures being determined by the resident careers advisor, John Doberman (I've given him a fictitious name). This gentleman was a well-know local bureaucrat who had undergone a successful charisma bypass and seemed to be in this job, like, forever. I'm betting that not one of the young bloods who darkened his desk over the years applauded him as an inspirational powerhouse who barked at them to get out there and 'shoot for the moon!'. I encountered him once, myself, at Prince Henry's Grammar School, just after taking my 'O' levels. Moreover, the previous evening, I had been to see the film *Deliverance*, a riveting yarn about men battling both the elements and their own inadequacies. All pumped up with a sense of derring-do I bounced into the career advisor's office, an embryo Burt Reynolds ready to overcome daunting odds and map out an heroic future for myself. I left twenty minutes later having lost the will to live. Irene Mackenzie must have harboured similar feelings in 1962 as he leaned over his desk, peered at her through his Roy Orbison headlamps and handed her a job interview card. "It's Beach's factory for you, young lady," he stated in a tone which seemed less to extol the benefit of employment as to seal her fate. Her friend Pat was presented with a card for interview at a certain nearby cinematic establishment where a Mr E.F. Highland required an usherette.

Pat's interview came first so Irene tagged along and they both sat in the back row of the stalls awaiting the manager. Ernie spotted Irene first and beckoned her over in his avuncular manner. The two girls shrugged at each other (they were only fifteen) and Irene toddled forth for an impromptu interview on the middle landing where Ernie offered HER the job as usherette. There was no bad blood over Irene's recent expulsion – you would have had to insult Elvis or the Queen for Highland to bear a grudge. All errant youth was eventually allowed back into the Regal. Ernie, first and foremost a businessman, realised that even bad boys made the till jingle.

Slightly bewildered, Irene tentatively broke the news to her friend. "Oh, that's okay, I'll take the Beach's job," said Pat Payne. Life was more straightforward in those days.

It was a strange turnaround for Irene. One minute she was getting the bum's-rush while Cliff crooned about teenage love, the next she was harnessed into an ice cream tray with her back to the screen. She went on to set the Regal record for uninterrupted full-time service of forty-one years,

Irene Mackenzie at the sweet kiosk in 1987

Elvis packs 'em in with **GI Blues** *in April 1964.*

having evolved from a naughty teenager, ejected by her mentor, to being a dedicated manageress of seventeen years, sadly having to witness the decline and fall of her beloved picture palace. Forty-one years is a long time, but I think it's fair to speculate that if the Regal had stayed in operation, Irene would still be prowling the marble stairs. Ironically, she says that she hated her first year in the place and determined to find alternative employment. But I suspect her efforts were half-hearted because by then, like her mother before her (manageress of the Clifton in the late 1940s and early 1950s – see Chapter Three), the cinema had begun to weave its magic and ensnared her for a further four decades. The Eagles once made a record called 'Hotel California' whose lyrics resonate with regard to the Theatre of Dreams: "You can check out anytime you like. But you can NEVER leave."

Elvis and the gypsies

I have no specific evidence of box office takings but the Regal's most bankable star in the post-war period was either The King, The Duke, The Man with No Name, a rubber-shark, a plastic spacecraft, a high school misfit, a bug-eyed alien, a short-arsed Aussie, an animatronic dinosaur or a sinking ship. Of these ten, however, none was regarded with more affection than Elvis and from 1957 to 1973, despite the dodgy quality of some of his thirty-three movies, he never had a flop at the Theatre of Dreams. *Flaming Star* in 1960 held the Regal post-war attendance record until surpassed by the 1967 Hayley Mills pic, *The Family Way.*

Irene Mackenzie was a huge Presley devotee who eventually became a fan club organiser. As such, Ernie Highland bought her a framed 12" × 9" black and white publicity photo which Irene proudly hung on the wall of the ticket kiosk in 1968 where

Irene Mackenzie with THAT picture of Elvis.

it remained until the new millennium. The King smiled through the glass at a third of a century of Regal fans. Apart from when it was cleaned, this picture only vacated the kiosk once when some unidentified heretic stole it, one winter's day in the 1980s. It turned up intact in a snowdrift by the Burford road car park two days later so Irene had to make a swift phone call to cancel the hit-man.

Irene has been a treasure-trove of information on the Theatre of Dreams and the very first question I threw at her when she agreed to contribute to this book was: "What happened to that picture of Elvis?"

She smiled, left the room and returned thirty seconds later with the sacred image and I finally got to hold it up close. It was better than discovering the Dead Sea scrolls. I just HAD to have the whole thing re-photographed.

Some of Elvis's biggest fans were the people of the travelling community and when Presley movies came to town on Sundays, gypsies from all over the Vale would arrive at the Regal en masse.

Ernie Highland had to be well organised and felt obliged to practise a type of segregation by reserving the front six rows of the stalls to accommodate them.[4]

The notion of segregation is now distasteful but during the fifties and sixties travellers tended to be a pretty unsophisticated group who evoked a natural enmity in conventional citizens. There is simply no ignoring that fact. So Ernie had his system and it worked – which was just as well because the gypsies were fantastic customers.

They were an awesome bunch as they massed in the foyer, dressed in Sunday best, parents giving the orders, tough young guys diligently chaperoning their sisters, and children knowing their place. They would descend on the sweet kiosk

4 In these appallingly politically correct times, readers may feel I am treading on thin ice with this subject matter. However, as what I am relating is the truth, it stands on its own merits and is treated in the same light-hearted, even-handed spirit as the rest of this book.

and spend a fortune on ice cream and joob-joobs leaving Violet Woodcock feeling like Old Mother Hubbard.

Highland's biggest headache in the early days of his tenure was the fact that many gypsies, particularly the young, were simply not used to indoor plumbing and, shall we say, there were a few accidents. This problem was eventually ironed-out (don't ask) and throughout the summer for more than twenty years the travelling community continued to keep the Regal ticking over during the periods when audiences were prey to other warm-weather distractions such as fetes, carnivals, Wimbledon, the World Cup or the Olympics.

So, for years, everything was cool. Elvis rocked for his travelling fans and there was little aggro. The worst incident on record was a barney between two gypsy women during a packed house. Predictably, it was over a man and it was nasty.
It resembled a leopard fighting a wolverine. Punches flew, stiletto heels slashed and long hair was wrenched out like mattress stuffing as the two gouging, biting females went at it to the death. Ernie Highland happened to be away and Iris Jordan was in charge. Iris and Irene had to act quickly before one killed the other, while running the risk of getting mashed themselves. With astonishing courage and strength Iris Jordan waded in, grabbed two handfuls of hair and banged their heads together. Hard. The combatants crumpled, to a mixed chorus of cheers, from them as like that sort of thing, and sharp intakes of breath from the more compassionate movie-goers wincing on impact.

"Girls, girls, girls," sang the King.

GRAND NATIONAL FILM DISTRIBUTORS present

BUSTER CRABBE

in, the death-defying, cliff-hanging adventures of...

FULL LENGTH
VERSION FOR
THE FIRST TIME!

FLASH GORDON

U

co-starring

JEAN ROGERS · PRISCILLA LAWSON · with CHARLES MIDDLETON AS THE MERCILESS "EMPEROR MING"

DISTRIBUTION BY

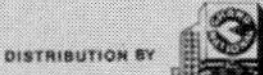

CHAPTER EIGHT

HIGHLAND GAMES

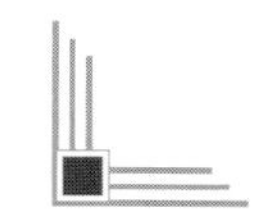

A Saturday morning Regal audience in 1956.

Best day of the week

People from every generation have fond memories of their favourite childhood events or activities. For late baby-boomers like me, these rose-tinted pastimes tended to be seasonal and/or traditional: Christmas, Easter, summer holidays, sports day, bonfire night, the mop, conkers, marbles, camping, swimming, football, tree-climbing, go-karting, etc. Sigh. But the one which I hold in greatest affection is Saturday morning pictures at the Regal. Those three hours from nine till noon had a particularly intense excitement. It's difficult to identify why. Perhaps it was the collective tension of around four hundred Vale kids, strangers from other villages who came together at this time to discover the fate of some hero last seen during a cliff-hanger moment in the weekly serial. Perhaps it was because it seemed like anarchy to our young minds, the very antithesis of school. And no homework. Or perhaps it was a sense of exclusivity, strictly no adults allowed, apart from Ernie and Auntie Iris and Auntie Vi and Auntie Irene. And they didn't count as your usual adults, 'cos they was fun!

Before the advent of sound in the cinema, most films, apart from more hard-hitting actioners such as *Battleship Potemkin* (1925), were easily understood by all age groups. Even teenies (under eights) could comprehend the likes of Chaplin or Keaton, which were not clogged with sophisticated dialogue and didn't indulge in gratuitous sex and violence. All this changed after the sound revolution as the breadth of expression in films exploded and the youngest cinema-goers were marginalised. Apart from early Walt Disney classics[1] the industry did not truly cater for children for two decades.

After World War Two, thought was given to how best to accommodate pre-teen audiences. It was, after all, a huge potential market. In Britain in 1951, the CFF (Children's Film Foundation) was formed with the aim of producing good-quality movies for the junior wing of the audience. These would typically be no more than one hour in length, so as not to exceed young attention spans, be adventurous and exciting without plots being too heavy or violent, with child actors prominent and adults kept largely in the background. These films showcased the burgeoning talents of many young actors who went on to become major stars of screen, stage and television: such luminaries as Jean Simmons, Anthony Newley, Susan George, Richard O'Sullivan, Olivia Hussey, David Hemmings (no relation), Dennis Waterman and Phil Collins.

Now that the industry was focusing on pre-teens, where better to corral this targeted audience than the local cinema on Saturday mornings? It worked wonderfully well for more than thirty years.

The CFF also produced serials in the same style as their films which would typically run for between six and twelve episodes of around twenty minutes each. The Americans had been producing these for years before the CFF came along, with heavyweight action heroes such as Flash Gordon or Buck Rogers being the order of the day. Screening serials was a fiendishly clever ploy because children would ponder for a whole week on the outcome of cliff-hanger endings and no power on earth would stop them from attending the next show (such innocent wonder would be compromised nowadays as most little smart-Alecs would trawl the Internet to discover the outcome).

When Ernie Highland arrived at the Theatre of Dreams in 1956 he re-branded this established children's matinee as the 'Saturday Morning Regal Chum's Club' (SMRCC) and boosted its popularity with all kinds of innovations which would transpire during the twenty-minute break between the serial and the main feature.

By 9.15 a.m. the lower deck was heaving with over four hundred children between the ages of four and fourteen. The lights would dim, cheers would ring out, the curtains would open, the serial would kick off and manic music would herald the conclusion to last week's cliff-hanger. Did our hero escape a terrible fate? You betcha – every single time. There was both a palpable sigh of relief and a sense of incredulity from the young fans, pleased on the one hand that the good guy was safe, but also just a tad cheated that the crisis had been averted in an implausibly simple manner. But no one complained just so long as the action kept thundering along

1 Even the Disney animated favourite *Snow White* originally received an adult certificate, primarily because of the very frightening scene where the wicked witch appears. It scared the Hell out of me.

until we were back on tenterhooks again, twenty minutes later. The excitement was obviously far less intense if the serial was a CFF effort as opposed to an American one. The Yankee offerings were more energetic and reckless with aeroplanes, cars and horses hurtling across the screen at breakneck pace. (I'm sure certain film sequences were speeded up by almost fifty per cent.) Fist fights could last two or three minutes without a drop of blood being spilled, a gentlemanly code of conduct dictating that if someone was punched and went down, his adversary would pick him up before punching him again. No one put the boot into a floored opponent. And perhaps the hairdressing the men used in those days had some adhesive quality because their bloody hats never came off. But I'm being picky from the vantage point of middle age. Young people can always be relied upon to suspend their disbelief. At the time it was marvellous.

Most of the American serials were produced by the long-defunct Republic company in the 1940s. Firstly, I remember *Flash Gordon Conquers The Universe* (rather an extravagant claim for its star, Larry 'Buster' Crabbe, who piloted a jet-powered dustbin which made a noise like a mozzie). Fantastic. Secondly, *King of the Rocketmen* (a zoot-suited hero played by the splendidly named Tristram Coffin, with a rocket-powered engine strapped to his back). Terrific. Thirdly came *Gene Autry and the Thunder Riders*. As far as I can recall this was a story about a cowboy who sang (Autry) battling evil robots. Possibly the most bizarre cross-genre blend in movie history. We lapped it up. Best of all, though, was the twelve-parter, *The Adventures of Captain Marvel,* starring Tom Tyler as the super-powered alter-ego of mild-mannered Billy Batson (played by Frank Coghlan Jnr). At times of peril, Billy would instantly change into the great man by uttering the magic word (all together, now):

Then heaven help the bad guys. There was a beautiful simplicity to these serial formats. The good guys oozed honour, were spotless, handsome and smiled – and always got the girl. Whereas the baddies, irredeemably evil, had pointy beards, wielded scimitars and grinned – and always came to a sticky end. That's the way it should be. Black and white film with black and white characters. Pre-teens can't assimilate subtle intrigue. There is no room in the junior psyche for complex, neurotic, misunderstood characters.[1]

Would Captain Marvel survive the stream of molten lava? Clang! The episode would end, the lights come on and the cycle of fascination was primed for another week.

All the American serials were male-orientated. The heroines (such as Dale Arden in *Flash Gordon*), although spunky gals, were usually peripheral. No avoiding it, this super-hero lark was a man thing and yet the young girls in the audiences enjoyed it every bit as much as the boys.

1 Imagine if Woody Allen had directed *Jaws*. He'd have probably cast himself as the shark.

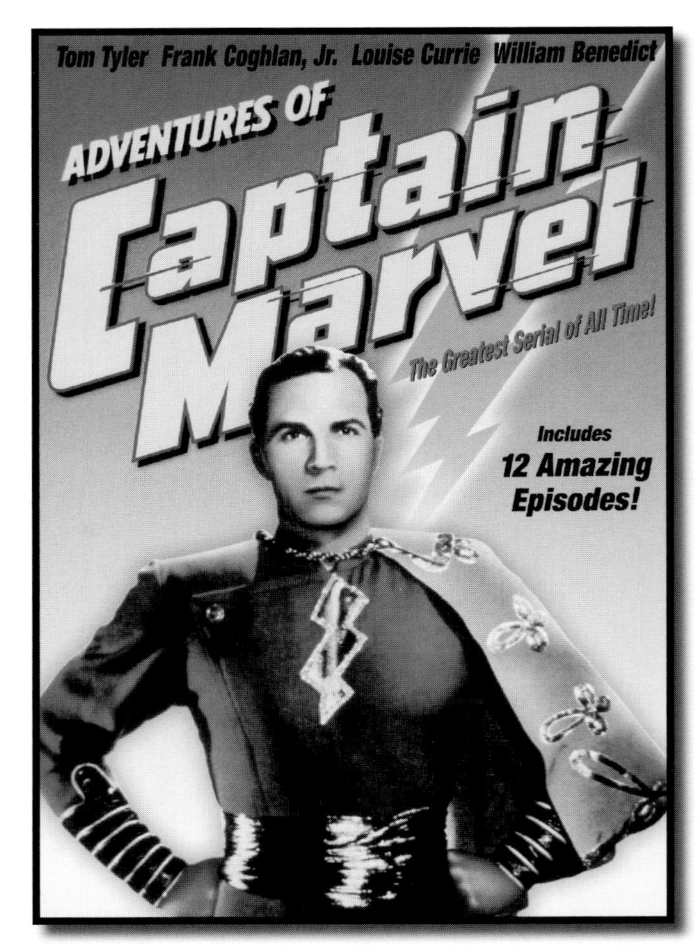

Captain Marvel. All together now: 'SHAZ ...

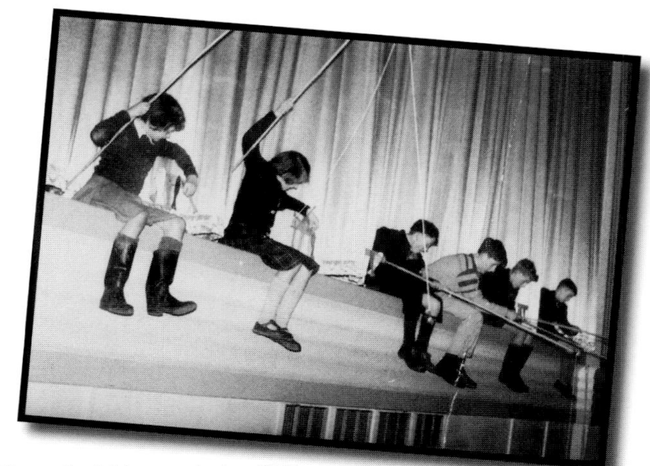

Magnetic fishing contest, c.1963.

When *Captain Marvel* concluded in July 1964 it was succeeded by a CFF serial *Dusty Bates* starring a very young Anthony Newley as the eponymous hero. After Captain Marvel's titanic dust-ups with his arch-enemy 'The Scorpion' I found the japes and scrapes of Dusty Bates a bit of a let-down and sulked for a couple of weeks. But the magic of the SMRCC remained undiminished, thanks largely to Ernie Highland.

During the interval of no more than twenty minutes between the serial and the main feature, all manner of fun was let loose. I suppose to an eight-year-old, twenty minutes is a long time and Ernie didn't waste it. He organised twisting and jiving competitions, fishing off the stage using magnets dangling from rods to catch metal fish from buckets, egg and spoon races (the two aisles, rear gangway and front of the stage made for a wonderful circuit and Hurley Robinson's dished floor saw many a young spooner kiss the deck). I remember once playing bingo, with Ernie drawing the balls. This was most unusual because lifelong cinema men despised the game, regarding it as an entertainment plague which was usurping the old picture palaces. Nonetheless, the winners collected a big bag of assorted joob-joobs. Come Easter time, a dozen or more young ladies would parade in their bonnets and in the run-up to bonfire night there was a best 'guy' competition. I witnessed one such event won by a young fellow whose effigy was rather pathetic, but it got the nod because he had had the nerve to 'borrow' his mother's new Silver Cross pram to transport it in.

I first went to SMRCC in 1963 as a seven-year-old, catching the bus to Evesham with my older brother Steve (he was eleven) and a group of his friends. First call in town, before nine, was Hamptons newsagent to buy something to read in the afternoon, usually an American horror comic. Three other Port Street shops held a fascination for us. If it was approaching bonfire night we would haunt Larners because it sold the biggest fireworks on the planet. I mean, these things looked like off-shoots from *The Manhattan Project*. We would press our noses up against the glass of the display case and drool at the sight of the dangerous beauties. Forty-five years on and it's incredible to think the law was so lax that if you had the cash nothing could stop you from laying your sticky little mitts on 'em. If Larners had ever suffered a fire and those monsters had all gone off, the resulting cataclysm would have levelled Bengeworth. Needless to say, we were not allowed to take them into the SMRCC.

If it was fishing season we would visit Escott Elsley's tackle shop. This place used to fascinate me almost as much as Larners. The vast array of floats, ledger weights and hooks seemed like jewellery and I wanted to own it all. (The wonder of childhood can never be overrated!)

Then there was always Franklin's pet shop from which my brother once bought a box full of day-old chicks (jewellery syndrome again). As we purchased our cinema tickets Iris Jordan confiscated them for the duration of the show, sensing, quite rightly, the potential for calamity.

The SMRCC also spawned some odd snack fads such as French sticks, purchased from Robbins' the bakers, next door to the cinema. A nice long French stick could perform several functions, only one of which was as food. You could deliver a gentle blow to the head of an enemy a full two rows in front, plus small chunks could be broken off and compacted to provide non-lethal ammunition. Cheap too, because no one in their right mind would have wasted a Malteser or Liquorice Allsort in order to settle a score. And does anyone remember those waxed paper tubes of red-coated popcorn? Manna from heaven.

Probably the only photo in existence of Ernie Highland spinning a free ticket into the young audience, c.1963.

Ernie Highland became a hero in his own right to us teenies, almost in the class of Captain Marvel. I got hooked on his ability to effortlessly spin free passes into the crowd during the interval; maybe half a dozen or so scattered evenly across the stalls. With a quick flick of the wrist, the tickets would soar and swoop above the hundreds of grasping hands. These passes were highly treasured because they allowed a whole family in free to see the major films. They were the coin of the realm. Very few were actually caught in mid-air and would land on the floor between the rows provoking a frenzied surge of bodies scrambling under the seats for the prize. The bigger boys usually won out and champion grabber was my brother. If any ticket landed within ten feet of us he would dive into the mêlée like a rat up a drainpipe and almost always surface victorious. Some days he secured two. If he hadn't taken up football, Steve might have become the world's greatest scrum-half. There even seemed to be a spirit of fair play, inasmuch as if rival mitts hit on the same ticket and tore it in half, the person with the lesser piece would invariably hand it over. I was that much smaller than my older brother and only twice dared to plunge into the seething ruck. Both times I was crushed under fifteen hundredweight of steaming brats, to emerge tearful and potless. Nonetheless, thanks to Steve's demon foraging, I can't recall our family paying for the pictures until the first moon landing.

Coin of the realm: a free pass.

My ambition to emulate my brother (or for that matter, scrap like Captain Marvel or ride a horse like Gene Autry) took second place to my desire to spin free passes like Ernie Highland. I would practise on Saturday afternoons with a whole pack of playing cards and never mastered the technique. (I am now fifty-two, have travelled the world, raised a family, am a fine upstanding member of society and after forty years of intermittent practice STILL CAN'T launch a four-by-four-inch piece of card.)

Nowadays, the 'nanny state' would prohibit much of this youthful anarchy. The staff would be crucified for promoting such irresponsible 'rough and tumble'. In my time at SMRCC the worst injury I ever witnessed was a skinned knuckle but times change and I guess these days our soft-shelled little darlings deserve protection.

Regal rockin'

Every few weeks from about 1958 onwards, the SMRCC's young devotees would get a special treat during the intermission, enjoying a twenty-minute session from one of Evesham's local pop bands. The three best outfits during this period (1958–64) were the Sapphires, the Wavelengths and Terry and the Trojans which all played undiluted rock 'n' roll until the style of pop altered when the Beatles made it huge in 1963.

Around this time, when bands did evening gigs at local venues such as Evesham Public Hall or the Lifford Hall in Broadway they could expect to collect a £15–20 fee. The deal with Ernie Highland was £6 for twenty minutes at the SMRCC. Alternatively, they would play free for the kids on Saturday if Highland allowed them to practise in the cinema on Sunday mornings. Plus, if they were ever spotted queuing for a film, Ernie would let them in free.

The Sapphires were formed in mid-1959 by Ian Findley and Dave Nicholls (who managed them from 1959–62) from Fairfield, both having previously been part of the Vale Five Rockets (which had disbanded some months earlier). They soon put together an excellent combo, with Dave (rhythm guitar), Ian (lead guitar), Pete Cresswell from Offenham (rhythm guitar), Roy Banks from Honeybourne (bass) and Barry Mellor (drums). Barry became Evesham's own Ringo Starr and was in big demand for more than one reason. Firstly, he was a real mean stick man who occasionally also played with the Wavelengths and the Trojans.

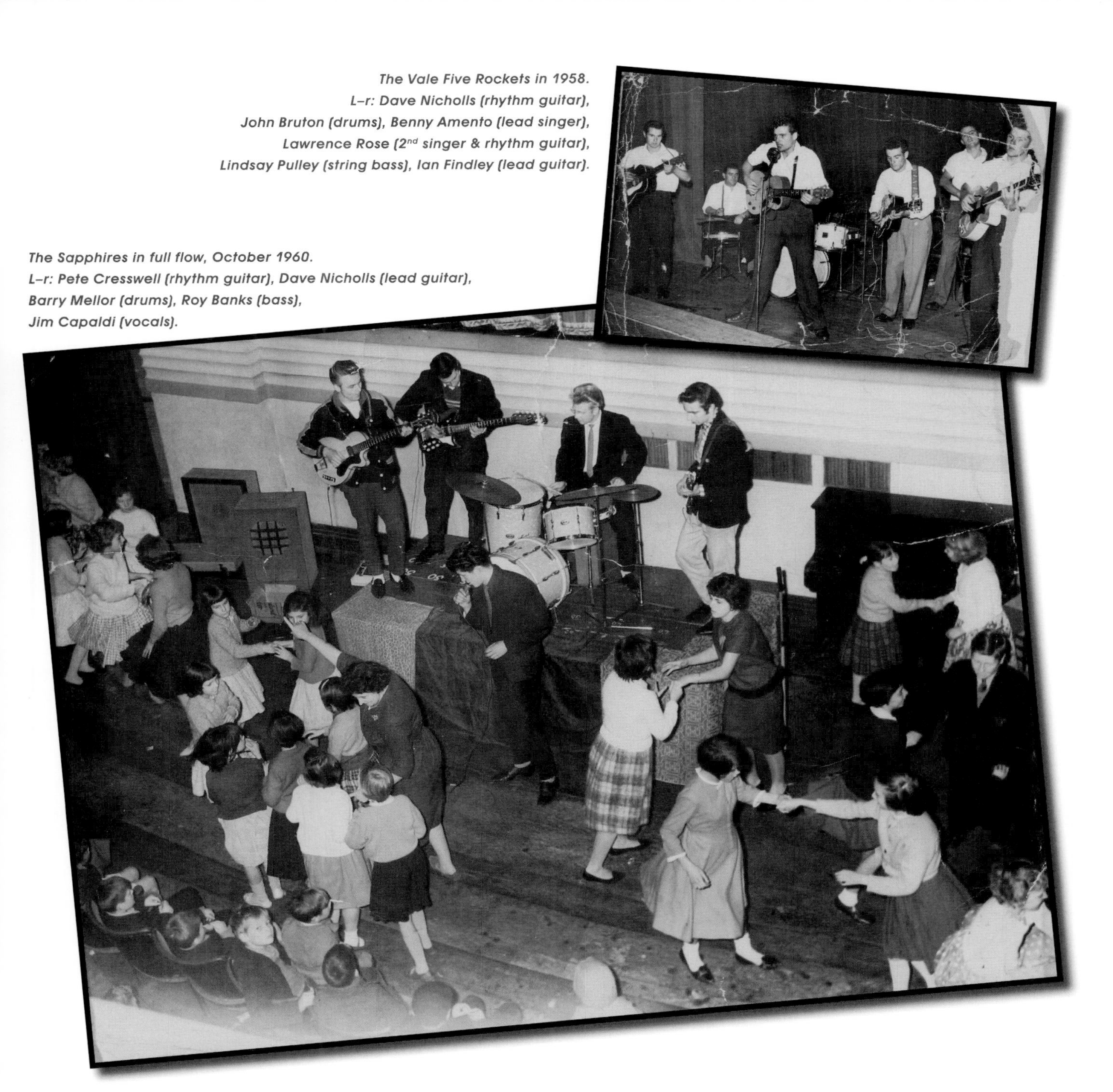

The Vale Five Rockets in 1958.
L–r: Dave Nicholls (rhythm guitar), John Bruton (drums), Benny Amento (lead singer), Lawrence Rose (2nd singer & rhythm guitar), Lindsay Pulley (string bass), Ian Findley (lead guitar).

The Sapphires in full flow, October 1960.
L–r: Pete Cresswell (rhythm guitar), Dave Nicholls (lead guitar), Barry Mellor (drums), Roy Banks (bass), Jim Capaldi (vocals).

Later, he even managed to join the Birmingham-based group the Fortunes, but with limited success. In the early days, however, as a cabinet maker at Gordon Russell Ltd. of Broadway he would hand-make amplifier boxes which, drumming skills notwithstanding, made him first choice for every new band around.

During 1959, the Sapphires needed a singer to complement their heavyweight line-up of musicians – someone who looked as good as Benny Amento (see photo of Vale Five Rockets) and sounded even better. They found one in the form of Jim Capaldi from the famous Evesham family overflowing with musical talent. Jim was the real deal, who could imitate anyone from Elvis to Dean Martin and fronted the Sapphires for the best part of five years until hitting the big time in the mid-sixties with the Birmingham group Traffic as vocalist/drummer. He was to become a respected performer and song-writer and even scored a chart number one in 1975 with a cover of the Everly Brothers' 'Love Hurts'.

I saw the Sapphires at the Regal a couple of times in 1963 and the excitement was tremendous. Okay, so I was only seven, but as with most things connected to the Theatre of Dreams, the memories get preserved in glorious Technicolor.

The October 1960 photograph on the previous page, taken from the balcony, sums up the excitement of the SMRCC. With Auntie Iris Jordan in the thick of it, the kids are giving it their all in a jiving competition as the Sapphires crank out 'Blue Suede Shoes'. And the contest results were as follows:

1st Alan Whittaker (from Elizabeth Road) and Betty Jury (Isbourne Crescent)
2nd Joy Clements and Judy Cooke (both Lichfield Avenue)
3rd Valerie Boswell (Aldington) and Yvette Harris (Badsey)

Another Regal favourite group, Terry and the Trojans, was also formed in 1959. The all-Evesham line-up was Terry Hyde (lead singer and rhythm guitarist), Brian Haywood (lead guitar), Ken Grove (bass guitar) and Brian Huxley (drums). They, too, played the rock and pop records of the day but diversified by updating old English folk songs such as 'John Peel' (nothing to do with the DJ) or 'Bobby Shafto', etc. by bolting them onto an eight-bar blues rhythm.

Terry and the Trojans, early 1964. L–r: Brian Haywood (lead guitar), Brian Huxley (drums), Ken Grove (bass guitar), Terry Hyde (rhythm guitar & vocals).

Guitarist Brian Haywood believed children to be the sternest of critics and as such, when they were due to perform at the SMRCC the band practised feverishly all week trying to perfect whatever was at the top of the charts. On 'House of the Rising Sun' Terry Hyde had Eric Burdon's vocals down to a tee – the only thing missing was Alan Price's frantic driving keyboards.

The Trojans found true affinity with the Dave Clark Five, however, whose two monster hits 'Glad all Over' and 'Bits and Pieces' were the most foot-stomping rowdy records of the time (Frank Ridge would have loved them) and their effect on

Evesham's mini boppers nearly gave Ernie Highland a heart attack. One time, when the group stoked up 'Bits and Pieces', most of the four hundred audience decided it would be fun to bounce up and down to it, on their seats. Half a minute in and Highland was hurtling down the aisle, the veins jutting in his skull with panic, his arms flailing like a demented windmill.

"Stop! Stop!" he yelled, above the beat and the cheers. The Trojans pulled up sharp as Ernie grabbed the microphone from Terry Hyde. "Pleeese, boys and girls. Don't jump on the seats, it's very dangerous!" pleaded Highland, as he mopped his brow with a hanky. It was dangerous all right – to the Regal finances. Ernie had just sweated blood for seven years in order to refurbish the place. To his horror, it was about to get trashed in the time it took to crank out a Dave Clark belter. But he was in the nick of time and the young audience descended from their trampolines. The stalls did not entirely escape damage, however, as more than a dozen seats were left in bits and pieces.

During one of the Trojans' Saturday sessions one young fan asked them if he could sing alongside them. For a twelve-year-old to front a four-piece band with four hundred contemporaries standing in judgement took some nerve but Colin Fisher proved to be one sweet little rock 'n' roller. He had a fine voice and belted out a very fair rendition of 'All Shook Up' which made a lot of people take notice. Colin wasn't content to leave it at that and by mid 1964 he and three of his buddies, Charles Marshall (bass guitar), Alan Bottomley (rhythm guitar) and Stuart Jobson (drums), all four of them only thirteen years old, had put together their own group, the Prowlers, who became a big hit playing for the SMRCC. In fact, they so impressed Ernie Highland that, the manager suggested they audition for *Opportunity Knocks,* the extremely popular sixties' television talent show. The young musicians leapt at the chance and with Ernie as their sponsor, they eventually found themselves sitting apprehensively in a Birmingham TV studio waiting for compère Hughie Green to grace them with his presence. Green, alas, had a reputation for being discourteous and the story goes that he was so obnoxious to Ernie and his young hopefuls that Highland pulled the plug on the whole venture, took the Prowlers straight home and set about sticking pins in an effigy of everyone's favourite talent jockey.

Sweet little rock 'n' rollers. The Prowlers in August 1964.
L–r: Alan Bottomley, Colin Fisher, Stuart Jobson, Charles Marshall.

Colin Fisher was to become one of the stalwart Regal fans of his generation and let rip with those tonsils any chance he could. When Irene Mackenzie decided to revive the Chum's Club in late 1992 Colin offered to help out for free. He can be seen in the Chum's Club Revival photograph, microphone in hand, entertaining a new generation of teenies.

Finally in the Chum's Club pantheon of early sixties rock greats came the Wavelengths who, like the Sapphires and the Trojans, cranked out all the meaty stuff of the time and went through numerous personnel changes. However, one of their original members was to reach similar heights of rock stardom as his

Chums Club Revival c.1990.

friend, Jim Capaldi. Luther Grosvenor was (still is) an ace guitar player and by the mid-sixties had left for the bright lights of London. He became part of the influential group Spooky Tooth (alongside Keith Emerson) but will be most fondly remembered for joining seventies' band Mott the Hoople and subsequently changing his name to Ariel Bender. Legend has it that in 1969 he was approached to join the Rolling Stones as a possible replacement for the late Brian Jones. This was just about the best available job on the planet at the time, and for reasons known only to Luther, he turned them down!

(Readers may feel that I have been insufficiently worshipful of the Sapphires, the Trojans and particularly the Wavelengths. However, as their combined history may just fill another volume I have had to cut them short. Many local groups were to play the SMRCC in the wake of the 'big three' and I apologise unreservedly for not shedding more light on the Zodiacs, the Jeebies, the System and the Eyesores, plus any other outfits, or for that matter individual performers, whose presence at the Theatre of Dreams I was unable to verify.)

Reptilicus: Terrifying Nonsense.

MPs: Monster pics and Members of Parliament

After the break came the main SMRCC film and on the whole, they were pretty good, ranging from 1950s westerns (things like *Tension at Table Rock*) and junior detective yarns, to tales of public school tomfoolery and, joy of joys, 'creature features'. Thirty years before CGI made us believe in the tooth fairy I sat through one film that terrified me, as a seven-year-old, more than anything since and crystallised my affection for monsters. It was called *Reptilicus* and although it is mandatory for giant lizards to smash up New York or Tokyo, this one was different – he did for Copenhagen. (Don't panic, the Little Mermaid survived unscathed.) So, praise be for the Internet. In 2005 I managed to track down a copy of both the Captain Marvel serial and *Reptilicus* on DVD and everything in life had to stop as I sat watching them for the first time in forty-two years. *Captain Marvel* clunked a bit but I made allowances and besides, when Billy Batson said the magic word, the hairs on my neck stood on end. *Reptilicus*, however, wasn't so hot. In fact, it made *Godzilla* look like *Citizen Kane*. On a one-to-ten scale of BAD, where one is BAD and ten is APOCALYPTIC DRIVEL, *Reptilicus* scored a seventeen, but this only emphasises the point that small children can 'suspend their disbelief' so readily and how valuable the SMRCC was for firing the imagination of pre-teens.

Ernie Highland propping up his MP's seat in March 1967.

If there was time after the main film, the Chum's Club would wrap up with either a cartoon or a perennial favourite short by Laurel and Hardy, the Three Stooges or the Little Rascals, then the doors would open and the lunch-time light stream in, as four hundred stimulated juniors streamed out to the bus stop.

A couple of times, the SMRCC played host to Sir Gerald and Lady Nabarro, who came to watch the show and preside over various events. The March 1967 photo (above right) shows the MP, in his capacity as President of the Bengeworth Traders' Association, presenting a bicycle to ten-year-old Peter Thompson, the winner of a local sports competition. At the same time he was made a member of the Chum's Club by a Miss Julie Thould, who pinned a badge on his lapel.

In late 1969 the Nabarros were in attendance again, presiding over a celebration of the local Girl Guides. The series of photographs overleaf shows Sir Gerald, who obviously modelled himself on Yosemite Sam, having a thoroughly spiffing time, while at the end of the morning usurping Ernie Highland's traditional job of stopping traffic as the children exited the Theatre of Dreams.

Another special guest was present on this occasion. Sidney Hall, the Regal's original manager (1932–34) and shareholder until his death in 1981, can be seen standing below the stage as Nabarro holds forth.

The legendary SMRCC fun continued into the late 1970s, until the irresistible march of Saturday morning television eroded the young audience, who seemed content to watch Chris Tarrant's *Tiswas* or whatever nonsense Noel Edmonds was serving up. The staff tried hard to keep the Chum's Club going, but it was an uphill struggle and tragically, by 1980, it had petered out.

In 1992, Irene Mackenzie, now the manageress, revived the SMRCC for almost two years, but times had changed and by 1994, with only a few dozen kids turning up each week, Irene knew the party was over. Young people were now more sophisticated, more demanding and prey to a million other distractions. Saturday morning flicks became a thing of the past, its social effect less relevant, its magic consigned to memory. The world had moved on.

It took more than a wintry Saturday morning in 1958 to discourage ardent Chum's Clubbers.

In August, 1972, he robbed a bank in New York.

250 cops, the F.B.I., 8 hostages and 2,000 onlookers will never forget what took place.

AL PACINO

An Artists Entertainment Complex Inc. Production

DOG DAY AFTERNOON

X

Also starring

JOHN CAZALE · JAMES BRODERICK and CHARLES DURNING as Moretti

Screenplay by FRANK PIERSON · Produced by MARTIN BREGMAN and MARTIN ELFAND · Directed by SIDNEY LUMET · Film Editor DEDE ALLEN

TECHNICOLOR® From WARNER BROS A WARNER COMMUNICATIONS COMPANY · RELEASED BY COLUMBIA-WARNER DISTRIBUTORS

CHAPTER NINE

A LEVEL PLAYING FIELD

Events of 1967 sum up Ernie Highland's dilemma as manager of a small-town independent cinema better than any other. For a start, midway through the year, original boss and managing director of forty-five years, Victor A. Morrall died at the age of seventy-seven. In many ways Morrall had been the perfect gaffer. He was never particularly 'hands-on' and didn't interfere in the day-to-day running, preferring to leave his managers with a broad field of operation. As long as they brought in the customers and the Theatre of Dreams made a profit, he was happy. The Regal Standard flew at half-mast for a fortnight, Vic's shares passed to his wife Stella and the business of trying to fill 847 seats each night rolled right along.

Into his twelfth year as manager, Ernie Highland was still searching for ways to circumvent the accursed 'barring system' (explained fully in Chapter Six) and bite into the lush fruit of big, early film releases. As I've touched on several times, the Clifton, as part of a cinema chain was looked upon with greater favour by the regional studios and could secure big films closer to their release dates.

Although the dynamics of the industry have altered dramatically during the last forty years, the overriding aim is the same: to cram cinemas with as many bodies as possible, all stuffing their faces with popcorn. Even in this day and age, with the assured knowledge that whatever movie appears it'll be on DVD within a month or so, the opening week at the pictures will still be the one which makes the money. And to emphasise its importance, one has only to glance at the takings during the spring/summer period in 2007, when blockbuster movies were tripping over each other to get onto the screen:

TITLE	America $ millions			Britain £ millions		
	OPENING WEEKEND	SECOND WEEKEND	THIRD WEEKEND	OPENING WEEKEND	SECOND WEEKEND	THIRD WEEKEND
300	70.9	32.7	18.0	6.45	2.90	1.89
Spiderman 3	151.2	58.1	29.0	11.84	6.86	2.24
Shrek 3	121.6	53.0	28.1	16.67	5.08	2.83
Pirates of the Caribbean 3	130.2	44.2	30.7	13.65	7.26	2.42
Ocean's Thirteen	37.0	20.2	14.5	3.80	2.03	1.29
Fantastic Four (Silver Surfer)	57.4	31.6	21.6	5.49	2.75	1.36
Transformers	70.5	36.0	20.5	8.72	2.33	1.39
Harry Potter 5	77.4	32.5	17.7	16.49	6.69	3.41
The Simpsons Movie	74.0	25.1	11.1	13.63	4.02	2.18

Cinema takings in the first half of 2007.

One can see that after the opening weekend bonanza, the second weekend drops off by more than fifty per cent and by the third week halves again. In the 1960s the system was much slower; nonetheless cinema managers knew what was in the pipeline and would put in their orders for films as early as they could.

At last: sixties' enlightenment

By the middle of the decade, the irresistible demand for harder-hitting entertainment triggered immense improvements in the industry, the dreaded Hays Commission in America (see Chapter Six) was scrapped and replaced by a far more progressive system of censorship and 1967 saw an explosion of wonderful movies from a wide variety of genres, tackling a slew of themes and thorny issues: *In the Heat of the Night* and *Guess Who's Coming to Dinner* (racism), *The Graduate* (adultery), *Poor Cow* (social realism), *Belle de Jour* (female sexual fantasy), *The Boston Strangler* (true story/documentary-style murder), *Thoroughly Modern Millie* (musical), *Far from the Madding Crowd* (literary classic), *Bonnie and Clyde* and *Cool Hand Luke* (the rise of the anti-hero). Plus a trainload of slam-bam actioners: *Point Blank*, *You Only Live Twice*, *Night of the Generals*, *The Good, The Bad and The Ugly* (the ultimate western) and *The Dirty Dozen*, the all-star World War II romp, which became the biggest grossing film of the year. Everywhere you turned there was a monster movie sneaking up on you. Even the recently departed Walt Disney was to have one of his biggest-ever hits with *Jungle Book*.

Ernie Highland became dispirited in the mid-1960s and, at one point, even considered throwing in the towel. However, the professional in him rallied and while waiting for the hottest movies to 'trickle down' through the system he utilised a standard ploy, which was to re-order a few of the Regal's most popular films then ballyhoo them in the *Evesham Journal* ("Back by POPULAR REQUEST! The enduring spectacle of *ZULU*"). If in doubt, Ernie would resurrect the battle of Rorke's Drift or *My Fair Lady* or rifle through Elvis's bag of iffy offerings. (The Clifton was often obliged to follow the same tactic, thus *The Bridge on the River Kwai* seemed to be playing every six months.)

(In fairness, this wasn't always hype. Many people besieged Highland with requests for films to be shown again. Ernie did have one unexpected success in 1967, when booking a little British film called *The Family Way*, starring Hayley Mills and Hywel Bennett. It was a gentle, post-kitchen-sink yarn about two newly-weds who couldn't consummate their marriage, yet it touched a chord with the public and became a smash hit. Highland held it over for a second week and it went on to break the Regal's television-era box office record (previously held by Presley's *Flaming Star*)).

If a movie is a must-see blockbuster, people always want to see it immediately. Not next year or next month – NOW! This was just as true of audiences forty years ago, despite their being far more parochial and disinclined to travel more than a few miles for their entertainment. For example, in 1965, even my mother, not a devout cinema goer, had no intention of waiting until *The Sound of Music* landed in Evesham. She packed the whole family into the car and made a trip to the now-defunct Scala in Worcester for her fill of nuns and Nazis. (The Scala was to screen it continuously for an entire year!) What on earth is it about Julie Andrews and seven yodelling brats? I have interviewed forty-odd people in the course of researching this book and asked each one, what is their favourite movie. Eight of them said *The Sound of Music* (three of them blokes!) with no other film being favoured more than once.[1]

1 I might give it a view if they remake it with Pammi Anderson as Maria, Wesley Snipes as Captain Von Trapp and Eddie Izzard as the Mother Superior.

Me? I'm a *Jaws* fan and first trekked to Redditch for a gawk at the Great White Rubber Cash Cow in late 1975, impatient of the fact that Highland couldn't secure it until March 1976. When it finally swam into Port Street I went to see it another three times, with crowds still enormous four months after its UK release. "We're gonna need a bigger cinema," said Ernie to Iris.

However, back in 1967, the so-called 'summer of love' was passing Highland by. The simple mathematics were that he had 847 seats to fill, three shows a day, seven days a week, yielding a maximum potential sales figure of 17,787 tickets per week. This target was almost certainly never reached, although individual showings would still occasionally hit 847. If approximately 5,000 tickets could be sold per week the Regal would be in profit, so obviously if Ernie could secure big movies before they faded from the public consciousness, ticket sales would increase considerably. So, how to improve the lot of the small independents?

Beating the system

Then in 1968 a ray of hope. Local solicitor John Darlington from the firm Smith and Roberts advised Highland on the feasibility of fighting the 'barring system' under the Monopolies and Restricted Practices Act. They put together a case against both the regional studio rental companies and the Clifton arguing that the Regal deserved a fairer share of available films on release (official case title: 'Application of Product before Kinematograph Renters Ltd.'). Alas, Ernie Highland's hopes were dashed when the tribunal in Birmingham rejected their case and, once again, he began considering his own future. But the Regal legal eagles held their nerve, kept Highland focused and prepared to lodge an appeal.

The next two years were a frustrating time for Ernie as a whole trainload of great movies were made which he couldn't take full advantage of. For example,1968 saw the release of: *Barbarella, Bullitt, Finian's Rainbow, Ice Station Zebra, The Lion in Winter, Once upon a Time in the West, Planet of the Apes, Rosemary's Baby, Shalako, Star, Yellow Submarine* and *2001: A Space Odyssey*. All of them money-spinners.

This trend continued through 1969: *Anne of the Thousand Days, Bob and Carol and Ted and Alice, Butch Cassidy and the Sundance Kid, Downhill Racer, Easy Rider, The Italian Job, Midnight Cowboy, On Her Majesty's Secret Service, True Grit, Where Eagles Dare, The Wild Bunch, Women in Love*… and in 1970: *Airport, Catch 22, Love Story, M.A.S.H., A Man called Horse, Patton, Performance, Ryan's Daughter, Woodstock*.

In late 1970, the Regal once again locked horns with the renters and the Clifton at the Monopolies appeal. This time the case was stronger. Firstly, sixteen miles was the accepted yardstick for determining the 'barring distance' between the Regal and its nearest city chain rival (the Scala, Worcester). So, Ernie Highland had asked the AA to measure the exact distance between these two cinemas using the shortest possible route. It was shown to be a fraction short of sixteen and a half miles, so technically the Theatre of Dreams should never have been penalised. This, together with other beefed-up arguments such as the economic importance of the Regal to a growing town economy, particularly the Bengeworth area, won the day and the tribunal found in its favour. Vic Morrall smiled down from his cloud. Ernie was elated and relieved, yet there was a poignant note to his victory. Highland's old adversary, Clifton general manager and film procurer Ken Jones was seriously ill during this time and upholding the case for his cinema at the hearing proved a dreadful ordeal.

Nonetheless, the battle was won and Ernie's Clifton counterpart David Johnson experienced a sinking feeling. It didn't necessarily mean that the Regal would always get things its own way but the increased potential for obtaining movies sooner rather than later was to improve audiences considerably.

During the first half of the 1970s, Highland steadily heaped pressure onto his High Street rival. The Clifton did secure a few 'biggies' such as *The Exorcist*, *Earthquake* and *Tommy* but the Regal mopped up just about everything else: *Dirty Harry*, *The French Connection*, *The Godfather*, *Cabaret*, *The Sting*, *One Flew Over the Cuckoo's Nest*, *American Graffiti*, *The Towering Inferno*, *Dog Day Afternoon*, and by the time *Jaws* smashed in early 1976 the Clifton shareholders began to see the writing on the wall.

This blitz continued throughout the latter half of the decade as the Theatre of Dreams showed almost all the hottest movies soon after their release: *Star Wars*, *Close Encounters of the Third Kind*, *The Omen*, *Rocky*, *Saturday Night Fever*, *Superman*, *Star Trek: The Motion Picture*, *Every Which Way but Loose*, *Alien*, *Jaws II*.

Each one made big money for the Regal but top of the tree in this period was *Grease*. Over the next ten years it regularly returned and, like *Jaws* before it, became less a film than a licence to print money. Of course, in between the blockbusters all manner of lesser movies continued to flicker. Some were flops, some did reasonably well and some were surprise smashes, the most astonishing of which was *Confessions of a Window Cleaner* in 1975. This could loosely be described as a British sex comedy, yet was so clod-hoppingly inept that it made the *Carry On* films look epic. (Guilty! I gave it a view.) It represented the very nadir to which the domestic movie industry had plummeted but frankly, my dear, Ernie Highland didn't give a damn. He was too busy pitch-forking the takings into a Securicor wagon.

Elvis has left the building

The year 1977 added a sad note to the 'chung-ching' of Irene Mackenzie's till. On August 16, The Regal's favourite celluloid son, Elvis, died at the catastrophically early age of forty-two. To make matters worse, it happened on Irene's thirtieth birthday – not something a dyed-in-the-wool fan relishes. The next day Ernie Highland ordered a couple of the King's best-loved films and showed them for a week to big audiences as a tribute to the great man. It was a shame the prints of *Blue Hawaii* and *GI Blues* sent from Paramount were of a poor quality, gooey Technicolor but no one complained. They merely sat entranced yet melancholy as the epitaph unfurled. Near the end of one showing of *Blue Hawaii*, as Elvis was rounding things off with the sentimental title song, a big gypsy stood up in the middle of the stalls. He was well over six foot, resplendent in powder-blue drape jacket and pink shirt, his black duck-ass hair piled high with Brylcreem. Wiping a tear from his Capo di Monte face, he began slowly clapping and was soon joined by five hundred other pilgrims. Rock 'n' Roll, Hollywood and the Theatre of Dreams – now wouldn't you say that's what it's all about?

Gone but not forgotten.
A double feature, 15th anniversary Elvis tribute.

The studios play hardball: goodbye Clifton

With the rise of the summer blockbuster, film booking practice had to change. Instead of ordering a film for a week (or even merely three days) with the proviso that it could be 'held over' for another week if it proved a hit, the mega-movies of the 1970s were secured for at least a fortnight. This was because the studios began asking for a higher percentage (up to ninety per cent), no doubt wishing to squeeze every last cent out of the public. Eventually, during the 1980s studios insisted that blockbusters were shown for up to a month. Fine, if the public interest in them was sustained, but the last week of a month-long run was usually poorly attended and managers preferred to screen a fresh movie. However, Ernie would have been unwise to complain because he realised the Regal was soon to become the only game in town. By the late 1970s the Clifton was really beginning to slide, and the owners were forced to take the drastic (some cinema men would say traitorous) step of selling out to, firstly, Essoldo, then the Granada chain, who promptly split the week into three days of films and four days of the great Satan, Bingo. Lord and Lady Clift's High Street pleasure palace was about to become extinct. Their manager of twenty-five years, David Johnson, retired as the new regime brought in its own staff.

Film choice at the Clifton became ever more dire. It was strangely prophetic that one of the last movies to feature was *Raise the Titanic*, Sir Lew Grade's monstrous white elephant which cost forty million dollars to make and took seven million at the box office. "It would have been cheaper to lower the Atlantic," wailed Sir Lew, after a harrowing session with his accountants.

The romantics amongst us would have wished the Clifton to go out in a blaze of glory with a non-stop twenty-four-hour whirlwind of classics: *The Sound of Music*, *Casablanca*, *Citizen Kane*, *Gone with the Wind*, *Stagecoach*, *Frankenstein* and *The Wizard of Oz*. So what did the new owners enthral us with? *A Force of One*, starring Chuck Norris – a crap film with an even worse actor. Philistines.

Back in Port Street, however, the mood was upbeat. The assistant projectionist, Michael Pulley, had received a bottle of champagne as a birthday present from his brother Arthur on the understanding that it was only to be opened on a special occasion. The demise of the Regal's great rival seemed special enough and the staff clinked glasses in the restaurant as young Michael shared out the bubbly. Ernie Highland, however, who didn't imbibe in the grape, was in a mood of sober reflection. He felt he should show a little respect for the passing of a fellow cinematic institution, left the revellers to it and retired to the privacy of his office. But it didn't take too long for reality to dawn. If the Clifts could have put HIM out of business, the Theatre of Dreams would have been history decades ago. So, Highland rubbed his hands together, Fagin-like, grinned a corn-cob grin and chortled: "Come to Poppa".

Lights out for the Clifton. Ernie Highland with one of the Regal's emergency gas lights.

One Stan and his dog

Ernie Highland could be a very generous man. 'Mr Regal' was often referred to as 'Mr Complimentary' because he would hand out perhaps a couple of dozen free passes a week to those he felt deserved them – the elderly, the infirm, those having a run of bad luck or anyone he might spot who was a keen regular. This wasn't quite as profligate as it sounds. Twenty-five individuals receiving free passes will, more than likely, bring along at least one other person, who will have to pay to get in and who probably wouldn't have visited the Regal otherwise. So, in theory, Highland's generosity would increase revenue, not to mention that it was wonderful public relations.

He would also organise occasional free film shows for various old people's homes or special needs schools and showed a sense of civic duty by raising money for such causes as the Vale of Evesham Swimming Pool Association (VESPA) in the 1970s.

However, like all good businessmen, 'Mr Complimentary' could also be 'Mr Parsimonious'. If the projectionists cranked up the 'maximum demand' meter too high in keeping the Westars, the lights and sound system going, Ernie would berate them about his electricity bill, particularly if the audience was thin on the ground. Any simple maintenance or decorating was usually done in-house, thus preventing the need for expensive tradesmen. Highland kept finances as tight as possible.

Ernie Highland and
Stan Jordan erecting an advertising hoarding
for perennial favourite **Jungle Book**. *November 1983*

So, it was most fortuitous that Ernie had a resident fixer in the form of Iris Jordan's husband Stan. From 1956, when Iris resumed work at the Regal, until his death in 1995, Stan Jordan was on hand to mend broken seats, hang doors, lay carpet, unblock drains or wield hammer and paint brush. Also, as a member of St John Ambulance he was the Regal's main first-aider. Stan was a useful guy to have around and during almost forty years of DIY saved the Theatre of Dreams a fortune.

Ernie and Stan would think nothing of erecting scaffolding from which to fix large film advertising hoardings over the front entrance. And, if this required them both to abseil down from the roof to achieve it, all well and good.

Stan himself was blessed with an ace four-footed sidekick named Pepi, who was every child's identikit of the perfect mutt. A Heinz variety shaggy mongrel, Pepi was no Brad Pitt Bull to look at but in the grey matter department he made Rin Tin Tin seem like Pluto. In January 1970 the *Evesham Journal* ran a feature on Pepi which made him a local celebrity. Stan Jordan would fix a small plastic jar containing money to Pepi's collar and send him off from his house along Burford Road, whence manager Highland would welcome him in through the Regal's doors. Pepi would then present himself at the kiosk, standing with front paws on the glass counter and Violet Woodcock would replace the money in the container with Stan's cigars. The amiable hound would then trot back home with his booty.

Stan taught Pepi to fetch and carry his tools while he effected repairs in the cinema and also to put up the seats at the end of an evening's show. Pepi did this by running along the rows and nudging each one up with his snout. If he could have sold ice cream he would have made three usherettes redundant.

By all accounts Pepi was the regular hound-about-town and sired many offspring. However, Evesham didn't need to fear an uprising of 'super-dogs' – nature doesn't work like that. Stan's next mutt was Pepi's daughter Tilly, who was similar in appearance but sadly lacking in brainpower. When Stan tried to teach her to fetch cigars like her father, she would hurtle down Burford Road, passing the Regal entrance like an exocet, only for the penny to drop twenty yards further on, whereby she would apply the brakes and leave ten-foot claw marks along the Port Street pavement.

"I blame the mother," mused Stan.

Pepi doing his master's bidding on a snowy day in January 1970.

CHAPTER TEN

'RITES OF PASSAGE'

The pulpit, the pub and the pictures

This is an appropriate juncture to look way outside the Vale of Evesham and consider the sheer SOCIAL importance of cinemas everywhere. From the 1930s to the 1960s, cities and large towns all over the world had several, or indeed many, picture palaces and even small towns of less than 5,000 population had a much-loved flea-pit. If we reflect on the range of entertainment available to people a couple of generations back it seems pretty limited to our avaricious twenty-first-century perceptions.

In Britain, the working week was probably five and a half days, with Sundays monopolised by the church. Best behaviour was required of adults and children alike as they attended worship. Perhaps twice on the Sabbath, people would listen to some charisma-free vicar bang on about the evils of drink and fornication. It must have been particularly rough on the kids as Victorian attitudes spilled over well into the twentieth century. Young boys could always join the church choir if they felt musically inclined and if rip-snorting gospel singing had been on the menu Sundays might have become halfway bearable. Alas, outside of the odd rousing chorus of 'Onward Christian Soldiers' there was precious little to stir the blood and in quiet moments many folks must have pondered the great question: "What's it all about, eh?"

Before the early 1950s in Britain, television was non-existent and the vast majority strived from day to day in a family-orientated existence. So, if you wanted to cut loose you could either cheer your team on at the Saturday afternoon match (blokes only) or strut off to the local shindig in the evening where young men would get ratted on mild and bitter while eyeing up the wallflowers lining the village hall, as the young ladies primped and pouted in the hope of attracting a future spouse.

Christmas, Easter and summer holidays were relished but they were distant islands in a sea of graft. This left things like local fêtes, the fair (infrequent), bonfire night or special one-off royal anniversaries on which the great and the good allowed plebs to remove their noses from the grindstone for a day.

Men, of course, could always go down the pub, an option closed to women unless they were chaperoned or hell-bent on building a reputation. The fairer sex always drew the shorter straw when it came to entertainment. Long before they could bray like asses at Anne Summers parties while necking a crate of Chardonnay they had to be content with baking, knitting, reading or mashing rusks.

(Yes, I realise I'm being cynical but it suits the premise of the chapter.)

Outside of this, travel was not aspired to, theatre too high-brow for the majority and social strictures inhibited the more eccentric avenues of behaviour which we nowadays regard as the norm. Both men and women could have hobbies and be creative but excessive fun was frowned upon (no nude bungee-jumping), sex only ever mentioned in hushed whispers and anarchy was off the menu altogether. The concept of the teenager as a creature of youth, shallow glamour and individual style was only recognised around 1950.

I've purposely painted a grey, post-Edwardian picture where society was still engineered to be uptight and people were expected to be grateful for their lot. However, one factor more than any other let fresh air and colour into this starchy world: the pictures.

Personally, I don't think the importance of the local Regal or Clifton or Ritz or Odeon or Gaumont or Scala or Majestic can be overestimated. During the era known as the 'golden age of Hollywood' (the twenties and thirties), through World War II, and right into the television era cinema brought so much benefit to the table. It was, indeed, the Jewel in the Crown of everyone's social life. Where else would you so willingly submit to someone else's fantasy creations? Where else could you experience a spectacle such as the parting of the Red Sea, in cinemascope and glorious Technicolor? You can't even create that NOW, outside of the local multiplex. The biggest plasma flat-screen television is only a tiny fraction of the size needed for that REAL buzz. And it was all new. What else provided such a glimpse of the outside world in those days as the Pathé and March of Time newsreels? Sure, there were newspapers but they were dry and certainly didn't appeal to kids. People enjoyed the radio, of course, but it still required you to paint images inside your head. In many parochial communities the flicks was the only place that showed people there actually WAS a wider world outside of the parish boundary.

In the early years (1900–1925) the sheer novelty of the medium packed cinemas. Once sound arrived in the late 1920s, so did the deco picture palaces. Some people went to the cinema almost every night. Most people went at least twice a week. If you didn't go to the flicks you were either dead, in prison, or your father was Oliver Cromwell.

When the Hays Commission came into force in 1934 (as discussed in Chapter Six) it had the effect of a legal 'cold shower' on film makers because of its harsh censorship, but the movie industry was a Pandora's box and boundaries of taste were still probed. However, Hays couldn't really dampen the social effect because all over the world people flocked to see just about anything.

From *The Public Enemy* (1931) to *Goodfellas* (1990), gangsters were gangsters. From *Stagecoach* (1939) to *Unforgiven* (1992), westerns were westerns. And from *King Kong* (1933) to *King Kong* (2005), monkey business remained just that. The basic ENTERTAINMENT factor was always in evidence, depending on personal preference and nothing else in normal life came close to the pictures in delivering people's dreams.

Breaking this 'thrill' effect down further, there were many categories of awareness which were highlighted by the cinema. People locked onto style, language, humour, music, fear, even history and geography, in a broad sense, plus, of course, sex. The local Theatre of Dreams was a kind of shallow university. American culture alone was of endless fascination, not just to Europeans but to people all over the globe. When Britain was still enduring rationing in the early fifties and the word affluence was never used, people would sit in the local picture house and drool over the Americans' fabulous Technicolor kitchens, their smart clothes, fantastic cars and backyard barbecues, all about twenty years before these goodies arrived here. Okay, much of it was make-believe because tens of millions of Americans weren't wealthy at this time but the images on the screen had a profound effect.

Celluloid idolatry

Alongside this came the impact of the stars themselves. People will always need heroes to worship, be they sports stars, politicians, artists, scientists, explorers or merely eccentrics. Hollywood gave us trailblazers by the truck-load. Of course, they were only actors, but people latched onto their style, courage, sexuality, humour – some talent or quirk that made them box-office winners. Consider some of the screen legends whose personas became part of the furniture inside our heads: Rudolf Valentino (the archetypal Latin lover), Mae West (the cheeky madam), James Cagney (the uncompromising thug), Humphrey Bogart (the cool loner), Lauren Bacall (the icy femme-fatale), Clark Gable, Errol Flynn and Tyrone Power (handsome rakes personified), Gary Cooper, Henry Fonda, Jimmy Stewart and the Duke (the embodiment of the courage, fairness, fortitude and decency that America cherished), and Spencer Tracy, Gregory Peck and Cary Grant (the last word in charm). There were any amount of macho characters such as Burt Lancaster and Kirk Douglas who showed young men the way it should be done. Hollywood's female stars poured from the screen like flocks of Valkyries: from Jean Harlow, Rita Hayworth, Vivien Leigh, Lana Turner and Betty Grable to Grace Kelly, Marilyn Monroe and Elizabeth Taylor. Not content with the role of sex symbol, Joan Crawford, Barbara Stanwyck and Katherine Hepburn gave us the ballsy babe who refused to be subordinate to men. The names and the images were almost endless.

(Of course, Britain had her own home-grown idols but they generally lacked the appeal of the Yanks. I'm not saying our actors couldn't do the business, merely that I wouldn't have bet on Michael Redgrave in a rumble with Victor Mature. Come to that, Gracie Fields didn't stack up too favourably against Hedy Lamarr.)

As the audience left the cinema, all kinds of thoughts would be swirling around in their heads. If not just the sense of exhausted excitement as the adrenalin began to ease, then the imagery of the stars and the subsequent desire to be like them. How many men have walked down the street emulating Robert Mitchum's moody strut? How many women thrust out their chests and walked with a wiggle? And how many of us have aped the lingo of the Yankee hotshots or the smoother, more erudite European stars (French and Italian ones in particular)? It only represents a small aspect of day-to-day life but it has always mattered. For over half a century the cinema made us think and act outside the box. Guys would emerge from a Theatre of Dreams and walk their girlfriend to the chip shop while mentally machine-gunning passers-by. Girls were more inclined to surround themselves with a force field of hearts and flowers, dead set on getting their hair done like Ava Gardner. The cinema was a potent force and whether people succumbed to the images or not, there was always a subliminal impact.

The finest examples of 'cinema effect' came after the mid-1950s when 'method' acting became prevalent in the industry. If you observed the audience as it emerged from *On the Waterfront* most of the males would be looking around moodily, eyes heavy-lidded, speaking in grunts and adopting Brando's rolling gait. The same happened after the first four Elvis movies,[1] except with a little more emphasis on hair combing.

Sometimes macho movies could have the adverse effect of causing the more over-stimulated fellows to butt heads on the cinema steps, or envious girlfriends might give their boyfriends or husbands merry hell for lusting after some screen siren.

1 His best ones. The next twenty-nine were roughly classifiable as crapola

Occasionally, an unlucky chap would have to deal with that most deadly of questions: "What's she got that I haven't?" The only possible response to this was (and still is) a benign expression and ABSOLUTE silence. It took me years of trying to be a smart-arse before I cottoned on. As a reasonably adept wordsmith I always felt that I could formulate a placatory reply. Alas, one simply does not exist. During my time I have stood outside three different cinemas in three different decades, offering three different replies to three different girlfriends demanding an answer to this bloody man-trap of a question. It was first prompted by my ogling Julie Christie in *Shampoo*, second, by Rachel Ward in *Against All Odds* and the third time by Sharon Stone in *Basic Instinct*. The first time, I chose to answer in the obsequious tones of Peter Lorre. The next time, I employed the lofty condescension of Noel Coward and thirdly, the dry, understated delivery of Clint Eastwood. Three times, I was mashed. So thank you, Julie, Rachel and Sharon.

My favourite example of the 'cinema effect' was in the late 1960s, a time when action films began featuring the obligatory car chase. As I wandered down the marble steps of my Theatre of Dreams after seeing the film *Bullitt*, I was aware of a guy on his own adopting the jauntiest of walks, priming his shoulders and doing the slow half-blink thing, complete with slack-jawed nonchalance. He was about five foot two with a Charles Hawtrey physique, a face reminiscent of Yasser Arafat and I knew he spent his working hours on the line in the local meat factory. Truly, he was one natural-born ticket collector but the movie had amped him up with so much sass that he was now a legend in his own mind as he swaggered out of the pictures and along the road to where his supercharged Ford Mustang was waiting. Moments later he exited the car park on two wheels, his rusty 1959 Austin Cambridge screaming like a banshee, and just for a second, everyone noticed his existence. Come the morning, an endless procession of offal would once more parade before his bleary eyes but he didn't care a fig because this night, yep, he was Steve McQueen.

On the wall of the Theatre of Dreams was a large mirror which all and sundry gawked in as they exited the balcony. I would also quickly scrutinise myself in it as I passed to see if I resembled Harry Palmer or Harry Lime or Harry Callaghan or Harry Black or Randle Macmurphy, Lucas Jackson, Popeye Doyle, Travis Bickle, Rocky Balboa, Spartacus or the Terminator.

"What are you rebelling against, Johnnie?"
"Whaddya got?"

In the fifties, with the recognition of teenagers as an economic force in their own right, two genres of movie provoked reaction more than any other. Firstly on its lighter side, the youth market was catered for by Elvis, a plethora of rock 'n' roll movies, such as the wonderful *The Girl Can't Help It* (1956) plus dreadful beach party efforts starring squeaky-clean starlets like Sandra Dee and hunky blond boys like Troy Donahue. It was kitsch style over substance but nowhere else could such shallow flash be witnessed by the boppers of the day. Most of this stuff looked as if it had been put together with two nails and a hammer but the music was usually good and kids sopped it up like sponges. Besides, amongst all the chaff lurked the King and that marvellous fidgety misfit, James Dean, who gave hope to every goggle-eyed, spotty dork who yearned to be a bad boy. All courtesy of your local Theatre of Dreams.

(On the subject of *The Girl Can't Help It*, this 1956 Technicolor 'masterpiece' contains a more concentrated blend of humour, sexuality and great sounds than anything previously. The music is classic rock 'n' roll by such magicians as Eddie Cochran, Little Richard and Gene Vincent, all at their peak. Both the humour and sexuality is provided by the pneumatic Jayne Mansfield in scenes such as the one where she dizzily questions her ability to be a good mother while absent-mindedly holding two bottles of milk under her epic breasts. The males in the audience didn't know whether to guffaw like hyenas or take a cold shower.)

Mirroring the real world

Some films of this time gave youth a solid platform, exploring serious issues such as delinquency, for example, *Mix Me A Person*, starring Adam Faith. And paralleling these were the so-called British 'kitchen-sink dramas', which were almost all fine productions showcasing a refreshing new trend towards social realism. They hit home due to the fact that they were more of a mirror than a fantasy image.

The themes were predictable but worthy and had real impact. First smash of the genre was *Look Back In Anger* in 1956 which gave elbow-room to the so-called 'angry young man'. It was a kind of grey version of *Rebel Without A Cause*, with Richard Burton coming across as some erudite incarnation of James Dean's uncle and he prompted not a few young bucks to give lip to their parents. Next came *Room At The Top* with Lawrence Harvey playing the louche central character fighting his way up the ladder of success. It was hardly fodder for teenagers but the guy did do 'obnoxious' with a certain panache.

Other hugely important social taboos were being explored in these particular movies, such as homosexuality (*Victim* starring Dirk Bogarde) and the dread spectre of unmarried pregnancy in an inter-racial relationship (*A Taste of Honey* starring Rita Tushingham). No other place but the local cinema could people experience the exploded emphasis on all these important issues. Easily the best of the bunch was *Saturday Night and Sunday Morning* (1960) which contained most of the usual themes plus marital infidelity, violence and abortion. It also catapulted the terrific Albert Finney into our consciousness, for my money the best working-class anti-hero British cinema ever coughed up. So young men gawped at him from the stalls and began to copy his belligerence and rebelliousness. Girls got hot under the collar at his brutish sexuality, their parents tut-tutted and the local picture house had done its job as social talisman.

Don't blink or you'll miss it

In more innocent times, curiosity and prurience drew people to the pictures like a magnet. Very often all it needed was a burst of publicity and subsequent outrage over a certain scene to ensure that audiences became sardines. As such, a predictable smash-hit was Howard Hughes' 1943 western *The Outlaw*. The studio advertising was loud and prolonged and seemed to intimate that its star, Jane Russell, actually got her tits out. This was not the case, alas, despite the censors' sombre mutterings. Instead, what was on offer was Ms Russell's impressive rack shoe-horned into a low-cut gingham dress and thrust up using a discreet brassiere purposely designed using Mr Hughes' own engineering expertise. "Don't miss *The Outlaw...*" ran the war-time blurb "...a big, bad, sexy movie!" Actually, it was neither big nor very sexy. Bad it was, however.

Occasionally, a scene would come out of the blue in a movie to both shock and delight the punters and guarantee that many of them would be in again next day for a second flash. One such scene transpired in the 1948 British movie *Good Time Girl*. It starred home-grown sexpot Jean Kent as the eponymous tart and the American 'B' picture actor Bonar Colleano, in his usual role as the Yank who forgot to go home after the war. They were getting acquainted in the back of a taxi with the appropriately named Bonar resting his hand on Jean's knee.

"We're gonna have a good time, baby," he stated, then with one unhurried movement proceeded to shove his mitt under her skirt, past her stocking top and right to the end of the line. Miss Kent jumped, rolled her eyes and the scene cut. Astonished members of the audience chorused, "Did you see THAT?"

We sure did, baby. How the censors missed it is anyone's guess.

Jean Kent and Bonar Colleano. "We're gonna have a good time, baby." (Illustrations courtesy of Michael Barnard.)

Mind the language

Stranger still, from our twenty-first-century, Quentin Tarrantino viewpoint, even a rude word in a forties' movie could spark tremendous curiosity, thereby guaranteeing its success. The 1948 Richard Attenborough film *The Guinea Pig* became a box-office smash on the strength of one scene in which young Dickie utters the immortal line, "You only want to kick me up the arse!" It's interesting to compare this with the kerfuffle over the 1989 movie *When Harry Met Sally*, in which Meg Ryan simulates an orgasm in a restaurant.

Much more fun were 'film noir' productions from the 1940s and 1950s, which were gritty and witty to make up for their lack of titty. Pity. They oozed menace and atmosphere and were laced with the most aggressive idiosyncratic scripting which often crashed through barriers of vocabulary, emphasising the old adage that Britain and America are separated by a common language. Consider the 1946 noir movie *The Dark Corner*, starring Mark Stevens as tough but beleaguered private eye Brad Galt and Lucille Ball as his sexy, hard-boiled yet utterly loyal assistant Kathleen. Our hero, Brad, finds himself tailed by a mysterious heavy, Stauffer, played by William Bendix, who wears a conspicuous white suit. Brad manages to shake him off and is holed up in a hotel room explaining events to a perplexed Kathleen. Now, how's this for some fantastic dialogue?:

Brad: *The guy in the white suit was shagging me again, tonight.*

Kathleen: *Oh, Brad, that's the second time he's done it this week. It's a good job you NOTICED him shagging you.*

Brad: *He WANTS me to know he's around, baby. That's why he's wearing those bright duds. Nobody goes on the shag in a white suit.*

Kathleen: *I'm up to my neck in this, same as you. Oh, Brad, do you reckon this guy will want to shag me as well?*

Beautiful. Alas, I must explain that in the USA the word 'shagging' is a term used in American football, meaning 'to chase'. However, I doubt if the good people of these islands were aware of that in the late forties, and curiosity would have dragged them into their Theatres of Dreams by the bus-load.

Occasional incidents at the flicks saw very different worlds collide, adding a strange complexion to the concept of 'rites of passage'. In 1970 my grandparents heard that *Woodstock* was showing at the Regal and decided to make it a Sabbath treat. Both keen historians, they mistakenly believed it to be about the life of Churchill. Go figure. (Hmm... interesting casting – Pete Townsend as Lord Randolph, Joan Baez as Lady Jenny and introducing Jimi Hendrix as the young Winston.)

They must have felt a sense of unease while nestling their Sunday-best-dressed selves into the red velveteen, surrounded by flocks of tie-dyed hairies in sandals drawing languidly on acrid-smelling cigarettes. Nonetheless Gran and Grandad sat through the whole junket. There were no rousing speeches, no Spitfires and no D-day celebrations, although they saw plenty of 'V-signs' (albeit inverted ones). Three and a half hours later they emerged into the fresh air, historically none the wiser, dreaming of nought but Ovaltine and aspirin.

Saturday night at the movies,
who cares what picture we see...
...when you're huggin' with your baby
in the last row of the balcony. (Courtesy of Atlantic Records.)

Many movie-nuts might dispute this, but as stimulating, wondrous and hypnotic as films could be, they were not the most important social benefit that the local picture palace had to offer. For over half a century the cinema provided sanctuary and intimacy to couples. These days it is astonishing to imagine just how difficult it was to find space to conduct a relationship in the decades before post-Beatles enlightenment. Cars were a minority luxury that belonged to dads and even if a young buck had a good job and could afford a hotel room he had to enjoy his manoeuvrings out of town because in close-knit communities, word would soon spread. Even young married couples were often obliged to live with their parents or in-laws alongside a gaggle of siblings.

With personal space at such a premium, the dark of the local cinema was extraordinarily important. The shenanigans in the back row have become a clichéd piece of folklore which underplays their significance. Either side of you could sit two strangers, yet you were inviolate within the boundaries of your seats. Sacred territory, a small personal domain where couples enjoyed contact. A microcosm of privacy. Many people came to appreciate the pictures as a place of GEOGRAPHICAL escape, every bit as much as the escapism of the films. Many cinemas even provided what were candidly called 'love seats'. Always placed in the back row, usually in the corners, they were either double seats or singles from which the centre armrest could be stowed in the back rest. Cosy. A little cramped perhaps, but so much better than the emasculated atmosphere of your future in-laws' living-room as you both sat there waiting for Daddy and the Dragon to bugger off upstairs.

Countless illicit meetings were conducted in the dark of the flicks. Cinema staff became inordinately observant with regard to surreptitious activity and would regularly spot two individuals entering the place down different aisles which led to opposite ends of the same row. Hawk-eyed usherettes might clock a town dignitary making his way along the seats while a young lady closed in from the opposite direction. As they nestled side by side the staff would study his furtive expression and note that she was sporting a little too much lippy. Alternatively, it could be a member of the WI gravitating towards a husky young gentleman who certainly didn't look as if he was into bottling fruit. Wonderful fun.

When all was said and done the local cinema could be a very sexually charged place with hundreds of couples and, no doubt, plenty of lone wolves, simmering together in a kind of carnal *esprit de coeur*. In more reserved times the simple static proximity of males and females sent a haze of testosterone and oestrogen swirling upwards to mingle with the smoke. Propinquity fuelled temptation and much groping ensued, whether desired or not. About twenty minutes into the main feature, young gentlemen would yawn, stretch and lazily float an arm along the back of their girlfriends' seat. If she was a 'good' girl, his subsequent fumblings could earn him a smack in the kisser, but if she was a friendly sort the guy might be allowed to slip his hand under her blouse and play 'safe-cracker' with her bra fastening. It has to be said that many guys developed watchmaker dexterity and became so proficient at 'springing the clip' they could have become design consultants for Playtex. There were (and still are), of course, more, shall we say, 'visceral' incidents in the back row of the flicks. And, dear reader, if you require elucidation, I refer you to a scene in the 1982 movie *Diner*, involving Ellen Barkin, Mickey Rourke and his collapsible popcorn box. (If this chapter appears to be lurching into the domain of schoolboy prurience, please do not expect an apology. R.H.)

In olden days, a hint of stocking...

Males are generally regarded as the voyeurs of the species yet there wasn't a woman in the land who didn't relish the nude wrestling scene between Alan Bates and Olly Reed in *Women In Love*. Not one of them would have been able to explain why they enjoyed it – this being long before the term 'homo-erotic fascination' was coined.

(For decades, film makers had been known to craftily infuse scenes with a homosexual sub-text, for example, in the 1948 western Red River in which the two young gunslingers, Matt Garth (Montgomery Clift) and Cherry Valance (John Ireland) compliment each other on their guns during a bout of sharp-shooting. There is a protracted scene of exuberant buddy-buddy contact between Charlton Heston and Stephen Boyd in *Ben-Hur*. The very heterosexual star didn't realise how it made him appear until director William Wyler explained about the mischievous choreography. Conscious of his macho image, Heston hit the roof. In *Spartacus*, Roman leader Crassus (Lawrence Olivier) is getting a back scrub in the bath from slave Antoninus (Tony Curtis). A vicious, camp Olivier quizzes Curtis on whether his preference is for 'snails or oysters'. (This scene was removed for more than twenty years.) There, I've ruined a few classics for you.)

The local cinema was the only place you could enjoy a hint of the naked form and then only from the 1960s onwards. There were always burlesque shows and underground strip-joints but these were just about impossible for teenagers to access and besides, such sleaze only existed in big city dives. Of course, you could try some arty revue such as Mrs Henderson's Windmill Theatre in London but just how erotic was that? There were also nude magazines to slaver over but they too were underground and probably consisted of photos of naked Germans playing badminton or skinny-dipping in some Black Forest idyll.

If you managed to lay your sticky mitts on a post-war *Health and Efficiency* magazine, the naturists' Bible, the chances are nipples and pubic hair were blanked out. This made things even more confusing for the sheltered parochials amongst us. Women, of course, had no such curiosity at this time (err... did they?). Finally, in the 1950s, Hugh Hefner turned up with *Playboy* and the concept of men's magazines began to gain acceptance. Mind you, if Mom ever found a copy under your pillow you were toast.

Nudity and explicit sexual activity on celluloid before the 1960s was virtually non-existent in American or British films. The French, Germans, Italians and Scandinavians were far more enlightened, but much of their output didn't make it past the censor this side of the Channel. (For example, the superb 1953 French thriller *The Wages of Fear*, often voted one of the greatest movies ever made, featured a scene showing a woman enjoying an outdoor shower, with no one batting an eyelid – apart from our moral guardians who immediately reached for the scissors.) Even the young Loren and Bardot were filmed topless in their native lands during the 1950s. No wonder Europeans pigeon-holed the British as a repressed bunch.

Finally, when kitchen-sink dramas arrived, along with a 'new wave' of directors such as Ken Russell, boundaries of taste began shifting and, of course, the pictures was the place to go to witness this revolution in social attitudes (television wouldn't catch up for years.)

Alongside sexual explicitness, violence and horror were becoming very graphic and foul language had its foot in the door. I was shocked to hear the F-word for the first time on the silver screen during the climax of *Dirty Harry*. It is only uttered once, by the villain, Scorpio, just before Clint blows his head off.

Sam Peckinpah became notorious for his bloodthirsty gun-ups and as the seventies dawned there was no going back. It was all hitting us in the face and no one could avoid it.

Bitten and smitten

One favourite cinematic genre guaranteed to deliver steady thrills were 'Hammer' horror films. From the 1950s this British company churned out good-quality gothic shockers, almost always starring Christopher Lee and Peter Cushing. (Lee's incarnation of Dracula is still unsurpassed.) For about fifteen years (between 1958 and 1973) if you fancied a good fright at the flicks, with plenty of gore, shivers and dust-ups, Hammer invariably produced the goods.

(They also had a sortie into bigger budget monster movies. With One Million Years B.C. (1966) they managed to corral no less a sex symbol than Raquel Welch into playing the lead. Her appearance in a fur bikini was ballyhooed as a stronger selling point than the dinosaurs yet even as a pre-teen I wasn't impressed. Although Ms Welch was groped by Neanderthals, chased by huge lizards and even carried off by a pterodactyl, her skimpy cozzy never so much as hinted at slipping off. Come to that, neither did her Estée Lauder slap.)

Over the years Hammer kept pushing the limits and with the exception of foul language their cheap British gems drew on just about all the cinematic taboos: obviously horror, violence and blasphemy, but also nudity and sex. They became must-see fare for any male with a pulse. In 1970 Hammer came up with *The Vampire Lovers* which was full of naked lesbian blood-suckers and starred a certain Ingrid Pitt, an eastern European actress with an astonishing chassis and seductive contralto. In terms of sex appeal she made Raquel Welch look like a tailor's dummy and remains to this day my perfect fantasy female. A year later Hammer came up with *Twins of Evil*, another vampire effort with a kinky twist. This one starred identical blood-suckers played by the beautiful Maltese twins Madeleine and Mary Collinson, who flashed their tits and fangs in roughly equal doses and had young men everywhere on their knees in praise of the local flea-pit.

In 1973, when *The Exorcist* was released, taking horror, plus all the other taboos to a whole new level, Hammer realised that the game was up. However, they checked out with their best-ever movie, one that has since become a cult classic and for me, is more enjoyable than *The Exorcist* itself: *The Wicker Man*.

During this chapter I have indulged myself in emphasising just how valuable the local picture palace has been down through the decades, in giving people privacy, a certain exclusivity, wonderment, knowledge, and allowing them to ignite and explore a variety of emotions. For me, as a seventeen-year-old with raging hormones and no concrete answers, my Theatre of Dreams served up a double bill that blew me away when they paired *The Wicker Man* with *Don't Look Now.*[2]

It's debatable which was the creepiest and which the sexiest but I always maintain that between them they added up to a kind of 'rites of passage' baptism. As I emerged from the cinema, cross-eyed with overload and mutating body chemistry, I wondered whether I would ever derive as much value from cinematic entertainment as I did that day. I still can't admit that I have.

As the decades passed and films progressed, the lovely naiveté of yesteryear receded. Audiences became worldly and almost unshockable. Special effects now allow us to witness beauty, horror and destruction to an unnaturally realistic degree. Even children are becoming desensitised to movies which, forty years ago, would have appalled the toughest adults. People now have the wherewithal to explore 'rites of passage' in any number of other fields worldwide and the coy, shadowy appeal of sex has been buried under an avalanche of crudeness. Wrecked by overkill.

The medium that gave us moral hot potatoes from *Sign of the Cross* (1932) through *From Here to Eternity* (1953) to *Women In Love* (1969) finally produced a thing called *9 Songs* in 2004. This was the first movie to show two actors having real intercourse in a main-line production. The result: absolutely nothing. There was barely a whiff of controversy because by then nobody gave a damn.

So now I mourn the loss of innocence of the cinema, where innocuous naughtiness once had such a wonderful effect. Where style and speech and fashion and novelty truly mattered to those generations who experienced the old picture palaces. I think we've all grown up far too much.

2 This movie is generally reckoned to have the most authentically acted love scene ever filmed, between Julie Christie and Donald Sutherland. They both hotly deny they were doing it for real!

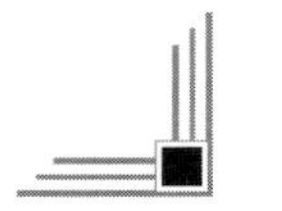

AUTHOR'S CONFESSIONS

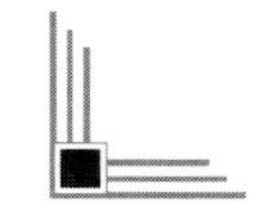

TOP TEN FAVOURITE MOVIES

1.	*Jaws*	1975
2.	*Thunderbolt and Lightfoot*	1974
3.	*The Wild Bunch*	1969
4.	*Lonely are the Brave*	1962
5.	*In the Heat of the Night*	1967
6.	*Dirty Harry*	1971
7.	*The Titfield Thunderbolt*	1953
8.	*The Wicker Man*	1973
9.	*White Heat*	1949
10.	*Zulu*	1964

TOP TEN COOLEST EVER CINEMATIC PERFORMANCES

1. Clint Eastwood – *Dirty Harry*
2. Kirk Douglas – *Lonely Are The Brave*
3. Albert Finney – *Saturday Night And Sunday Morning*
4. Sidney Poitier – *In The Heat Of The Night*
5. Steve Mcqueen – *The Thomas Crown Affair*
6. Elvis Presley – *Jailhouse Rock*
7. Orson Welles – *The Third Man*
8. Jack Nicholson – *Five Easy Pieces*
9. James Cagney – *White Heat*
10. Al Pacino – *Heat*

TOP TEN CINEMATIC SEX SYMBOLS

1. Ingrid Pitt
2. Jeanne Moreau
3. Faye Dunaway
4. Liv Ullman
5. Sophia Loren
6. Jayne Mansfield
7. Nastassia Kinski
8. Lee Remick
9. Dahlia Lavi
10. Julie Christie

All lists are subject to occasional revision.

A SYDNEY POLLACK Film

ROBERT
REDFORD

MERYL
STREEP

CHAPTER ELEVEN

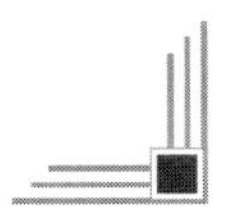

HALF A CENTURY NOT OUT

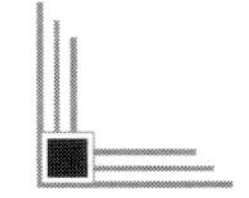

Regal V. technology

By 1980, after twenty-four years of sterling service, Ernie Highland should have had the movie business sewn up. He could order the hottest movie almost always on release, the cinema-going public had never been so affluent and his great rival, the Clifton, was defunct. The Regal should have been a cinema nirvana, but two factors conspired to make the early years of the decade a torrid time for the Theatre of Dreams. Firstly, by late 1979 Britain was heading into one of the worst recessions since the war, and when people lose their jobs they cut back on creature comforts such as nights out at the flicks. Secondly and more significantly, technology had coughed up the latest 'must-have' toy.

Video just had to happen. If we are honest, it was the invention we had all been yearning for. To finally be able to record films and television programmes and select any movie of your choice to play in the comfort of your own home, night or day – start, stop, freeze, rewind, fast-forward, pre-programme – there was loud cheering at the church of the couch potato. The video recorder appeared to be a greater threat to the industry in 1980 than television had been in 1953 and, as then, many cinema owners panicked at the writing on the wall.

The Regal still had several factors in its favour, however:

(a) She was now the only game in town and with Highland's price-pegging policy, which kept the cost of a ticket considerably lower than those at the cinemas in Worcester, Redditch or Cheltenham, she could still entice reasonable numbers through the door to escape the domestic round and the horror stories of redundancy and hardship so prominent on television at the time.

(b) Movies themselves were continuing to evolve as they always had and hopefully always will. The early 1980s produced ever more hard-hitting entertainment across almost all film genres, catering for world-weary tastes which longed for heightened sensation. Violence and shocks hit new heights with *Alien*, *Scarface*, *The Terminator* and *Sudden Impact*. Domestic dramas such as *Kramer vs Kramer* and *Ordinary People* shared the Oscars with modern history epics such as *Ghandi* and *Reds* while *The French Lieutenant's Woman* had us blubbing into our hankies.

(c) Initially video was limited to supplying movies twelve months after their release, which allowed for a good tour of the cinemas. Plus, when they finally made it onto cassette, the quality of some copies, after numerous hirings, was sub-standard, making true buffs question the value of their conversion to the couch. Many times have I sat with bated breath awaiting the pleasures of a video film, only to be infuriated by grainy images and duff sound.

(d) This period also saw the rise of the big movie franchise. Films in decades past often generated sequels, for example, *The Magnificent Seven* had three and *In the Heat of the Night* had two, but they were almost all pale imitations of the original and bombed at the box office.

However, in 1974 *Godfather II* was hailed as being every bit as brilliant as (many said better than) the 1972 original and the concept of the sequel began to receive a fresh appraisal. By the early 1980s the hunger for sequels was having a positive effect on cinema business, which circumvented video because the audience couldn't wait to see them. *The Empire Strikes Back*, *Superman II*, *Star Trek: The Wrath of Khan*, *Rocky II and III* and even the *Jaws* follow-ups, with their ever-more bendy fish, became box-office gold. Most extraordinary, some said unwise, were two 1980s sequels to the 1960 classic *Psycho*, still starring the increasingly loopy Anthony Perkins. The franchise which came to sum up this trend better than any other, however, was Steven Spielberg's *Indiana Jones* actioners (there is yet another one due out in 2008!). When *Raiders of the Lost Ark* smashed in 1981 it was trumpeted as an updated version of the old Saturday morning matinee serial. Video could never offer such a dynamic.

Besides the pull of sequels and drag factors inherent in video, other events have been known to either kick start a film's appeal or kill it stone dead. For example, when the Regal screened *Chariots of Fire* on release in 1981 the audiences were feeble. In early 1982 the film garnered five Oscars and blew up a storm of interest centred around the possible revival of the British Film Industry. Ernie Highland re-screened it and the place was packed. A similar thing happened in 1982/3 following the eight-Oscar triumph of *Ghandi*.

Extraneous factors can also have a negative effect, as in 1987 when Highland screened *Rambo: First Blood Part II*. The film had been a smash in America and consolidated Sylvester Stallone's standing as the biggest star of the day. However, the Hungerford massacre in September of that year brought public consciousness into sharp focus on the subject of gun control and the Rambo character was demonised. Sly's movie attracted only a few dozen customers to the Theatre of Dreams. With regard to sequels, many near-geriatric stars were compelled to continually resurrect their career-defining characters. Think Bruce Willis in the recent *Die Hard 4*, Sly Stallone in *Rocky Balboa* and Harrison Ford in the soon to be released *Indiana Jones 4*. Also, despite the scorn heaped upon Rambo in the late 1980s, pensioner Stallone has breathed new life into his one-man-army-ego-trip in 2008 with *Rambo 4: First Dribble*.

Despite its advantages over the burgeoning video culture, overall Regal audiences nose-dived, so during the recession period 1980–82 Ernie Highland had a fight on his hands. With box office certainties such as *Raging Bull* or *On Golden Pond* accounting for perhaps only fifteen of the fifty-two weeks in a year, he was forced to plumb certain depths to swell the coffers.

Fleshing out the audience

It has to be recognised that one of the major attractions of video was the influence of the growing pornography market. Since the mid-1960s, in mainland Europe (especially Scandinavia, Germany, Holland and France) the hard-core industry had become virtually socially acceptable and despite ferocious opposition in the USA in the 1970s, porn was establishing a huge underground market. Britain was much slower to catch on and with our severe laws on the import of obscene material it was difficult to obtain hard-core videos.[1]

1 During the 1990s most types of pornography were decriminalised in Britain. This was probably a necessity because with the rise of the Internet and the subsequent surveillance culture our courts would have been permanently clogged with curious peepers.

While Britain lagged behind in terms of the social acceptance of explicit material Ernie Highland provided a stop-gap for the droolers in Asum. Unless a major movie was doing the rounds, Sundays were put aside for a double bill of soft-core titillation. These would either be some of the atrocious *Confessions* films or dubbed, emasculated European romps. Having to resort to screening this trash must have dented Ernie's professional pride but the prospect of seeing sagebrush swirl around an empty cinema galvanised his actions.

These Sabbath flesh fests appeared to fill the social chasm created by the death of Elvis for many gypsies, albeit only the men. They would often provide half the Sunday audience during this period and without wishing to sound totally patronising I found it sad that without The King movie-going travellers appeared to have lost their moral compass. This said, I'll drop the subject as the words kettle, pot and black spring to mind.

The softer end of the rumpo market began to achieve a modicum of respectability through one film in particular, *Emmanuelle* (yes, yes, I did see it) which eventually sashayed into Port Street in 1978 and packed the place to the rafters. It spawned (if you'll pardon the expression) numerous sequels, all successful and all garbage, but they began to bridge the gap between main-stream cinema and the adult market.

With the liberalisation of laws and cross-border trade, DVDs and particularly the Internet, the worldwide porn industry has become so profitable that it now dwarfs Hollywood and Bollywood combined. The whole culture is so tiresome, crude and 'in your face' that I long for those far-off days of youth when to sit in the Theatre of Dreams and glimpse a naked Julie Christie *(Darling)*, Ursula Andress *(Perfect Friday)* or Glenda Jackson *(Women in Love)* provoked a volcanic hormonal experience. I can hear the ghost of Ernie Highland yelling: "Don't forget Jenny Agutter!"

Oddly, with so much nudity and sex on television and the web there appears to have been a considerable drop in both in mainstream movies. Which is a blessed relief to those of us fed up with seeing the likes of Tom Cruise having to mount his leading ladies in all his celluloid outings.

To further aid finances, the Regal restaurant was leased to a variety of ethnic incarnations for over thirty years. The most popular was probably the Maharajah Indian but it proved a mixed blessing because it often made the cinema reek of curry.[2]

Recession or not, with true Highland bloody-mindedness Ernie opted for extensive refurbishment during this hungry period. At the end of the 1970s he had reduced the total seating capacity from 847 to 700 by removing two rows of seats each side plus the complete row attached to the rear gangway partition in the stalls. This complied with modern safety regulations and made the lower deck far more accessible from all directions. The balcony capacity remained unchanged.

During the 1981/82 refit the capacity was reduced still further to 540 with the removal of the upward-facing seats at the front of the stalls (the first six rows). These were more prone to damage than the rest, had never been particularly safe or

2 The Regal was one of the founder members of The Bengeworth Traders' Association and many of their meetings were convened in Ernie Highland's office.

comfortable and were finally deemed unacceptable. Alas, the charm of architect Hurley Robinson's dished floor had to concede to economics and the modern spectre of claims for personal injury. It left a large bare slope of floor between the new front row and the screen but this was unavoidable. Another much-loved (at least by me) feature was altered at this time. The exterior wooden display cases which had been exhibiting stills from current and forthcoming movies ever since the early 1950s were replaced with modern illuminated single-poster Perspex cases, which remained until their removal in 2007.

The cost of the refit was £22,600, which included seats, carpet, a new screen and upgraded sound system. It was not such a reckless use of funds because Highland may have spotted the first inklings of a strange reverse trend that video was generating in the industry.

A new film-hungry generation was growing, having been turned on to the medium purely because the ease of access to movies through their VCR was making them addicted. A true couch potato might wade through two or more cassettes a day, thus it was logical that many of these new film junkies would opt to experience the thrills as they were originally intended – on a thirty-foot screen. This was by no means everyone, but a significant number of sofa loafers were changing their habits to create this noticeable increase in cinema takings. By late 1982, with the recession just beginning to ease, Ernie could see the light at the end of the tunnel.

E.T. brings home the bacon

Also, in 1982, one film took the industry by storm. *E.T. the Extra-Terrestrial* proved to be the perfect film for all cinema goers, young and old, broke all box-office records worldwide and dethroned *Star Wars* as the most profitable movie in history. Ironically, when it opened at the Theatre of Dreams it was a damp squib, barely filling two hundred seats. However, sleepy Evesham soon cottoned on and for the next month, *E.T.* made more money for the Regal in four weeks than the cinema had taken in any FOUR MONTHS of the previous year on the way to topping the best attendance figures of *Jaws* and *Grease*. No mean feat, considering the reduction in seating capacity since the two seventies' blockbusters, although *E.T.* was screened for at least a week longer.

E.T. was one of the few major films which didn't appear on video after the usual time had elapsed. Steven Spielberg was particularly patriarchal about his little spaceman, stating that it was his favourite creation and so refused to put him on the shelves for over a decade until E.T. had enjoyed a couple of (very profitable) re-issues on the big screen.

Fifty years of dreams

The year of 1982 was indeed memorable as, on Sunday, 10 October the Theatre of Dreams reached a half-century. On Monday 11, as part of a night of celebrations Highland screened the 1938 black and white musical *Alexander's Rag-Time Band* (obtained from MGM) as fitting entertainment. A large souvenir programme, which mirrored the 1932 original was printed to commemorate the anniversary. It contained glowing tributes to Ernie and the Regal staff from Reg Wilkes of Evesham Chamber of Commerce, Ed Cohen representing Bengeworth Traders' Association and from Mayor and Mayoress John and Marjorie Kay.

Much ceremony was enjoyed on the night attended by various worthies who made affectionate speeches awash with nostalgia. The Mayor and Mayoress drew the tickets for a grand raffle of £1,000-worth of prizes and proceeds from the evening went to Brook House home for the mentally handicapped. This event may well have been the pinnacle of Ernie Highland's career and long-time Regal devotee Tony Goodwin was present to record the emotional manager thanking his special guests, his audience, his staff, Evesham, Hollywood and the Lumière brothers for giving him the best job in town.

Soon after this, several students from the BBC Training Centre at Wood Norton produced a ten-minute video about the Regal which shows it as we all choose to remember it. It includes interviews with Ernie Highland and Iris Jordan and even now, a quarter of a century further on it can make the true fan go misty-eyed.

Meanwhile, back in the box

By the 1980s many top movies were exceeding two hours of running time so a new device known as the 'tower' was installed (by Western Electrics) in the projection room to accommodate their length. It was a tall metal structure holding four very large upright reels, two either side, one above the other. The upper reel could be loaded with many hours of film, particularly as the new thinner polyester material was now in widespread use, and would be connected through the path rollers of the nearest Westar in such a way that after projection of the image it would by-pass the machine's own spool-box and rewind onto the lower reel of the tower. This avoided the risk of exceeding the limited capacity of the Westars and ended the need for an intermission (unless the film was so long that it was courteous to insert one). The operators set the tower up onto a lateral-running rail so that it could be easily shifted from side to side to access each of the Westars.

At the same time the old arc lamps were finally replaced by modern Zenon ones which emitted a constant brilliance without the need for the operator to keep adjusting the carbon electrodes inwards as they wore down.

Projectionist David Stride with a BIG movie on the tower around Christmas 2002.

From 1971 to 1982 chief projectionist Brian Houghton was working part-time due to family commitments and a number of other operators kept the Westars rolling during this period. Once again, I apologise for being unable to expand much on some of these characters. Scotsman Norman Yarr was the main man for most of the 1970s until moving on and being replaced by Peter Bennett, who had been in the film industry since 1938. Sadly Peter died soon after the Regal's fiftieth anniversary and Brian Houghton was persuaded to take the helm full-time again. He was ably assisted at various times throughout the 1980s by Tony Goodwin, Ray Houghton (no relation), Michael Pulley and Martin Bennett (no relation to Peter Bennett).

Martin Bennett, who was second operator for several years during the middle of the decade, caught the Regal bug as badly as Tony Goodwin. I visited him at his house in Redditch to glean any anecdotes or information about the old fun factory and to my intense delight discovered that he had actually built a mini-cinema in his garage. And neither was it a half-hearted effort. A large screen festooned the rear of the garage door, the floor was carpeted and nine plush red cinema seats were arranged in rows of three to accommodate a select gang of friends. Best of all, however, an extended section at the rear of the garage served as his projection room and housed two lovingly-restored Westars, primed and ready to show Hollywood's finest creations. Martin kindly gave me a demonstration (I wasn't budging until he had) and within a few minutes of him 'lacing-up' I was transported back to 1964 and drooled with nostalgia as a compilation of old Regal advertising films extolled the refreshing taste of Kia-Ora, the delicious crunch of Butterkist and the cool satisfaction of Consulate. Sigh. Martin tells me that he now only requires an original usherette's ice cream tray to seal the authenticity of his little Theatre of Dreams and, of course, supply his nine guests with Mivis. What he didn't specify was who might be harnessed into it, resplendent in short gingham uniform, black stockings and a Veronica Lake 'peek-a-boo' barnet.

Martin Bennett (with Brian Houghton) taking a break between movies in the 1980s. Not content with having worked in the Regal, Martin has actually built his own Theatre of Dreams at home.

The changing world of the mid-1980s

By the middle of the decade the Regal was still cruising along nicely, coping with the increasing effect of video ownership and appearing to still be a highly relevant facet of Evesham's social scene.

The Regal Super-Cinema Company Ltd. now had only four shareholders: Stella Morrall, wife of the original owner Vic, Eileen Bowerman, daughter of the Regal's long-time accountant Walter Dix, Ernie Highland and Jane Peatfield, daughter of original manager Sydney Hall. This group symbolised both the continuity and family ethos of the Theatre of Dreams. Nonetheless by 1985 Stella Morrall and

Received of Regal Super Cinema (Evesham) Limited Certificate No. 159
Ordinary Shares.
for
Date 19
Signature

No. 159

Regal Super Cinema (Evesham) Limited.

(Incorporated under the Companies Act 1929)

CAPITAL - - £20,000

Divided into 20,000 Ordinary Shares of £1 each.

This is to Certify that MRS EILEEN, AGNES MARY BOWERMAN, of FOREST HOUSE FOREST HILLS, SANDWAY, NR NORTHWICH CHESHIRE is the Holder of ONE THOUSAND TWO HUNDRED & SIXTY SIX Ordinary Shares, fully paid, of £1 each, numbered [illegible] inclusive, in the above-named Company, subject to the Memorandum and Articles of Association thereof.

Given under the Common Seal of the Company, this [illegible] day of December 1980

Directors.

Secretary.

No transfer of the whole or any portion of the above Shares can be registered without the production of this Certificate.

(Wound up)

Regal share certificate.

Eileen Bowerman, sensing the radical changes in the industry opted to sell their shares to the other two. Entertainment options were beginning to expand and a new 'bad witch' was about to make its impact felt. In 1985 the first 'multiplex' cinema opened in Milton Keynes.

These were designed to package films in bulk, showing perhaps a dozen features on a dozen screens at any one time. Compared to the glamour and decorous excitement of the old picture palaces, they resembled giant soulless arcades providing punters with quick turnaround viewing and obscene amounts of fast food. Ernie Highland appeared philosophical in the face of this new threat by stating that at least multiplexes were still picture houses, albeit in a vulgar, updated form, and that Evesham itself had once supplied twelve films a week for decades when both the Regal and the Clifton had each screened double features three times a week. "So what's the difference?" said Ernie.

Highland's real ogre of the future was Sky television. "Once that gets established, with hundreds of channels to choose from, I think the Regal is a dead duck," he confided to Irene Mackenzie.

After almost thirty years at the helm, Ernie regarded the Regal as his baby and, as such, it had to survive at all costs. As he told the *Evesham Journal* in 1983: "The cinema is an addiction. It fills your life and becomes something to live for." Even so, events transpired which would begin to make him feel his age.

Firstly, teenagers were becoming less respectful and more troublesome. Friday nights, in particular, could be nightmares for the staff because of rowdy conduct, with fights breaking out, kids running from seat to seat and usherettes suffering verbal abuse. The yobbos would never seem to settle down to enjoy a movie until Arnie or Sly was sending blood and guts all over the screen. Extended dialogue or subtlety in film was a bit too much for some tiny minds and the Neanderthals in the stalls would become restless if there was no mayhem being served up. The so-called 'dumbing-down' syndrome appeared to be taking effect and would eventually give rise to such trash entertainment as *Big Brother* and similar dross, untaxing to feeble mentalities. With the rise of these moronic elements, several pleasant traditions had to fall by the wayside. It was now deemed too risky for an usherette to dispense goodies from trays while standing against the balcony balustrade, in case jostling nutters sent her the quick way down to the stalls. Thus, from the early 1980s, ice cream was sold from a table in the rear gangway by the balcony exit.

I'm sure that the trouble-makers were in the minority (just) but this aspect of the business was giving even a mighty manager like Highland a Jurassic headache. The crunch came in 1985 when, in his inimitable style, he chose to eject two hefty gypsy boys for causing aggro. He was to receive a salutary lesson in how deference to authority was becoming unfashionable. On the steps leading down from the stalls' gangway to the Port Street exit one of the miscreants took exception to being given the bums-rush, turned on the manager and landed Ernie a meaty one round the side of the head, then for good measure, followed up with one in the kisser. Highland was left stunned and sat for a few minutes on the bottom step longing for the genteel days of yore. At seventy-two he realised his physical prowess was on the wane and now was the time to contemplate his future seriously. The incident left Ernie depressed for several weeks, his staff and friends becoming increasingly concerned for his well-being.

In late 1985 a conversation with his friend Barry Willis, a fellow cinema manager who owned the Majestic in Bridgenorth, was to give Highland fresh impetus. Willis persuaded Ernie that selling up was his best option and then actually made an offer for the Theatre of Dreams of close to £100,000. Ernie pitched the idea to fellow shareholder Jane Peatfield, who was agreeable but thought they could do better than Barry Willis's offer. It was decided to advertise the Regal nationwide via Conrad Ritblat Estate Agents and by early 1986, with the post-recession property market looking rosy, tentative offers began drifting in. Ernie and Jane also decided to keep schtum about the sale. They didn't need ferocious resistance from Irene, Iris, Brian and the rest while any deal was being struck. Whether or not this can be regarded as underhand is debatable, but Ernie and Jane were the owners and as such, could do whatever they wanted. Besides, Highland knew that if he didn't alter his life soon, the stress of running the Regal would do him in.

With this fresh change of direction Highland once again seemed energised, but his core agenda would never alter: The Regal had to remain a cinema at all costs. The very thought of its metamorphosing into a bingo hall, bowling alley, amusement arcade, apartments or, God forbid, a Macdonald's made him break out into a cold sweat. So he took what steps he could to ensure its survival.

The first two houses in Burford Road had belonged to the Regal since its construction and were traditionally available for any projectionists who needed a roof over their head. Many operators took advantage of this down the decades. Highland decided it was prudent to sell them at this time, firstly because in a rising property market they would raise capital for investment and secondly (and most important to Ernie) a new owner would be unable to get overly creative with regard to the original structure of the cinema. Even when the place was being built, thought had been given to flattening numbers 1 and 3 Burford Road to accommodate a larger, comfier auditorium. Therefore, in 1986, the possibility of demolishing the cinema AND the two houses in order to create a huge space for redevelopment must have registered with all the speculators.

Highland's viewpoint can, of course, be regarded as most unbusinesslike, but having poured his soul into the place for thirty years the thought of his deco palace being destroyed or disfigured was unbearable. Every Regal fan in the world would have concurred with his sentimental rationale.

Guardian Angel?

During late 1985/early 1986 several parties were taking curious nibbles at the bait. The front-runner proved to be Angel Leisure Ltd. bossed by Hampshire businessman John Angel, who owned cinemas in Cirencester and Devizes and was, therefore, no newcomer to the industry. However, Angel was also a fair-sized bingo impresario with halls in Boscombe, Bulford, Chippenham, Swindon and Toton, a fact which rang warning bells in Highland's head. Jane Peatfield, on the other hand, was less sentimental about the Regal so didn't fret too much over what was in store. There was now a firm offer of around £150,000 on the table and with John Angel appearing to be making the right noises, Jane pressured Ernie to accept.

During negotiations, Angel had mooted splendid ideas on installing two or more screens by dividing either the stalls or balcony or both. This seemed to finally soften Highland's intransigence over development, perhaps because it was an indicator of Angel's definite commitment to the preservation of the place as a picture house. An interview with the *Evesham Journal* in early 1987 appeared to show Ernie's enlightened stance: "I'm looking forward to working under the new ownership but there are going to be some big changes. It's likely the cinema will split in two and the loss of the circle will be sad," he said.

Whatever the future had in store, John Angel seemed as rosy a prospect as could be secured, so in December 1986 the offer was agreed which gave Angel Leisure controlling interests with Highland staying on as manager. Jane Peatfield retired from the scene completely, thus severing the final link with the Regal's origins. After fifty-four years of success, the Regal Super Cinema Company Ltd. ceased to exist.

The 'gang of four' in late 1986. Between them, Iris Jordan, Ernie Highland, Brian Houghton and Irene Mackenzie served the Theatre of Dreams for 160 years.

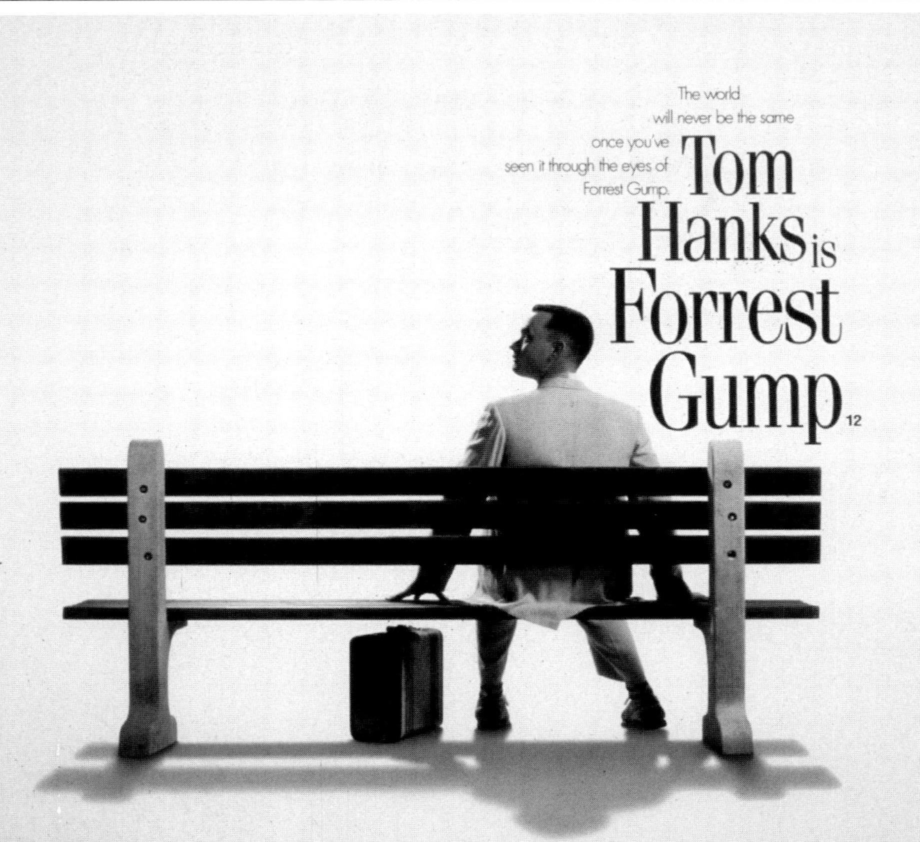
The world
will never be the same
once you've
seen it through the eyes of
Forrest Gump.
Tom
Hanks is
Forrest
Gump
12
Paramount Pictures presents a Steve Tisch/Wendy Finerman production a Robert Zemeckis film Tom Hanks Forrest Gump Robin Wright Gary Sinise Mykelti Williamson and Sally Field Charles Newirth Joanna Johnston Alan Silvestri Joel Sill
United International Pictures
Arthur Schmidt Rick Carter Don Burgess Winston Groom Eric Roth Wendy Finerman Steve Tisch Steve Starkey Robert Zemeckis
SPECIAL VISUAL EFFECTS BY INDUSTRIAL LIGHT AND MAGIC

CHAPTER TWELVE

'HEEERE'S JOHNNY!'

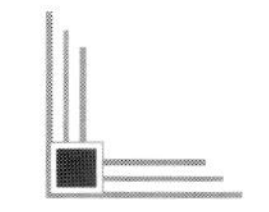

By January 1987, with the Regal under new ownership, Ernie Highland and the rest of the staff felt a mixture of fresh optimism tempered by a healthy suspicion. With the ink still drying on the exchange contract, the year kicked off on an upbeat note as the Theatre of Dreams had one of its biggest ever post-war smashes, *Crocodile Dundee*. This appeared to set the seal on the Regal's health during the post-recession period, in which so many fine, money-making movies had been produced that even die-hard sceptics could believe the cinema industry was on firm ground:

1980 *Alien, American Gigolo, Any Which Way You Can, The Empire Strikes Back, Ordinary People, Raging Bull, The Shining*

1981 *An American Werewolf in London, Atlantic City, Chariots of Fire, The French Lieutenant's Woman, On Golden Pond, Raiders of the Lost Ark, Southern Comfort*

1982 *Annie, Blade Runner, E.T., First Blood, Ghandi, An Officer and a Gentleman, Reds, Tootsie*

1983 *Jaws 3-D, Return of the Jedi, Scarface, Sudden Impact, Terms of Endearment, Twilight Zone, War Games*

1984 *Amadeus, Ghostbusters, Indiana Jones and the Temple of Doom, The Karate Kid, The Killing Fields, A Passage to India, Romancing the Stone, Splash, The Terminator*

1985 *Cocoon, The Colour Purple, Commando, Out of Africa, Prizzi's Honour, A Room with a View*

1986 *Aliens, Cobra, The Colour of Money, Flight of the Navigator, The Jewel of the Nile, Platoon, Top Gun*

Add to these the lucrative franchises finding purchase during the decade, some of which would come through with a new instalment each year: *Friday the Thirteenth, Halloween, James Bond, Nightmare on Elm Street, Police Academy, Poltergeist, Star Trek, Superman.*

Video had been accommodated, DVD was yet to happen, Sky was in its infancy and with people becoming more affluent the creative output from the industry was surely enough to secure the future of the Port Street fun factory – or was it?

The honeymoon period with John Angel appeared short-lived as he immediately applied for a bingo licence, apparently intent on marginalising the showing of films. However, despite securing the licence he was to hit a major snag. Essoldo, his bingo rival in the High Street, were not enamoured with the prospect of competition and countered by threatening to recommence showing movies if Angel began spinning balls in Port Street. So he backed down pronto and let Ernie Highland carry on with business as usual. At the same time, the proposed idea of dividing the Regal into a multi-screen facility was kicked into the long grass.

John Angel in 2000.

I have attempted to track down the now retired John Angel, but much of the time he decamps to Thailand so, as I'm not Alan Whicker, it has not been possible to record his thoughts on the Regal story during the period of his ownership (1986–2001). I have therefore attempted to present a balanced account of these fifteen years from the point of view of both the uncompromising fan and the pragmatic businessman.

Whether Ernie Highland was naïve or not in selling to Angel Leisure and expecting the Regal to drift sweetly on as it had since 1932 is irrelevant because ANY new owner would have immediately assessed its potential for change. This was 1987 and Thatcher's super-heating economy was just beginning to send the land/property market into orbit. No businessman could have been expected to ignore the possibility of converting an old cinema into either a residential or an office development. When the stock market crash of 19 October 1987, the so-called Black Monday, sent distraught yuppie traders swallow-diving from their tenth-floor office windows, John Angel would have been as concerned about his future as the next shark.

End of an era

Ernie Highland's last year as manager of the Theatre of Dreams, under the ownership of Angel Leisure, was an unhappy time. He was too old to change his ways, fretted about the long-term future of the place and frequently clashed with John Angel. Highland confided to Iris Jordan and Irene Mackenzie that he regretted selling and several months on, he even offered to buy the Regal back, but to no avail. The chances are that in 1987 any new owner would have adopted a similar mercenary attitude and the simple truth was that Ernie had been unable to sell it to a younger version of himself.

By mid-1987 Highland had had enough and asked deputy manager Iris if she fancied taking the reins, but she, too, was disillusioned and at sixty-seven, needed the stress of pandering to the new regime like a hole in the head. The two of them decided this would be their final year and asked Irene Mackenzie to be the new skipper. Irene was cagey at first but, as her love for the old place was no less great than that of the other two, she decided to grasp the opportunity. Ernie and Iris spent the next six months prepping Irene on those facets of the business she was unsure about (which wasn't many) with a view to her taking over at Christmas. John Angel was agreeable to this move, no doubt glad to off-load the old guard and start afresh.

On 19 December 1987, at the end of the evening's work, Ernie and Iris were asked down to the Regal restaurant[1] and were ushered into a surprise retirement party where the long-serving couple posed for the local newspaper and, if the truth be known, both breathed a sigh of relief.

Iris was presented with a cut-glass rose bowl and Ernie a new typewriter as retirement gifts, together with a crystal glass horn of plenty and a trophy projector on a stand each. Iris intended to join her sister Violet Woodcock (who had retired a few months earlier) in taking advantage of the Cinematic Benevolent Fund (CBF) retirement homes on the south coast.[2] However, for the next couple of years Iris was always around to cover for Irene during holidays and emergencies.

1 When Angel Leisure bought the cinema it included the restaurant and the Maharajah Indian ceased to be.

2 Iris Jordan died in 2002, just short of her eighty-third birthday. Violet Woodcock died the following year, aged ninety-five.

Ernie and Iris with staff and friends at their retirement party. L–r: Helen Spiers, Samantha Spiers, Iris Jordan, Eva Turski, Ernie Highland, Simon Kenshole, Irene Mackenzie, Brian Houghton, Kate Seabrook, Jessica Sinclair.

Ernie was to stay on in an advisory capacity to Irene for the next few months and would probably rue the fact that he was too emotionally attached to the Regal to make a clean break.

On Thursday, 12 May 1988 Ernie arrived to take Irene to the première of the movie *Beetlejuice*, showing at The Picture House, Monmouth. In the car were John Angel and his assistant Chris Epps, whom Ernie had just collected from the Evesham Hotel. There had obviously been bad blood between Angel and Highland because the old manager was in a barely contained rage for the whole evening. Irene never did discover the exact cause of their bust-up but the smart money was on Angel confessing that he intended selling the Regal to either Wimpy, Bovis or Redrow Homes. In mid-1988, with developers feasting on the hottest property market since the war, no one could blame John for taking a long, hard look at the possibilities of unlocking his potential gold-mine.

After the show there was a dreadful silence as Ernie drove the four of them back to Evesham. Angel sat hunched up in a giant sulk, his pal Epps next to him with the face of a man witnessing Armageddon. Irene Mackenzie tried her best to shrink into the passenger seat as an enraged Highland, his blood pressure off the clock, floored the gas pedal of his Honda.

Next day, Friday, 13 May, the stress finally caught up with Ernie as he suffered a heart attack and spent the next two weeks in hospital. Irene went straight to see him where he conceded that he wouldn't be going back to work at the Theatre of Dreams. "You must book *Beetlejuice*," he instructed.

Both 1988 and 1989 proved to be good years for the Regal. People were still flocking to see quality stuff such as *Born on the Fourth of July, The Accused, Dangerous Liaisons, When Harry Met Sally, A Fish Called Wanda, The Untouchables, The Bear,* and *Batman*. Irene Mackenzie was doing a fine job in the hot seat albeit while half-expecting John Angel to announce that the bulldozers were outside. But it never happened. Angel may have been deflected from pushing for redevelopment of the Regal, having both purchased another cinema in Daventry and set his sights on acquiring the old Clifton premises from Essoldo to satisfy his bingo ambitions in Evesham.

On May 8 1989 Ernie Highland suffered another massive heart attack and died at the age of seventy-six. His funeral was a big affair with representatives from all sections of the cinema industry in attendance. The Regal flag flew at half-mast for a fortnight and Ernest Frederick Highland's place as a local legend was secure.

Highland had spent the previous twelve months typing his memoirs but they were incomplete. Thus, it is both a thrill and an honour for me to write *SHAZAM*, which, although nothing like as detailed as Ernie's tome would have been, I'm hoping will serve as a fitting tribute to the gentleman known affectionately as 'Mr Regal'.

The nervous nineties

By 1990 John Angel had acquired his latest cinema in Daventry (also named the Regal) just as the storm-clouds of recession were gathering. This latest economic clout was to do far more damage in Port Street than the one of a decade previously.

Angel came up with the bright idea of asking Irene to commute to Daventry to get his latest folly ticking over properly. The experienced Mackenzie was the ideal person to ramrod the Daventry Regal through the economic downturn, even though she fancied neither travelling everyday nor the thought of being away from her own 'Theatre of Dreams'. Soon, Irene also found herself overseeing the fortunes of John's Cirencester operation but conceded that a change was as good as a rest and it did put some distance between her and the increasingly erratic owner.

John Angel's next stroke of genius was to draft in another of his employees, Paul Wills from Huntingdon, to take over as manager in Evesham. Young Paul, although a nice man, was to prove that Marx Brothers comedies are not necessarily confined to the silver screen. Angel's remit for Wills was simple enough: don't get creative with the maintenance and don't let the studios rip you off with huge percentage takes from movies. The maintenance part was easy – Paul simply ignored anything more complex than changing a light bulb or having the cleaners vacuum up spilled popcorn. Stan Jordan barely needed to lift a finger and although both he and Iris were long past retirement age, it did pain them to see their Theatre of Dreams begin to fall apart.

Paul Wills' true incompetence, however, was in film choice. Instead of going all out to secure the big money movies, he booked many lesser ones from which the studios either demanded a one-off fee, or merely a small percentage (perhaps twenty-five to forty per cent as opposed to seventy-five to ninety per cent for smash hits). Basic abacus training would have showed Wills that a twenty-five per cent loss from fifty customers is not as profitable as a seventy-five per cent loss from four hundred. Not to mention the cash those extra sweets and ice cream would rake in.

John Angel's next mistake was to allow Wills to remove the tiled, rendered façade from the front entrance. The local authority had insisted that the worn shuttering be improved, so instead of re-tiling and painting it, Wills tore down the whole shebang to reveal the original pillars. In theory, a nice idea, creating a retro look to the cinema. The snag was that when the façade had been erected in the sixties, the Cotswold stone fluting on the tops and bottoms had been shorn off, plus the pillars were full of drill holes. As Angel wasn't prepared to stump up for a decent renovation, the exposed entrance simply looked tatty.

By the middle of 1991, with Regal audiences way down, the lower deck was falling into disrepair. Paul Wills decided to lock the stalls' entrance doors and for several months used the bottom deck as little more than a store room. Meanwhile, with the recession at its height John Angel, like all business people, was under pressure and appeared to be losing the plot. He had let the Regal's hard-won bingo licence lapse and seemed to be turning a blind eye to Paul Wills' cack-handed stewardship. Angel finally had a Damascus moment while driving past the Odeon cinema in Cheltenham on the evening that *Terminator II: Judgment Day* hit town. It was, by far, the biggest film of the year, with a queue of people stretching round the block and off into the wide blue yonder. Angel rang Wills and demanded to know why the Regal wasn't screening it. I believe Paul's single word reply was "Duh?" John immediately contacted Irene and asked her if she would kindly sort out the Port Street fiasco and get a piece of Arnie's action.

Paul Wills (centre) after removing the entrance façade. Big mistake.

"I'll be back," stated Miss Mackenzie.

Back in the saddle

First job, back at the Theatre of Dreams, was to locate Stan Jordan and have him cut the padlock off the stalls' entrance doors. The place smelt dank and the presence of small scurrying shapes in the gloom indicated that Irene's next phone call would be to Rentokil. Later in the day with the stalls rodent-free, Irene had every cleaner, usherette, projectionist and volunteer within a five-mile radius vacuuming, dusting and polishing the entire cinema, even as a van hurtled up the motorway carrying a copy of James Cameron's mighty sequel. Irene then harangued the *Evesham Journal* for a stop-press advert. The message quickly got through to the locals and for three weeks, five hundred red velveteen seats took a profitable pounding (twice by me).

The whole farce had infuriated Irene Mackenzie but didn't really surprise her. She informed John Angel that she would no longer commute to Daventry and was staying put in Port Street. Angel could hardly complain and they both knew it was the end of the line for Paul Wills. He headed home a sadder, wiser chap, leaving the running of the Theatre of Dreams to an expert.

However, getting her old job back didn't quite cut it with the feisty Mackenzie who wanted her pound of flesh over the shambles. She refused to book films and Angel was forced to bring in an experienced old pro named Len Stirling to deal with the studio reps. For the next year Port Street was to see good business with a string of smashes: *Beauty and the Beast*, *Scent of a Woman* and *Howards End*. Sterling also had to play catch-up with a few biggies which Wills had missed out on such as: *Ghost*, *Goodfellas* and *Dances with Wolves*. Sadly, likeable Welshman Len passed away after eighteen months in the job, so Irene relented and once more shouldered the responsibility of bookings.

As 1993 dawned Britain was finally surfacing from recession and in Port Street business was reasonable, yet John Angel refused to invest in the place. Extracting money from Angel Leisure for essential repairs was harder work than actually running the cinema. This may have been because John had finally secured the prize he had coveted for years when he bought the bingo hall in the old Clifton building from Essoldo. It immediately became his favourite toy and the Theatre of Dreams its poor relation. The fact that he also sold the Daventry Regal indicated that movies were not his first priority.

In late 1992, after a break of fifteen years, Irene revived the Saturday Morning Regal Chum's Club (see Chapter 8) and although this only sustained for eighteen months it did aid the cinema finances until the recession was past.

Then 1993 saw a true monster of a film doing the rounds. *Jurassic Park* superseded *E.T.* as the biggest money-spinner in movie history and for a month the Regal ticket machine roared. Hard on its heels came *Schindler's List* and in early 1994 *The Lion King*, two more enormous hits. With the cinema's immediate future once more looking prosperous, Irene and the staff could have reasonably expected John Angel to address the jaded look of the interior. One can only conjecture as to why he refused to invest more in the upkeep of the building. Perhaps he was overstretched financially, or he was simply no longer interested. More likely, he was negotiating with Wychavon over its redevelopment. The only positive thing he did was have a more robust walkway installed in the roof for safer access to the ceiling lights.

In 1995 Stan Jordan died and his presence was greatly missed. It came home to the staff just how valuable the Regal's own 'Mr Fixit' had been. There was now no one on hand to effect minor repairs or splash paint around. In particular, the seats in the stalls were getting shabby, under constant pressure from the youth of the day. The arm-rest squabs almost all had flock stuffing poking out through myriad rips. With John Angel unwilling to unchain his wallet Irene came up with the idea of stripping the arm-rests down to the bare wood and staining them. Cheap and effective.

A worse problem than this was the Regal's stone-age heating system. The old boiler had become temperamental and the pipes were so furred up they probably only channelled half their original capacity. "No money available," Angel kept parroting to Irene whenever she pestered him over the fact that the only customers turning up were Eskimos.

One particularly chilly evening in November 1996, the ancient boiler was to throw a sicky, which earned the Theatre of Dreams a mention on national radio. The audience numbered less than a hundred but was producing enough icy breath to mimic an old London fog and one of them was none other than the disc jockey John Peel. No one wanted the embarrassment of seeing either him or anyone else bale out before the end due to frostbite. Fortunately Irene hit on a stroke of genius. She ordered her staff to grab every cup and mug in the restaurant and to serve free tea and coffee to all the hardy souls risking pneumonia. The constant relay of hot drinks, evoking the spirit of the Blitz, played well with archetypal Englishman Peel, who lovingly related the experience on his popular Radio 4 Saturday show *Home Truths*.

Humiliation was avoided but Irene had had enough of pleading with the Scrooge-like Angel to act every time the thermometer dipped below the legal health and safety limit. An exasperated Mackenzie decided to pull a crafty flanker while John Angel was away for a fortnight so contacted John's sister June Thompson, the 'Angel Leisure' accountant, and explained the dilemma in no uncertain terms. June proved to be most understanding and accessed the firm's coffers for a new boiler, which was installed within a week. When John returned and spotted the hole in his balance sheet he stormed into a balmy Regal and remonstrated with his manageress. Irene let his rant wash over her. There wasn't much Angel could do and by this time Irene was getting numb to his cavalier attitude. More importantly, her feet and hands were warm again.

Little horrors

During the 1990s, chief projectionist Brian Houghton and his deputy (from 1990) David Stride may have allowed themselves a smug chuckle as they sat toasted by the Westar Zenon lamps while the rest of the Theatre of Dreams shivered. But their cosy reverie was being frequently disturbed as both the behaviour of youths and the state of the building began to worsen.

At the beginning of one show, the lights dimmed and the hushed audience held their breath as the curtains parted. Well, that is to say, the starboard 'tab' opened while the other stayed put due to a split cable on the winding mechanism. Brian Houghton noticed the crisis, arrested the film and high-tailed it down the stairs. To hoots of derision a breathless Houghton clambered onto the stage, hauled open the offending drape and was rewarded with a sarcastic ovation plus a shower of ancient dust.[3]

The next morning found Brian teetering on a twelve-foot ladder reconnecting the winding cables while grumbling down at Irene Mackenzie. Her apologies and thanks gushed in equal measure and she promised (once again) to broach the dread subject of maintenance with John Angel. Alas, true to form, his wallet remained impregnable.

One-off disasters such as the broken winder could be dealt with in-house but when it came to customers' thuggish behaviour John Angel was even less inclined to act. When it was suggested that he employ a thickset gentleman as security officer to maintain order in the stalls he merely grunted that it would be like using a sledgehammer to crack a nut. So, more and more, it fell to Brian Houghton to leave the projection box and help keep young miscreants in check, particularly at the weekend. His imposing frame was an asset to five-foot-two-inch manager Mackenzie until the time he told a young blood of around fifteen to curb his nonsense and received a sock in the jaw for his pains. Now, Brian is a big guy and in a perfect world, or even a previous generation, he would have had scant difficulty dragging the little darling into the rear gangway and administering chastisement prior to ejection but these were

3 After this incident Brian Houghton took it upon himself to clean the curtains regularly (this was once a specialist outside job).

litigious times and the kid had plenty of witnesses. Apoplectic with rage, Houghton stomped back to the box and locked himself in vowing to concentrate on the job he was paid for.

One maniac let off a firework in the stalls during a film. It was a real whiz-bang job which flew up to the ceiling and exploded in a rainbow shower, terrifying hundreds of people. A shocked manageress hit the buzzer to the projection room and Brian Houghton stopped the film. Irene Mackenzie marched up front, incandescent with rage and fright and bellowed about the stupidity of such an act. The culprit had hotfooted it out of the place and evaded identification.

When Irene did manage to catch and ban mischief-makers it was possible she could suffer repercussions. Three ejected thugs made a hoax call to the fire brigade, causing a major interruption to one show.[4]

An undesirable side-effect of the *Rambo* movies and perhaps *Crocodile Dundee* was the glorification of carrying a knife. There were at least two unpleasant incidents during the nineties involving youths packing blades. One managed to cut part of the screen, then exit the cinema before anyone could stop him. Another, a certain Peter Eastwood, decided it would be a hoot to slash his seat to ribbons. (This is not his real name. He's now probably a fine, upstanding thirty-something, undeserving of being outed as the 'velveteen vandal'.)

Irene caught Eastwood, confiscated his knife and gave him a lifetime ban. However, the situation was complicated by the fact that Mackenzie was a friend of his family, who also had a long connection with the Theatre of Dreams. So Irene made a wise judgement call by informing young blade-runner that if he paid for repair of the seat within a month she would desist from telling the law and his family. Plus she MIGHT reconsider his lifetime ban. It's interesting to conjecture as how Ernie Highland might have handled this situation a generation before. I suspect he would have been less liberal-minded and more inclined to spiflication. Young Eastwood certainly had a brass neck. Twice he turned up at the ticket office hoping Irene would relent and let him in and twice he was sent packing with a flea in his ear the size of a pterodactyl.

Three weeks after his misdemeanour he again faced the ferocious glare of the manageress but this time greeted her with an envelope full of fivers and an apology – plus a request for a job! Irene marvelled at his cheek but sensed his contrition and was also swayed by some compelling logic. "I know all the trouble-makers in town," he stated. "If you make me an usher I can point them out to you. They know me and won't want to get fingered."

Irene heard herself agreeing to his request, made him swear that he wasn't going to target any reprobates for boxing practice, then told him to arrive Monday lunchtime in his best bib and tucker, when he was given a torch and a month's probation. For once, there was a happy ending. Young Peter's presence considerably lessened the weekend monkey business and when he moved on to pastures new eighteen months later the Regal staff were sorry to see him go.

4 Several organisations obtained permission to use the Regal for varying purposes. It was invaluable to the fire brigade for training in how to deal with emergencies in a blacked-out building (obviously, only when the cinema was empty). Guide dogs were taught how to negotiate stairs and seating and BBC students from Wood Norton would regularly haunt the cinema, testing out cameras and sound equipment.

Big horrors

Whatever pranks children get up to, they usually pale into insignificance when compared to the mischief of adults. In the mid-1990s John Angel decided that a late Friday night screening of *The Rocky Horror Picture Show* (*RHPS*) would be a splendid idea (it had never been to the Regal). This film was a flop on initial release, but soon gained cult status and has regularly done the rounds ever since. It tends to attract the more, shall we say, theatrical types, who dress outrageously in accordance with the theme and know every word of every dopey song. In 1975 I was dragged(!) along to see it in Birmingham by an artistic girlfriend and afterwards we had a huge row. She thought the make-up and costumes were wonderful. I thought the whole thing was the Emperor's new clothes. She said the music was imaginative and exciting. I said the music was shallow bubble-gum. She INSISTED it was a creative masterpiece. I INSISTED it was hogwash. We didn't speak to each other for a week. We were only nineteen.

Now, at last, the *RHPS* had minced into Port Street and with it came its attendant hordes of drag queens and transvestites and little androgynous painted creatures. Some customers made it seem like a wannabees convention of gay icons: Quentin Crisp, Freddy Mercury, Shirley Bassey, Lisa Minelli (as she was in *Cabaret*) and Fenella Fielding (as she was in *Carry On Screaming*). The heady mix of perfume made the Theatre of Dreams smell like a Transylvanian knocking shop. As they poured through the doors, Irene Mackenzie and her usherettes stood goggle-eyed with culture shock, while Brian Houghton and David Stride thought it prudent to barricade themselves into the projection room. John Angel beamed with delight.

Midnight movies at the Regal were a rare event so, as closing time was called in Port Street's various watering holes, several dozen regulars exited the Bear, the Swan and the Talbot intent on prolonging their evening's entertainment at the Theatre of Dreams. As the beery tribe lurched up the marble steps, the sight of so many alien transsexual Frank N. Furter clones must have seriously promoted a yen for temperance. Having negotiated the foyer they huddled together for safety on one side of the stalls, longing for the times when Friday nights merely sent forth pink elephants.

Once the place was full, John Angel climbed onto the stage to a chorus of whistles and catcalls, thanked the eclectic bunch for turning up and complimented them on their gay dress sense. However, the audience wasn't entirely composed of freaks and drunken red-necks. A few conventional, smart, sober individuals had decided to see what the *RHPS* was all about and on a visit to the downstairs lav, one such customer stumbled upon a sight which hadn't been included in the programme. He immediately sought out Irene Mackenzie and furiously demanded that she 'curtail the shenanigans in the bog'. Now, formidable character that Mackenzie can be, no threat of death or torture would have made her peek around the door of those toilets. So, it was a mad sprint up to the projection room for some masculine assistance.

> *"There's something nasty happening in the stalls toilets," she panted at Brian Houghton and David Stride. "Which one of you two is going to deal with it?"*
> *"You're the manager. Why don't you sort it out?" suggested Brian Houghton hopefully.*
> *"No chance! Look, I'm ORDERING one of you to get down there and chuck 'em out."*
> *Irene's voice had risen three octaves in desperation.*

Houghton and Stride looked at each other with expressions fuelled by the anticipated horror of what they might be witness to. Stridey got his case in first: "Brian, you're twice as big and ten years younger than me," and Houghton suddenly found himself out-numbered two to one.

So the chief operator stomped down to the stalls, clenching and unclenching his fists to steady himself for the task ahead. Irene Mackenzie hurried behind him determined to offer what (vocal) assistance she could from the cinema side of the toilet door. Houghton reasoned that hesitation might break his nerve and so charged straight in, assegai raised.

> *"Right!" he boomed, "Break it up and...*
> *Aww Judas Priest... (heavy blink) ... Everybody out! Now!"*

Ten seconds later a scarlet-faced Brian Houghton exited the toilets in the wake of four exotic specimens sporting sickly grins. He ignored Irene Mackenzie's enquiries, trudged wearily back to the projection room, switched on the kettle and slumped in a chair. He looked for all the world as if he had clapped eyes upon the Gorgon.

Over the years the *RHPS* had developed the tradition of the flour fight. I have no idea how this evolved but near the end of the film many Rocky Horror groupies began producing bags of self-raising from stocking tops, bras or other unmentionable hidey-holes and suddenly, anarchy reined. Very soon the Regal stalls resembled a remake of *The Belles of St Trinians* as directed by Wes Craven. One of the local inebriates, awoken from his alcoholic torpor by the burgeoning madness, decided it was time to split and lurched towards the exit only to be hit full in the face by a pound of Homepride. Enraged, he retaliated by taking a wild agricultural swing at a small transvestite. He was subsequently flattened by a haymaker from a basque-clad lesbian with slaughterhouse shoulders and alarming tattoos. The violence might have escalated if not for the fact that the flour fog became so dense, no one could make out who to attack.

Irene Mackenzie and John Angel stood in the rear gangway observing the carnage. She glared at the owner – after all, it was his idea to screen the *RHPS* – and advised him that it was going to require ALL hands on deck to clean up the frightful mess. "They certainly have had a lot of fun," he cooed thought gritted teeth, and began moving in the general direction of away.

Eventually, the colourful audience dispersed into the night, back to their homes, belfries and coffins, and so began the big clean-up. 1991 had seen the nationwide smoking ban in cinemas on health and safety grounds. What the heck was the point, thought Irene, when lunacy like this was permitted?

The Regal staff worked until 2.30 a.m. then resumed at 10.00 a.m. It was 2.30 p.m. before the dozen or so weary workers finally stowed their vacuums and brushes. Irene phoned John to suggest that a little overtime pay was in order for her staff. He flatly refused on the grounds that whether the cleaning took five minutes or five hours, that's the job – so tough titty. Angel certainly wasn't making any friends.

Regal horror stories

1. When the Regal screened *Psycho* in 1960 no customers were allowed in after the start.
2. Every Christmas Eve, a small wooden door (an access panel to some electrical wiring) high up in the wall of the foyer would mysteriously open.

3. The 1963 British horror classic *The Haunting* was set in a large country house near Stratford-on-Avon. The owners came to the first showing at the Regal where they sat in the middle of the front row of the balcony.
4. One clairvoyant usherette swears the Regal is haunted by a former cleaner and claims to have watched the spectral Mrs Mop moving from seat to seat in the balcony wielding a duster, during a full house.
5. A bat began roosting in one of the organ vents and decided to fly around the cinema while *Dracula has Risen from the Grave* was showing. Some wag christened it *Lee*. It was in residence for a week.
6. The Regal flagpole once broke free of its bracket on the roof parapet and speared through the roof of Pat Wyld's greengrocer's van which was parked below in Burford Road. This was reminiscent of the famous scene in *The Omen*; however unlike Patrick Troughton, Pat Wyld wasn't skewered.
7. There was only one recorded death at the Theatre of Dreams, when an old gentleman passed away in the stalls just before the start of a children's movie. It was a full house, but the show was halted as the impeccably discreet usherettes informed parents to leave quietly with their children, until the body had been dealt with.

The late 1990s: more rocky times

By the late 1990s John Angel was certainly falling out of love with the Theatre of Dreams and Wychavon weren't about to hand him *carte blanche* with regard to redevelopment. Again, I can only conjecture as to the dynamics of the relationship between Angel Leisure and the local authority but, as with all business dealings, it no doubt came down to money, intention and politics. Angel expected Wychavon to contribute various grants towards the Regal's redevelopment because of its status as a local asset. Understandably, however, the council weren't prepared to pick up the tab for an entire re-vamp, particularly as later plans included such unorthodox innovations as building apartments on top of the place. Some of the designs put forward seemed reasonable enough but planning is a necessarily pragmatic and pedantic field and the ball never started rolling.

What did keep rolling were the movies and even here, John Angel could feel aggrieved over what he perceived as static from the local Watch Committee. Take for example the 1993 smash-hit *Mrs. Doubtfire* which, although ostensibly a broad-based comedy, received a 12 certification from the British Board of Film Censors – the same as the terrifying *Jurassic Park*. Apparently, this decision was based on one 'inappropriate' scene in which Robin Williams is wearing ladies' tights and knickers. It seems ridiculous that nineties' teenies needed shielding from such innocuous nonsense as forcefully as they were denied seeing a lawyer bitten in half by a Tyrannosaurus Rex. Whatever the pros and cons, the decision to award a 12 certificate threatened to clobber the Regal's potential takings from the second biggest film of the year.

John Angel contacted the local authority to explain that there was enormous interest in the movie from under-twelves and the parents who would accompany them. To bar them would represent a considerable loss to the cinema. However, Wychavon had no option but to concur with the BBFC decision and Angel was left fuming.

However, rules do not always engender blind obedience so, suffice to say that a considerable number of extremely young-looking twelve-year-olds appeared in the audience. So many, in fact, that every spare seat in the office, rest room and restaurant was utilised to accommodate the overflow in the stalls. Okay, Irene Mackenzie was guilty of colouring outside the lines, this one time. So what? Business is business and boy, did her beloved picture house need the revenue.

This kind of issue was becoming a real nonsense. By 1993 kids only had to wait a few months before every movie appeared on video. The whole panoply of sex, violence, blasphemy, degradation, foul language and Keanu Reeves' crap acting was available to any age group, just so long as teenies could sneak cassettes past discerning parents.

On this occasion, as with many others when hugely popular children's films hit town, Irene had to order extra amounts of profitable joob-joobs from Tarry's, the Evesham confectioners, because the younger the customer, the sweeter the tooth.

On the subject of teeth, as if the pressure of the ailing cinema wasn't enough to contend with, John Angel arrived at the Regal one lunchtime cradling his mouth, which sported an impressive fat lip and a yawning chasm where several of his tusks should have been. Apparently, while checking on the high street bingo operation, he had berated a female member of staff within earshot of her proprietorial boyfriend, who then proceeded to reveal the chivalrous side of his nature by socking Angel in the cakehole. To hell with pictures, planning and profits, at this point John must have been yearning for his Hampshire retreat.

In 1998 the Regal enjoyed its final giant movie of the decade when the phenomenally successful *Titanic* steamed into Port Street. For a solid month attendances rivalled all other post-war smashes (*Flaming Star*, *The Family Way*, *Jaws*, *Star Wars*, *Grease*, *E.T.*, *Crocodile Dundee*, *Jurassic Park* and *The Lion King*). Ironic, indeed, that the previous film to feature the famous liner, *Raise the Titanic* in 1980, was an unmitigated flop which heralded the demise of the Clifton, whereas Leo and Kate's effort, despite becoming BY FAR the biggest money-spinner ever, made little difference to the fact that the Theatre of Dreams was badly shipping water.

By 1999 Angel Leisure had progressed no further in its plans for developing the cinema and each year John would howl that Wychavon were moving the goalposts with regard to mandatory licensing. He complained bitterly that his annual renewals were being refused by ever-more stringent regulations concerning the roof, the equipment and overall safety matters, all of which necessitated the unchaining of his wallet.

Either Angel was being too lax with regard to the upkeep of the place and Wychavon were, quite rightly, taking him to task OR the council had some shadowy agenda afoot. I think the former is much nearer the truth but also suspect there to have been a marked lack of communication and diplomacy on both sides.

Whatever the machinations between the parties, with DVD and the multiplexes beginning to bite into the cinema market, the industry was now an unforgiving battleground and as the new millennium dawned, the Theatre of Dreams found itself teetering on the brink.

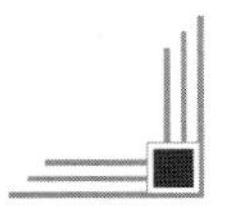

THE REGAL ROLL OF HONOUR

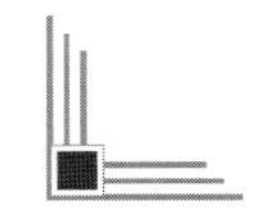

MANAGERS

SIDNEY HALL 1932–34
FRANK RIDGE 1934–41
JOHN HACK 1941–50
EILEEN BUTLER 1950–56
ERNEST HIGHLAND 1956–87
IRIS JORDAN (DEPUTY) 1956–87
IRENE MACKENZIE 1987–2003

PROJECTIONISTS

BRIAN HOUGHTON
JOHN HACK
BOB WEBB
MAURICE BERRY
NORMAN ROBERTS
NORMAN YARR
PETER BENNETT
MARTIN BENNETT
MAURICE DORE
SIMON KENSHOLE
REG BIRCH
TONY GOODWIN
JOHN KILBY
DENNIS BROWN
ALEC GRANT
CHARLES LOUDON
LES BROWN
HILTON GREEN
MICHAEL PULLEY
BASIL CARE
NORMAN HOLLY
LES ROBERTS
ALAN COOK
RAY HOUGHTON
TREVOR SKAYSBROOK
BASIL COOK
CYRIL KEEN
DAVID STRIDE

USHERETTES

CRISTY ALCOCK
CLAIRE GREEN
JEAN RICHMOND
KAREN ALCOCK
QUEENIE HALE
IRIS JORDAN
JAYNE ANDREWS
JULIE HARRELL
JOAN SANDERS
TRACEY ANNIS
BARBARA HARRISON
BONNIE SCARROTT
SUSAN AYLETT
DOROTHY HERITAGE
SHARON SCARROTT
HILDA BANDY
DAPHNE HERMAN
KATE SEABROOK
EMMA BEAUMARIS
DAWN JONES
SARAH SEABROOK
KATY BUCKLAND
MARILYN JORDAN
JESS SINCLAIR
STELLA BUCKLAND
MARY KEEN
CLAIRE SPIERS
ALISON BYRD
LOUISE KENSHOLE
HELEN SPIERS
PAULINE CANDY
JOAN KNIGHT
SAMANTHA SPIERS
TRICIA CLARKE
PHYLLIS KNIGHT
BARBARA TAYLOR
BARBARA DOLPHIN
CHRIS KYTE
ELSIE TANDY
BARBARA EDEN
BARBARA LAMPITT
EVA TURSKIE
RACHEL EVIS
MARGARET LAMPITT
LYNNE WATTIE
ANNA FORTEY
NINA LANE
SANDRA WESTMACOTT
MARIA FORTEY
TRACY LEIGHTON
JOAN WESTWOOD
TINA FORTEY
IRENE MACKENZIE
ELSIE WILLIAMS
EILLEN GRIFFITHS
MARY MAJORS
CYNTHIA WILSON
and VIOLET WOODCOCK

CLEANERS

MRS BENNETT
MRS MALLEY
MRS BUXTON
MRS MOFFATT
MRS DAVIES
MRS SALMON
MRS DOBBINS
MRS SPRING
MRS HEMSLEY
MRS SMITH
MRS JOHNSON
MRS UPTON
MRS LOWE
MRS WESTWOOD

COMMISSIONAIRES

LES CRABTREE
BOB FISHER
CLIFFORD HAINES
VIC LIPETT
FRED MARSHALL
TED NEWBURY
STAN PEDDAR

Most years of full-time service: IRIS JORDAN (nee SALE) 43 years
Most years of full and part-time service: BRIAN HOUGHTON 45 years
Most years of continuous full-time service: IRENE MACKENZIE 41 years
Special mention: STAN JORDAN – the REGAL'S own Mr Fixit for 40 years

Sincerest apologies to all the people I have not been able to include in this list.

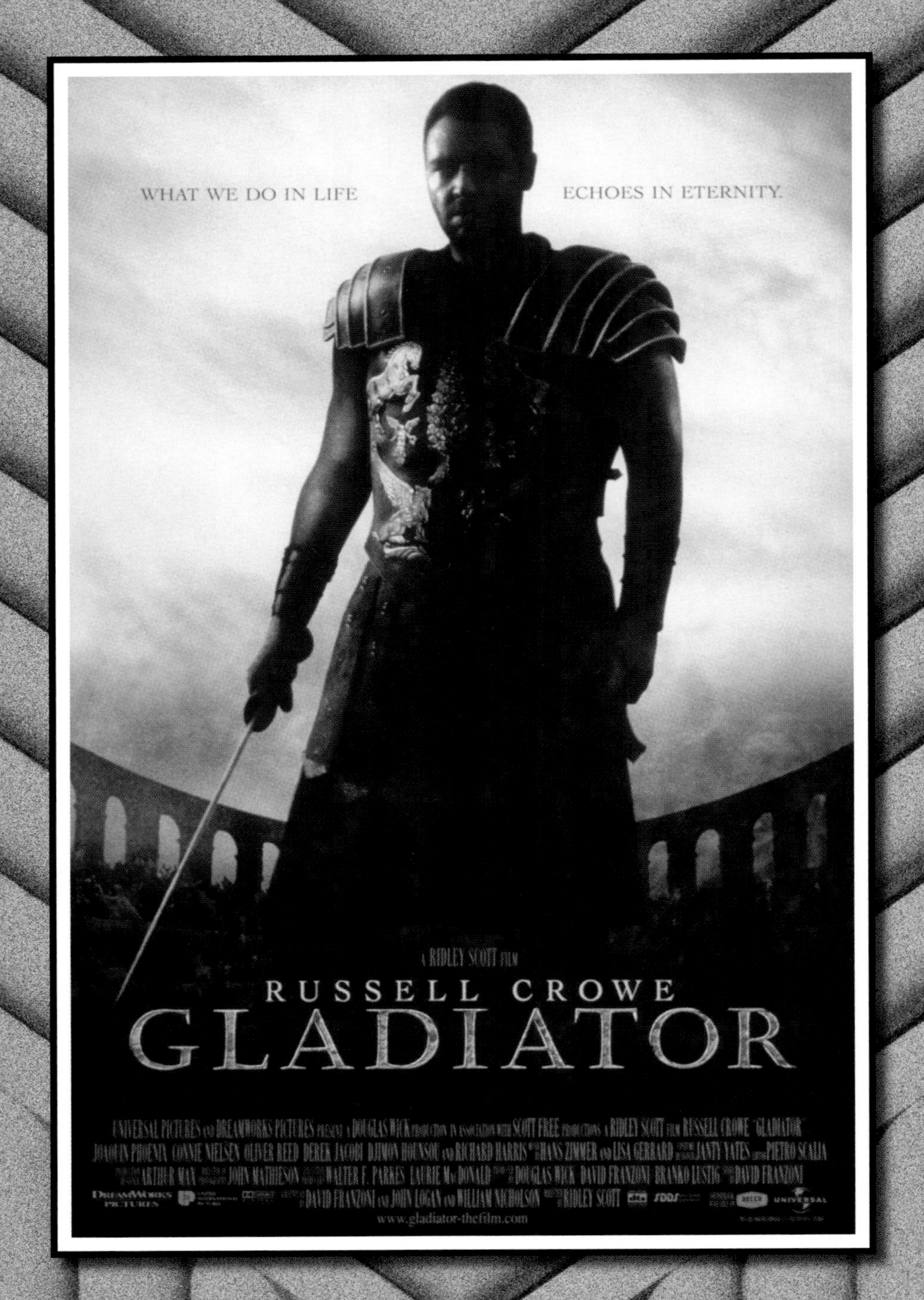
WHAT WE DO IN LIFE
ECHOES IN ETERNITY.
A RIDLEY SCOTT FILM
RUSSELL CROWE
GLADIATOR
www.gladiator-thefilm.com

CHAPTER THIRTEEN

THE LAST PICTURE SHOW

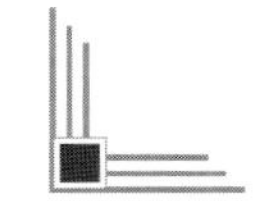

During the early months of 2000 John Angel's agenda became clear. He wanted out of Evesham, fancying retirement in the sun, and the ongoing battle to keep the Theatre of Dreams afloat was a thorn in his side. John simply would not throw any substantial cash at the place to bring the electrical wiring up to spec or repair the shabby roof. The property market was once more becoming buoyant and it seemed logical to offload the cinema before it became a money pit. The obvious prospect of it as a site for complete redevelopment would surely attract someone.

With Wychavon on his case to effect repairs in order that the licence be saved, Angel chose to shut up shop for six solid months in order to concentrate on finding buyers for both the Regal and his High Street bingo operation. As the Theatre of Dreams fell silent there were grumblings of discontent all over the Vale, the loudest ones coming from inside the cinema itself as Irene Mackenzie and Brian Houghton had to wander the aisles kicking their heels with nothing to do. The owner had stipulated that they both come to work regardless of the situation. There was certainly no mention of redundancy pay. So they both sat in there day after day, gawking at a blank screen and taking it in turns to make the tea. It wasn't long before the strain began to tell. Brian was not enjoying the best of health as it was, without having to endure this nonsense. Irene meantime was suffering badly with stress. Just HOW badly became clear on a visit to the doctor in the early summer, when her blood pressure was taken at 220 over 105. The doc gave it to her straight: "If you don't get out of that bloody cinema you could go the same way as Ernie Highland at any time." Mackenzie had no choice but to take sick leave.

Something worth fighting for

Meanwhile, the good people of Evesham began to mobilise. The Regal's plight came to the attention of local businessman Martin Hammon, known to all as 'Tom the Barber' (for 'tis his profession) who began organising the 'Regal Action Group' which quickly garnered local support. Hammon also brought more than just hot air to the table by putting his money where his mouth was and ponying up £1,000 towards a fighting fund. Things began to roll and both Wychavon and John Angel took note.

Irene Mackenzie also began pulling strings behind the scenes. The manageress was fuming over her treatment by the owner and determined to exact payback that would yield a practical benefit to the cinema. Obviously, while still in the employ of Angel Leisure she was obliged to watch her step, thus she discreetly contacted local cinema fan Willy Ford and together they put forward a proposal to English Heritage for the listing of the Regal. Small-town deco picture palaces were now such a rarity that the application hit a chord and was given priority status. It worked. A glowing report from the sympathetic adjudicators at the Heritage office effectively barnstormed the Theatre of Dreams to a Grade II listing within two months and Irene Mackenzie slept the sleep of victory as her ongoing nightmare about the wrecking ball faded into the ether.

It's reasonable to assume that John Angel felt smug as he trousered a reported half a million clams for the sale of his High Street bingo business. He must, therefore, have been brought down to earth with a bump on realising that while he was preoccupied on the other side of town, the Regal had been dipped in aspic.

As 2000 ended, the cinema was valued at around £300,000 and although it's debatable whether the new listing affected its intrinsic value it did put the kibosh on the more outlandish ideas for redevelopment and almost certainly made it problematic to market.

A matter of trust

Meanwhile the Regal Action Group had hardened into the Regal Trust and was campaigning to secure the cinema for the town by running it as a charity. Several meaty ideas were broached for expansion of its use which wouldn't compromise its status as a cinema. For example, there was interest in installing a Wurlitzer organ, from them as likes that sort of thing, plus the screening of themed all-night shows ranging from silent movies to horror, art-house, sci-fi, etc. In fact any number of nostalgia-fests which would promote the place as a 'regional centre for the appreciation and study of cinema and recorded media in general'. It all sounded highly feasible. There were a few dissenting voices (ain't there always?) who moaned that it would be a waste of public money but, overwhelmingly, folks were for it and it began to attract local celebrity interest. First along was the actor Chris Jury from Blockley, best known for playing Ian McShane's side-kick Eric Catchpole in TV's *Lovejoy*. Jury was certainly smitten with the idea and in November 2000 enthused about it in the *Evesham Journal*. He immediately picked up on the vision of a renovated Regal at the heart of a rejuvenated, pedestrianised Port Street. Furthermore, he contacted his friend, heavyweight film director Anthony Minghella, also a fan of the traditional small-town picture palace, who added his weight to the campaign. Things were suddenly looking rosy and by early 2001 actors John Nettles (from TV's *Bergerac* and *Midsomer Murders*), Robert Llewellyn (Kryten from the sit-com *Red Dwarf*) plus impressionist Alistair McGowan were voicing their support. Alistair in particular was (and still is) most passionate about the resurrection of the Theatre of Dreams. As a local boy he spent as much time in the place as anyone and, like the rest of us junkies, the Regal seeped into his soul.

Actor Chris Jury drumming up support.

By late 2000 John Angel had made sufficient repairs to breathe life back into the licence and the Regal limped into the winter with its new listing and a huge groundswell of local support for its survival. There was optimism for a flicks renaissance and John must have felt the heat of public desire burning his ankles. Irene was once again able to organise the free pre-Christmas show for senior citizens which had long been a tradition.

Evesham Journal reporter Pat Smith hands out the sherry.

Usherette Katy Buckland hands out mince pies.

Once more for old times' sake

2001 was to be the final complete year of operation for the Theatre of Dreams. I had been living away from the Vale for several years and fancied a private trip down memory lane one Sunday afternoon during April. Having followed the fluctuating fortunes of the cinema in the local press I reasoned that this might be one of my last chances to see, feel and smell the old place. On arrival, there was no queue along Burford Road and moreover, not one other living being in the foyer until Irene Mackenzie appeared from the stalls to press the magic button in the kiosk. 'Chung-ching!' sang the ticket machine – that sound hadn't altered in forty years. Neither had Irene, I remember thinking. I ascended the marble stairs to the balcony, soaking up the timeless atmosphere, and had a good gawk in the posing mirror on the middle landing. Yep! Still super-cool. As I stepped through the balcony doors there was no usherette to clip my ticket, no music and no muffled chatter as people nestled themselves into their red velveteen seats. Apart from Irene and whoever was prepping the Westars, I was the only soul in the building. It was a strange feeling, a mixture of eeriness and exclusivity. Oddly enough, with all three hundred-odd seats beckoning, it took a couple of minutes of ambling along the aisles until I chose one – four rows down, bang in the middle. I was in a most nostalgic mood and sat there reflecting on when, as a sixteen-year-old, I had watched one of the best films ever, in Port Street, *The Last Picture Show*. Beautifully shot in retro monochrome, it was the archetypal 'rites of passage' movie, with all the ingredients designed to impact on the juvenile psyche: teenage angst, black humour, pathos, mischief and the deflowering of Cybill Shepherd, all set against the backdrop of a crumbling hick-town flea pit. I felt as if I was making a guest appearance in it, thirty years too late (and minus Cybill Shepherd, alas).

The movie I had come to see was *Jurassic Park III*, ideal fare for a lifelong monster fan and yet I have to admit to feeling bored with it. The beasties were wonderful, even if the acting was tripe. However, the real problem was the atmosphere in my Theatre of Dreams. I suppose being all alone simply didn't feel right. It's interesting to contrast this occasion with sitting in a packed Regal as a ten-year-old, spellbound at Ray Harryhausen's jerky creations in *One Million Years B.C.* which fired my imagination for weeks.[1]

1 This film contains one of the all-time-great cinematic piss-takes during the scene where Raquel Welch, while helping a stricken caveman, is suddenly menaced by an enormous sea-turtle. Terrified, she squeals "Archelon!", the only discernible word in a screenplay consisting wholly of grunts, growls and finger-pointing. 'Archelon' is the modern scientific name for this extinct creature and being a quality young dino-nerd I picked up on it straight away; almost certainly the only person in the cinema to do so. How sad it that?

The Jurassic frolics finished, the lights came on and I wandered out alone, never to return. Shame on me.

The author and his final Regal movie.

By June 2001 John Angel was bleating in the local press about needing financial help both to pay for new equipment and to ensure a satisfactory safety inspection. Understandably miffed about having the listing foisted upon him and with the Regal Trust shoving its foot in the door, John was obviously seeking to explore Evesham's commitment to the cinema. With both eyes on retirement it made no sense to him to splash out large amounts of cash on a building he wanted rid of. Wychavon were being as cautious as usual but it was reasonable to imagine that the Trust might intervene and save Angel the job of raiding the bank. His protestations of penury were pure cheek, but John couldn't be blamed for testing the water. From Angel's point of view, if the local authority HAD simply marched in and purchased it, problem solved. Well, his problem, at least. He could then go off to wallow in the Indian Ocean and (I'm sure) fret about Evesham's community charge going stratospheric.

Wychavon had given Angel until the end of August 2001 to effect suitable repairs to the roof in order for it to pass a safety inspection. (The cost of a complete roof refurbishment was estimated at upwards of £50,000.) He refused to spend another farthing and warned that the Regal would close down unless financial assistance was forthcoming. Things looked dire until a gentleman arrived to discreetly hand £1,000 in cash to Irene Mackenzie for a temporary roof repair adequate for inspection purposes. He wishes to remain anonymous and there was considerable local speculation as to his identity (I'm saying nowt), with many people believing him to be a bespectacled lad with a wand. So, celluloid continued to whirr in Port Street.

As 2001 wore on, the Regal Trust began to run out of steam. Despite applying for grants from English Heritage and the National Lottery, the well-attended public meetings and the visionary business plans, the Trust had only managed to raise £20,000. Martin Hammon was sagging on the ropes with the strain of campaigning, and trying to secure financial backing from Wychavon was like pushing water uphill. The councillors, understandably, were conscious of the huge criticism that would be forthcoming if they bankrolled what amounted to a seven-figure project. Hammon and the patrons made a final few pleas, conceding that what was needed was a benevolent millionaire who happened to be crackers about movies. Alas, none was forthcoming and the Regal Trust dissolved. Unsuccessful though they were, I think their attempt to turn the Theatre of Dreams around should be applauded and in particular, the vision and energy of Martin Hammon deserves much praise. It was a bloody good try.

The various celebrities attached to the Trust came in for some serious criticism over the issue of funding, particularly local boy Alistair McGowan. People didn't seem to appreciate that jobbing actors and entertainers, although high profile, are not Richard Branson. If you have an established career, you can't just abandon it to subsume yourself in the task of purchasing, renovating and managing a cinema. This is the job of businessmen whose *raison d'etre* is accruing wealth, not doing a season in panto.

2002 dawned, with Irene Mackenzie still nursing the geriatric picture palace from day to day until February, when John Angel suddenly announced his intention to close the cinema in order to concentrate on securing a buyer. The few dozen fans who showed up to watch Tom Cruise in *Vanilla Sky* were turned away. This time, Angel struck pay dirt and in May the Regal keys were handed over to its new owner, Amberleaf Properties.[2]

Wow! If only...

During the months that the Theatre of Dreams was in mothballs, much had been happening behind the scenes. Amberleaf had submitted plans for a £1m face-lift and the artist's impression which appeared in the *Evesham Journal* in October 2002 had the whole town buzzing. The new Regal was to comprise a two-screen cinema and leisure facility including a bowling alley and roof-top restaurant. Even to a die-hard traditionalist like me this new image looked wonderful and I applauded the melding of minds between Wychavon's chief planner, Jack Hegarty, Amberleaf's architect and English Heritage. The proposed rebuild enhanced the original art deco feel (to the exterior, at least) and a display area was to be created to house some of the Regal's original fixtures and fittings, most notably the two Westars. Councillor Martin Jennings waxed lyrical about the upgrading of Port Street and optimism in Evesham hit the roof. I have to confess that while gawking at that sumptuous colour picture of the 'new-look' Regal, I began to believe in the Phoenix.

Harry Potter and the Theatre of Dreams

It appeared that the potential of the old cinema had enticed a real 'mover and shaker' to Evesham in the form of Amberleaf boss Alan Redpath. A successful developer, he had actually been circling Port Street warily for a couple of years. When he finally committed to the project it seemed that progress would be swift. In late 2002 the Regal re-opened on a six-month lease to Lee Allwood, a long-time movie man from Orion Cinemas who kept the original staff and immediately secured the hottest movie of the time: *Harry Potter and the Chamber of Secrets*. At advance showings from Friday 8 to Sunday 10 November the queues of young Hogwarts aficionados stretched right down to the Burford Road car park and just for a while it felt as if the clock had spun back half a century. Irene Mackenzie grinned like Julia Roberts.

2 In fairness to John Angel, despite the steady degeneration of the place since the mid-1990s, he had kept the Regal open in its original form for fifteen years and in 1986 there were plenty who would never have predicted that happening.

The boy wizard turns back the clock.

Alan Redpath's strategy appeared to be to keep the place ticking over until the spring in order to dot the 'i's and cross the 't's with regard to the plans while attempting to secure whatever grants were available from such sources as English Heritage or Wychavon's proposed economic regeneration scheme for Port Street. Then, full-scale renovation of the Regal would commence.

Swan song

As the first half of 2003 wore on, the Harry Potter effect didn't sustain and the lack of tlc left the Theatre of Dreams too decrepit to appeal to a healthy customer base. The original plan to commence rebuilding work in the spring of 2003 didn't materialise and the reasons were never specified. Lee Allwood's lease ran out on 1 May and with insufficient bodies going through the door leaving the cinema trading at a permanent loss, he chose not to renew it.

After six months of fresh hope the Regal's Indian summer was over. Long-time projectionist Brian Houghton had retired several months before on health grounds and it fell to his replacement, veteran operator Norman Holly, to spin the last miles of celluloid.

On May 1 2003, four people were on hand to watch the final frames of the Al Pacino movie *The Recruit* flicker past the lens. In seventy years it was the very last of more than ten thousand titles to be shown in the Port Street picture palace. The manageress, her two projectionists Norman Holly and David Stride, plus cinema historian Peter Thackery stared dewy-eyed at the blank cinemascope screen, still illuminated by the Zenon lamps. Then the power was switched off, the Westars fell silent and the four friends walked down the marble steps for the final time.

"That's all, folks."

Money, money everywhere and not a drop to spend

Since that day, hopes of the great revival have been repeatedly dashed. Amberleaf's 2002 plans looked so good it's a crying shame they never came to fruition. During the latter half of 2003 Alan Redpath decided to reconsider the plans in order to make the project more profitable. Can't blame him for trying. They were redrafted to include a third cinema screen plus ten flats on top of the roof. While this was happening, Wychavon announced that an £84,000 grant from their Port Street 'Heritage Economic Regeneration Scheme' (HERS) was available, on condition that Amberleaf showed them the colour of ITS money by commencing an agreed £650,000 worth of restoration work.

Naturally, with the rejigged plans under consideration, nothing kicked off and Redpath may have considered it a crafty ploy to catch the planners napping while the pressure was on to make an impact in Port Street. Whether or not it was his intention, all it succeeded in doing was creating a log jam. The Regal stood festering for a whole two years before common ground was reached with regard to the renovation. In April 2005, to no one's surprise, the plan for the addition of ten flats was rejected. The owner quickly returned with a scaled-down plan incorporating a mere five flats. Finally, this compromise satisfied the planners and received their rubber stamp in June 2005. Redpath now had his flats, plus a promise of eighty-four grand on condition that he get his act together, pronto. Yet, another six months elapsed with the owner doing precisely squat.

In January 2006 complaints flooded in about guttering falling from the rotting building. Wychavon insisted the owners pull their finger out and secure the cinema exterior. Two deadlines for the initiation of work had passed and the powers that be were now considering cancelling the heritage grant if this inertia persisted. It persisted. Finally in May 2007 builders were sent in to clean up the worst of the mess inside and remove the exterior wiring serving the display boxes. But since then – zilch.

I had a chance meeting with Alan Redpath on Easter Saturday 2007 and asked him to update me on the Regal situation. When I told him I was a writer, he became quite suspicious and grumbled on about bad publicity in the local press. Understandably cagey after having been besieged by critics and campaigners for more than three years, Redpath did let slip that his plans were still on the table if the local authority would just hand over the promised eighty-four grand. After that he clammed up. "If you want to know about the history of the Regal, go and talk to John Angel," he suggested. "Give me the plane fare to Thailand and I will," I retorted and for a few seconds we shared a chuckle.

As no more information was forthcoming and with his air of injured innocence sticking in my craw, I wished him *adios* and boogied. I couldn't decide whether Redpath was playing at brinkmanship with Wychavon or whether he could no longer give a toss.

AUTHOR'S LOG, STARDATE: 30/04/2008

Following my recent tense, though diplomatic, encounter with the Regal Empire leader, I have located and surveyed the abandoned hulk of flagship *Theatre of Dreams*. Damage is considerable but not irreparable and the Westar drive still fully functional. I am forwarding recommendation of its complete rebuild and return to active service. Priority sub-space message dispatched to Wychavon High Command urging renewal of dialogue with Empire leader while adhering to the terms of the Treaty of Bengeworth. Am now heading out of Neutral Zone on course to observe star clusters in the Hollywood nebula.

This is Captain Robert J. Hemming, commanding officer of the dreamcruiser SHAZAM, signing off.

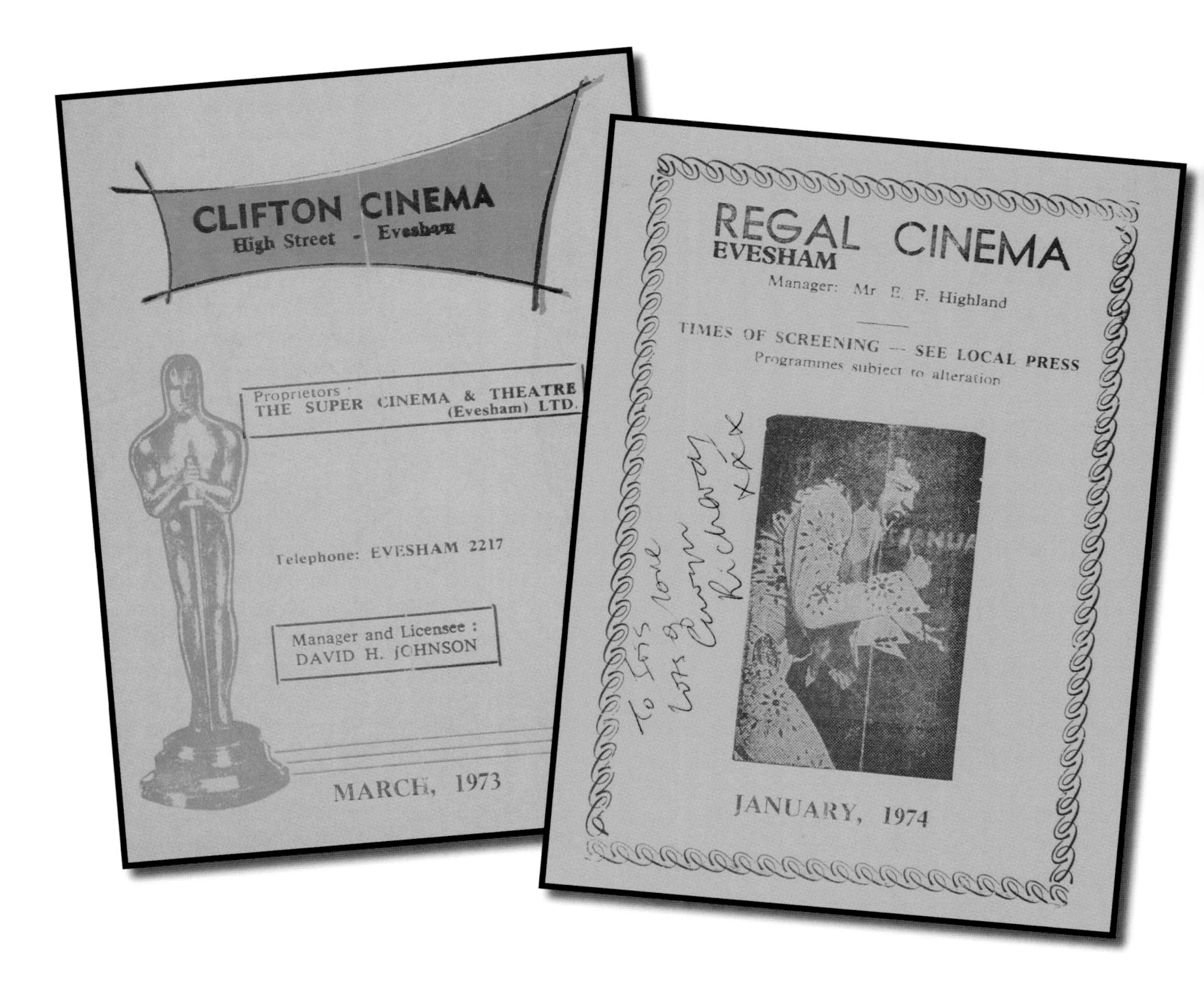

Eveshams's rival cinemas each produced monthly programmes and like all throwaway printed articles, these are now highly collectable.

An Invitation
The Regal Chum's Club
invites you to bring
Your Parents
to any performance of a
suitable programme
ADMIT THREE

REGAL CINEMA
PORT STREET, EVESHAM
presents
A SPECIAL
50TH ANNIVERSARY
SHOW
THE 1930'S FILM
"ALEXANDERS RAG TIME BAND"
STARRING: TYRONE POWER & ALICE FAYE
PLUS – BILLY DAVIES ON THE CINEMA ORGAN !
Monday October 11th 1982 at 8.0 p.m.
Admit One 5/- (25p)

The
SAPPHIRES
Rhythm and Rock Group
Enquiries to—
D. NICHOLLS
78 BATTLETON ROAD
EVESHAM
WORCS
Featuring—
Jimmy Capaldi

'Honey I Shrunk the Kids' packs the Regal in 1989. Lets hope this happens again one day.

A rear view of the cinema in 2006

John Angel presents Ernie Highland with his retirement gift. Sadly, Ernie never completed his memoirs.

The marble staircase to the gods as seen through the stalls door.

The changing look of the front entrance.

1967

1980

WALT DISNEY
JULES VERNES
20,000 LEAGUES UNDER THE SEA
KIRK DOUGLAS
JAMES MASON

1985

1993

"I'll have some Payne's Poppets, Spangles and an Aztec Bar, please."

Kiosk c.1995.

Kiosk c.1988.

"I'll have an industrial-sized bucket of popcorn, please."

Film connected from the Tower spools through the Westar, December 2002.

Norman Holly in December 2002, who began spinning celluloid in the late 1940s.

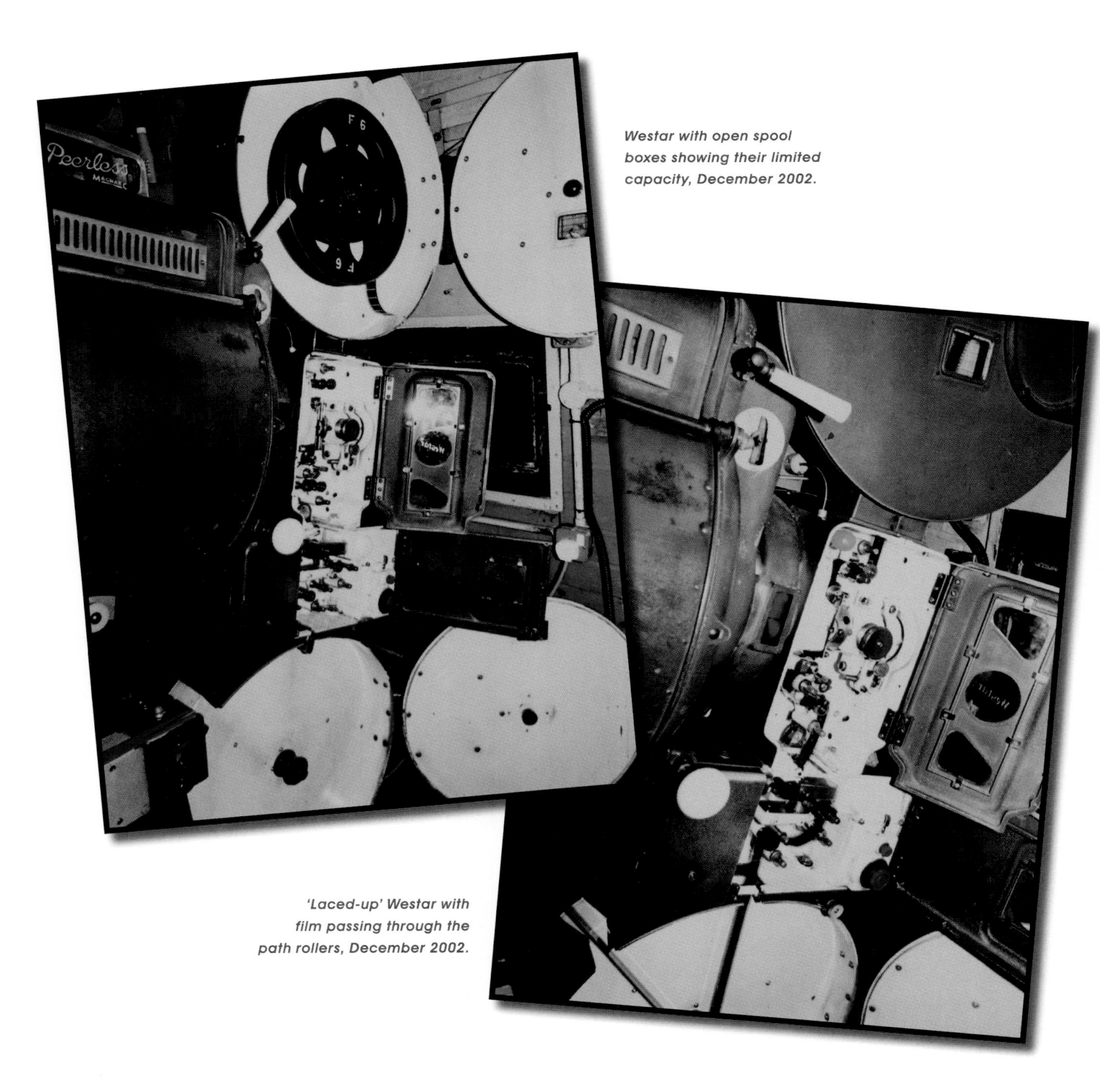

Westar with open spool boxes showing their limited capacity, December 2002.

'Laced-up' Westar with film passing through the path rollers, December 2002.

Members of the Cinema and Theatre Association pay a visit, 19 September 1993.

Octagonal ceiling light. Bulbs were replaced by reaching down into them while lying on a walkway inside the roof.

Original 1930s lights.

A contrast in styles.
The sharp angles of this art-deco corner design (left) contrast wonderfully with the sumptuous rococo scrolling of the cornices (below).

The chosen colour scheme of dark blue, turquoise, red and gold was a stroke of genius.

Right and left view of the front lower deck showing the beautiful symmetry of the Theatre of Dreams.

With no organ ever installed, the decorative organ vents actually served little purpose.

The art-deco seat lights give a true Picture Palace feel.

The rear gangway of the balcony. Before cinema crowds began to wane and safety laws were tightened this provided standing room for dozens of people.

Detailed view of the balcony balustrade. It was re-designed in 1955 when cinemascope was installed.

A front view of both decks of Evesham's own Picture Palace.

Hurley Robinson's dished floor is clearly visible. Upward-facing front seats in the stalls were more prone to damage and several rows were finally removed in the early eighties.

The stalls in the early 1990s. The seat backs have seen better times.

Balcony with newly re-covered seats in the 1980s.

The beautifully ornate organ vents (pictured here in 1989) blended art-deco with rococo styling. They were never put to practical use but remained the stand-out feature in the Theatre of Dreams.

The famous Ward clock was installed for the 1932 opening by young apprentice jeweller Les Jobson, who lovingly maintained it for the next seventy years. Its whereabouts are now unknown.

The cinemascope screen. The lights dimmed, the audience chatter receded and the faint whirr of the curtain motor was audible as three hundred square feet of viewing pleasure appeared. All one had to do was look, listen and soak up the thrills.

FRIDAY NEXT
FOR
6 DAYS

REGAL
JAWS
SUNDAY NEXT
ALSO
The Sheepman

FRIDAY NEXT
FOR
6 DAYS

AFTERTHOUGHTS

In 1957 British Lion produced a comedy film called *The Smallest Show on Earth*, set in a tiny British cinema which, even then, had seen better days. It is inherited by a naïve young couple (Bill Travers and Virginia McKenna) who determine to make it profitable again. The whole place is a rag-bag of comedy clichés: the heating system malfunctions wildly, the electricity is dodgy, the décor tatty and to cap it all the cinema, named the Bijou, is built next to a main railway line so that when trains pass, the building shakes as if suffering an earthquake. Add to this the magnificent Peter Sellers as a moth-eaten, drunken projectionist and you have the very image of the 'flea pit'.

Yet the point is this: no matter how hopeless the cause of trying to make the place workable, or even merely habitable, no one watching this film will want to see them fail. It would be unthinkable for any member of the audience to desire the Bijou's destruction in favour of a more economically viable development. I like to think that the same affection is felt for Evesham's own Theatre of Dreams. We love her, don't we?

At the time of writing, the Regal cinema is a very sad sight indeed. The front doors and kiosk are boarded up, the windows rusted and cracked, and where six-foot shuttering has been nailed to cover the whole length of the former restaurant, some local Rembrandt has given us 'SAVE R CINNAMON!' all along the boards. (By the way, I know who did this, but he needn't worry about me disclosing his identity because it made me howl with laughter and such off-beat genius must be protected.) I'm assuming his spelling is meant to project a sarcastic irony after the style of Woody Allen, aiming a pointed critique at both the town fathers and the mercenary tactics of the current owners. Either that or our Bengeworth Bard is a bloody imbecile.

Sarcastic irony?

Funnier still, and this I truly applaud, are the printed mock-ups which appeared in 2006 based on *Star Wars: Return of the Jedi*. *Return of the Cinnemon* will now star Alistair McGowan as Darth Vader, thus giving his acting career a stellar boost.

Coming soon, we hope.

But it's all irrelevant. The old Theatre of Dreams seems doomed unless a Hollywood-sized miracle is forthcoming. On Friday, 4 May 2007, while passing the Regal, I noticed that the place had been opened up by workmen sent in to clean whatever health hazards had been left by various unsavoury visitors who had forced their way in through unsecured accesses. They kindly let me have a good look around the entire building, which, although fascinating, I can't say was my happiest visit to the pictures. The seats and carpets were relatively unscathed but the ceiling was hanging in tatters. Much of the glass panelling along both the stalls and balcony walkways was smashed and the place was as rank as a tomb. Both the famous Ward clock[1] and the middle landing posing mirror had vamoosed, and one of the beautiful gold, red and turquoise organ vents was vandalised.

Worse still, virtually sixty years to the day after their installation, the two Westars were standing silently in the dark of the projection room gathering dust, rust and pigeon shit when they should have had *The Fantastic Four* whirring through them. The *coup de grâce*, however, was the ghastly sight of the cinemascope screen, which some unspeakable cretin had slashed to ribbons. It summed up the demise of the whole institution. With a lump In my throat and spooks closing in from all sides, I got the hell out of there.

Many people believe the owners are waiting for the building to become hazardous and will apply to have its Grade II listing removed, demolish the place and build flats, a nightclub or some other commercial development. If, by chance, Wychavon were to achieve a belated meeting of minds with Alan Redpath, we might just glimpse the Phoenix. However, as this seems as likely as Joan Collins winning an Oscar, don't hold your breath. Alas, the dream of renovation is remote (unless I win the Euro lottery) and Port Street's pleasure palace remains an eyesore. Still, you never know…

1 This clock was installed for the Regal's 1932 opening by then apprentice jeweller Les Jobson, who lovingly serviced it throughout the life of the cinema.

Our techno-gadgetry is now making us a nation of couch potatoes. How inert are our lives, as machines give us home entertainment at the touch of a button or the click of a mouse? People's sense of occasion is diminishing rapidly, with fewer and fewer fans dressing up and going out to see a film at the local cinema.

But perhaps I'm being too old-fashioned and overly critical of the effect of technology. I suppose eventually, in order to survive, cinema will have to become a whole different experience from sitting in a smoky space gawking at a huge flat screen. Soon we may be able to 'sit inside' a movie, due to the advance of holographic wizardry, and perhaps even interact on some creative level. All sorts of magic will be ours to indulge in. Once this is available in the comfort of your own home, you won't even dream of anything so quaint as buying a bus ticket or queuing in the rain, and if it kills off the movie medium which I love so much, well that's my cross to bear.

But I believe in the old adage 'what goes around, comes around' and prefer to think in terms of re-awakened interest in the small local cinema – a resurrection of the old style. Imagine the scenario: it is the year 2032 and the Centenary Mega Digital Regal Cinema opens for business, a thousand people lounging in comfort to watch the greatest star of the day (no doubt some two-headed transsexual Martian who talks in a well-wicked supra-Americano patois which makes Will Smith sound like Neville Chamberlain) strut his/her stuff on the giant silver screen as the ghosts of Hitchcock, De Mille, Disney, Kubrick, Scorsese, Spielberg, et al. smile approvingly from the Gods.

Rob Hemming

APRIL 2008

SHAZAM!
THE HISTORY OF
A
REGAL
PICTURE PALACE